Derrida on Exile and the Nation

Derrida on Exile and the Nation

Reading Fantom of the Other

Herman Rapaport

BLOOMSBURY ACADEMIC
LONDON • NEW YORK • OXFORD • NEW DELHI • SYDNEY

BLOOMSBURY ACADEMIC
Bloomsbury Publishing Plc
50 Bedford Square, London, WC1B 3DP, UK
1385 Broadway, New York, NY 10018, USA
29 Earlsfort Terrace, Dublin 2, Ireland

BLOOMSBURY, BLOOMSBURY ACADEMIC and the Diana logo
are trademarks of Bloomsbury Publishing Plc

First published in Great Britain 2021
This paperback edition published in 2022

Copyright © Herman Rapaport, 2021

Herman Rapaport has asserted his right under the Copyright, Designs
and Patents Act, 1988, to be identified as Author of this work.

For legal purposes the Acknowledgments on p. vi constitute
an extension of this copyright page.

Cover design by Charlotte Daniels
Cover image © Herman Rapaport

All rights reserved. No part of this publication may be reproduced or
transmitted in any form or by any means, electronic or mechanical, including
photocopying, recording, or any information storage or retrieval system,
without prior permission in writing from the publishers.

Bloomsbury Publishing Plc does not have any control over, or responsibility for,
any third-party websites referred to or in this book. All internet addresses given
in this book were correct at the time of going to press. The author and publisher
regret any inconvenience caused if addresses have changed or sites have ceased
to exist, but can accept no responsibility for any such changes.

A catalogue record for this book is available from the British Library.

Library of Congress Cataloging-in-Publication Data
Names: Rapaport, Herman, 1947- author.
Title: Derrida on exile and the nation : reading fantom of the other / Herman Rapaport.
Description: London ; New York : Bloomsbury Academic, 2020. |
Includes bibliographical references and index.
Identifiers: LCCN 2020033898 (print) | LCCN 2020033899 (ebook) |
ISBN 9781350163096 (hb) | ISBN 9781350169814 (epdf) | ISBN 9781350169807 (ebook)
Subjects: LCSH: Derrida, Jacques. | Nationalism.
Classification: LCC B2430.D484 R365 2020 (print) |
LCC B2430.D484 (ebook) | DDC 320.54–dc23
LC record available at https://lccn.loc.gov/2020033898
LC ebook record available at https://lccn.loc.gov/2020033899

ISBN:	HB:	978-1-3501-6309-6
	PB:	978-1-3502-3329-4
	ePDF:	978-1-3501-6981-4
	eBook:	978-1-3501-6980-7

Typeset by Integra Software Services Pvt. Ltd.

To find out more about our authors and books visit www.bloomsbury.com
and sign up for our newsletters.

Contents

Acknowledgments   vi

Introduction   1

Part 1   Nationalism, Cosmopolitanism, Exile, and Return

1   Of Philosophical Nationalism and Cosmopolitanism   17
2   What Is German? Adorno's Homecoming   47
3   Universalist Tendencies in Tocqueville, Adonis, Schlegel   63
4   World and Worldlessness: Arendt and Wittgenstein   83

Part 2   *Geschlecht* as Social Relation: Nation, Sex, Race, Kith, and Kind

5   Das Geschlecht   103
6   Retreat into the Inceptual   135
7   Of Promise and Return   193

Bibliography   235
Index   240

Acknowledgments

I wish to thank the staff at the UC Irvine Critical Theory Archive for enabling me to work with Derrida's manuscripts during my various stays in Southern California. In addition, I am grateful to the University of Southampton (United Kingdom) for a developmental leave and to the Reynolds Foundation at Wake Forest University for generously supporting my work. I am also grateful to UC Irvine's Spanish Department and Critical Theory Institute for providing me with office space at various times. I thank Jade Grogan, editor for Bloomsbury, for facilitating my project, as well as Peggy Kamuf, Gerald Bruns, Jack Caputo, David Weinstein, and, for her hospitality and ironical encouragement, Marjorie Perloff. Thanks, as well, to Lambert Stepanich, Kurt Ozmunt, and especially Alexander Gelley, who took such a strong interest in my researches at the Archive. I am grateful to the four outside evaluators of the manuscript for their helpful comments and advice and for the encouragement of colleagues in my academic department. I also extend thanks to my wife, Angelika Rauch Rapaport. Last, I wish to remember the late Hans Breder, of the University of Iowa, who was an inspiration. His many artistic projects in video, photography, and painting led by example.

Introduction

This is a study of Jacques Derrida's lecture course, *Philosophical Nationality and Nationalism: Fantom of the Other* (*Nationalité et nationalisme philosophiques: Fantôme de l'autre*), that was given under the auspice of the École des Hautes Études en Sciences Sociales (EHESS) during 1984–85.[1] The manuscript for the course is archived at the Institut Mémoires de l'édition contemporaine (IMEC) and the Critical Theory Archive in the Langston Library, University of California at Irvine. Currently there appears to be no immediate undertaking to edit and publish the entire course in the series Bibliothèque Derrida that is published by Éditions du Seuil, though significant parts of the course are currently in print. Given the erratic history of publishing Derrida's lecture courses, it is impossible to predict when an integral publication of *Fantom of the Other* will appear. A considerable delay would be unfortunate, given this course's significance.[2]

In the preface to the book *The Politics of Friendship* (1994), Derrida talked about the possibility of redacting a multivolume work comprising lecture courses grouped under two general titles, *Philosophical Nationality and Nationalism* and *Questions of Responsibility*. Courses belonging to the *Nationality* rubric included *Fantom of the Other* (1984–85); *Mythos, Logos, Topos* (1985–86); *The Theological-Political* (1986–87); *Kant, the Jew, the German* (1987–88); *The Politics of Friendship* (1988–89); and *Eating the Other (Rhetorics of Cannibalism)* (1989–90). Courses belonging to *Questions of Responsibility* included *Answering for the Secret* (1991–92); *Testimony* (1993–95); *Hostility and Hospitality* (1995–97); *Perjury and Pardon* (1997–99); *Death Penalty* (1999–2001); and *The Beast and the Sovereign* (2002–03).[3]

Mentioned first, *Philosophical Nationality and Nationalism: Fantom of the Other* not only begins the cycle of courses that follow but can be considered foundational to them. Notable is that this is the first course Derrida gave upon accepting a position at the EHESS where he assumed the post of full professor.[4] Retroactively, one notices that a new phase in Derrida's career had been made possible at the EHESS wherein *Fantom* and following courses were more closely linked as an overarching project than courses of the past given at the École Normale Supérieure (ENS). The decision to give a series of courses on philosophical nationalism that would consider the social relation from the perspective of the national and the international (or what Derrida calls the cosmopolitan) set the stage for a number of inquiries, among them, an inquiry into race that would be retroactively amplified in the course of the following year in which racism in Plato would be examined. Also noticeable would be Derrida's increased interest in the topic of "the Jew, the German," which has an important thematic inception in *Fantom of the Other*. That Derrida had initiated what would be a twenty-year inquiry into topics such as philosophical nationalism and nationhood is hardly surprising, given his position at an institution of higher learning devoted to social science.

Meanwhile in America, where Derrida had been guest lecturing for years as a figure associated with Paul de Man and others of the Yale School, he had become typecast as a literary-philosophical critic concerned with the aporias of formal, textual analyses divorced from politics—activist politics in particular. By the mid-1980s Derrida had already been so much debated in the United States that most people on the left had come to agree with Fredric Jameson's famous dismissal of Derrida as a brilliant thinker locked in a "prisonhouse of language," whereas most people of a more conservative cast of mind, Walter Jackson Bate of Harvard University among them, had concluded publicly that Derrida was too hermeneutically extreme.[5] Given that Derrida was so much in the spotlight relative to debates about methodology, the political incorrectness of close reading, and whether Yale suppressed social critique, no one was paying attention to the fact that back in France Derrida had launched a bold new lecture course that was investigating social and political issues concerning nation, nationality, and nationalism. Nor had hardly anyone paid attention to Derrida's political activism in Paris as a founder of a new type of university, the Collège Internationale de Philosophie that was started in the early 1980s and of which Derrida was the head for a brief period. Indeed, awareness that Derrida might be a social thinker engaged in the sort of political analysis relevant to Americans schooled in social-political thinking was not imaginable for most until well into the early 1990s when readers of Derrida's *Specters of Marx* and *The Politics of Friendship* saw a social-political thinker at work with considerable depth that had been gained over many years of researching and thinking.

In fact, well before "race theory" became an area study in American universities, Derrida was already developing this line of inquiry in *Fantom of the Other* as well as in the lecture courses in the following years. In the course *Mythos*,

Logos, Topos, which immediately followed *Fantom* in the fall of 1985, Derrida was probing the xenophobic foundations of Western nationalist thinking in the writings of the Ancient Greeks, in particular, within the genre of the Athenian funeral oration in which one can detect the problematic ancestors of notions such as *Vaterland* and *Heimat*. Was it the case that Nazism was inscribed in the letter of philosophy since ancient times? It is a hypothesis that haunts Derrida's inquiries from time to time and one that Derrida affirms, to some extent, when he points out that Nazism was not born in a desert, but has been nurtured in a European clime for many centuries.[6]

One of the nurseries for National Socialism, closer to the twentieth century, that Derrida would explicate near the outset of *Fantom of the Other*, was Johann Gottlieb Fichte's *Addresses to the German Nation* which straddles both nationalism and cosmopolitanism, given the influences on Fichte of Enlightenment thinking and Napoleonic conquest in the name of France. Essentially, Derrida treats the *Addresses* as a major resource for the study of philosophical nationalism. Throughout the *Addresses*, Fichte prominently repeats a word, central to *Fantom of the Other*, that will have a role to play in National Socialism, namely the word "*Geschlecht*," as in the sentence "*Eines neuen Menschengeschlechtes müsse zu allererst von Deutschen an Deutschen angewendet werden* ... (A new race of men must first be applied by Germans to Germans)."[7] *Geschlecht* is a "complex word," to use William Empson's locution, that means not only race but kind, type, sex, stock, tribe, imprint, and generation, not that this exhausts the list (which will be discussed in detail later). Whereas in the quotation above Fichte probably means humankind or mankind when he invokes the word *Menschengeschlecht*, the National Socialists heard something else, namely "race of men," which, interestingly enough, is how Gregory Moore renders it in the English translation provided above from the *Addresses*. As it happens, Fichte's own project is to consider the education of a new man, the German, in the context of a nationalist transformation whereby loosely confederated provinces would be turned into a centralized nation state populated by *Germans*, as opposed to just Germanic peoples.

Fichte considers education key to such a nationalist transformation because by means of embracing Enlightenment notions of national identity, purpose, and international fraternity, future generations of people in Germany could by means of identitarian consciousness-raising view themselves as German nationals, just as Frenchmen could view themselves as French nationals, and Englishmen as English nationals, and so on. Once again the slippery word *Geschlecht* comes in handy, because it conveys not just a sense of mankind or humankind in general but of generations as distinct age groups, as in *"das Heil der künftigen Geschlechter* (the salvation of future generations)."[8] Here national generational identity is given the religious nimbus of apocalyptic salvation. Compare that, however, to an interrogative locution such as *"wie könnte sonst jemals ein besseres Geschlecht beginnen?* (how else could a better race/generation ever begin?)" wherein the key term is again more unstable, though Moore translates it as "race" in order to show that generation and race can be improved for salvific ends, an idea compatible with Nazism.

In the first two lectures of *Fantom*, Derrida investigates Fichte's *Addresses* because they are a sort of witches' cauldron of nationalist rhetoric that is idiomatically problematic in a way that had made it possible for later generations of Germans to suit Fichte to their own agendas. The Nazis, ever sensitive to language, exploited the German language's philological past in order to recover what they considered to be an originary state of Germanness in which language could be viewed as a direct expression of a racial stock apart from genetics per se. For them, *Geschlecht* was important as a philological *idiom* showing that Germans in the past, supposedly more Aryan than Germans in the present, took for granted that sex, race, kin, and generation are more identical than not. This idiomatic expression of the past conflicted with modernized German in which *Rasse* and *Sexualität* were categorically separated in the fields of medicine and the sciences more generally. Whereas *Fantom* initially situates the term *Geschlecht* in the context of Fichte, *Geschlecht* will be the topic of main interrogation in the last eight lectures of *Fantom* in which Martin Heidegger's historical appropriation of this idiomatic word is key. Heidegger also wants to retrieve the term *Geschlecht*, though for purposes that are and are not compatible with a National Socialist agenda, given that Heidegger's aim is to do battle with a nationalist metaphysics, which National Socialism uncritically embraced.

Fantom of the Other consists of thirteen lectures that could be conceived as falling into two parts. The first part (lectures one to five) covers the following main figures: Fichte, Karl Marx, Friedrich Engels, Karl Grün, Friedrich Schlegel, Alexis de Tocqueville, the Arabic poet Adonis, Theodor Adorno, Hannah Arendt, and Ludwig Wittgenstein. The second part (lectures six to thirteen) is entirely devoted to Heidegger. My title, *Derrida on Exile and the Nation*, refers to the overarching theme of nationalism and exile. A significant portion of *Fantom*'s first part treats figures who hold on to or struggle with nationalistic attachments while living in voluntary or forced exile in a foreign land. Of special importance are the Jewish figures Theodor Adorno, Hannah Arendt, and Ludwig

Wittgenstein, though Derrida also devotes lengthy commentary to the Arabic poet Adonis, living in exile in Paris, as well as to Alexis de Tocqueville with whom Derrida puts himself in relation as a Frenchman living and working overseas in America. In all of these cases, language poses the possibility if not inevitability of a return to one's native national homeland. Indeed, Adorno and Arendt's public interviews, broadcast in post-war Germany, discussed the question of the need for such a return in much detail, despite considerable psychological ambivalence and conflict, given the events of the Holocaust.

In the second part of *Fantom*, it is the last six lectures that concern nation and exile, this time in the context of Martin Heidegger's exceptionally enigmatic essay "Die Sprache im Gedicht" on Georg Trakl whose untranslatable title has to be left in the original. Heidegger's main thematic throughout the essay is that of exile, presumably that of the poet, his relation to language, and return to a homeland. Put into question, however, is whether this homeland is to be thought of in terms of nation or as something less well defined, the Occidental (*Abendland*). Apparently, it was Derrida's aim to contrast Heidegger, a German with a National Socialist history, with mainly the exilic German-Jewish figures, Adorno and Arendt. Ironically, in Heidegger's text the return from exile leads to a dissolution of the nation and the national, whereas in Adorno and Arendt, return from exile motivates them to uphold familiar conceptions of nation and the national.

In Heidegger's reading of Trakl, the word *Geschlecht* posits an erasure of the social relation that justifies the poet's exilic retreat to an ontologically inceptual place within central Europe wherein objectified social categories do not yet obtain. Even gender dissolves. In the earlier lectures of *Fantom*, *Geschlecht* is mentioned explicitly, as in the case of Fichte's *Addresses*, but is also to be inferred, as in Adorno's question "What is German?" wherein he is asking what kind of person (*Geschlecht*) does one identify as German. Tocqueville's inquiry into what makes up the American national type speaks to *Geschlecht*, as well, though once more we have to infer this. Mention of Arendt and Wittgenstein concerns the Jew as a bad sort of *Geschlecht*, however ambivalent that is for Arendt and less ambivalent for Wittgenstein. Not surprising is the precarity of the social relation for exiles. This speaks to an undercurrent that runs throughout *Fantom*, namely the effects of exile relative to understandings of nationality and nationhood.

Much of *Fantom of the Other* is currently available, albeit not integrally. Lecture one was edited and translated as "Onto-Theology of National-Humanism (Prolegomena to a Hypothesis)."[9] Lectures six and seven have appeared as "Geschlecht II: Heidegger's Hand."[10] Part of lecture seven, a revision of lecture eight (dubbed the "Loyola Typescript"), and lectures nine to thirteen have been published by Éditions du Seuil as *Geschlecht III* (2018).[11] Most of the first part of *Fantom* is only accessible in manuscript form in the archive. Care has been taken to focus on major points of interest in the course as a whole. This includes some heavy stress on background information, mainly with respect to the texts Derrida was examining, given that he often cited them by way of intervention rather than by way of considerable exposition, if any at all. Because readers will require the contexts Derrida was hinting at and at times amplifying, my reading has the function of relating content seminal to Derrida's writings from 1984 onward that are put into perspective, both in terms of *Fantom* itself and Derrida's broader philosophical itineraries that are so often kept tacit.

Among the reasons there has long been an intense interest by Derrideans in *Fantom of the Other* is that it was known to contain materials that were never reworked into "Geschlecht III," the essay on Martin Heidegger's reading of Georg Trakl that Derrida had announced forthcoming at a conference in Chicago in 1985. In the book *Phantoms of the Other*, David Farrell Krell set out to (re)construct the four-essay monograph on *Geschlecht* that Derrida had announced and abandoned, despite having published three chapters of it separately: "Geschlecht I," "Geschlecht II," and "Geschlecht IV."[12] Given this incompletion, and Krell's interest in Heidegger and Trakl, he set himself the task of reconstructing Derrida's entire *Geschlecht* project, which required him to investigate and explicate the then unpublished lectures eight to thirteen in Derrida's *Fantom of the Other* (which I spell with an "f," in line with Derrida's spelling, and in order to distinguish from Krell's text). Given that an issue for Krell was really the larger project of reconstructing what Derrida probably had in mind for the major study of Heidegger that never came together on *Geschlecht*, Krell had to include materials in Derrida's *Of Spirit* that borrowed text from the *Fantom* course. The extent to which Derrida compressed materials in *Of Spirit* that derived from and amplified *Fantom*'s lectures on Heidegger and Trakl clearly posed difficulties of explication that Krell boldly tackled and that readers are strongly encouraged to survey. Of course, in order that Krell could most efficiently do the work of reconstruction, it was to his advantage not to take all of the *Fantom* course into consideration. My study, by contrast, attempts to relate the *whole* of the *Fantom* course's lectures and to contextualize them in terms of one another, Derrida's published corpus, and the texts Derrida expected his auditors to know. If in fact the entire manuscript of *Fantom* is made available to readers, this will not alter the fact that the course is not sufficiently self-explanatory and that therefore an explication of main features of the course is very much required in order to see connections and relationships that Derrida leaves tacit.

To that end, I conclude this introduction with commentary on some major themes that recur with some frequency throughout the course, leaving aside the theme of *Geschlecht*, since it has already been discussed.

1. **Idiom.** Derrida asks whether philosophy is or isn't inherently idiomatic and therefore nationalistic, given that philosophers are writing in a particular national language or mother tongue. The question is highly debatable, Derrida acknowledges, though he clearly sides with the case for idiomaticity. Far from being a universal language that ought to be expressed formulaically in terms of symbolic logic, philosophy is not dissociable from the mother tongue of the thinker, a view shared by Heidegger, Nietzsche, and Fichte. That Derrida should seize upon the idiomaticity of the mother tongue in relation to philosophy at this point in his career is not too surprising, considering that foundational to all of Derrida's work has been the question of whether philosophy is translatable from one language to another. Not merely a theoretical or speculative question, it is one that pertained rather pragmatically to his own translation into French of Husserl's writings on geometry back in the early 1960s, as well as to his numerous critical inspections of various French translations of German or Greek philosophical texts, all of which he finds to be productively problematic. At issue in the earlier and later lectures of *Fantom* is the philosophical occurrence of the word *Geschlecht* as an idiomatic marker for a nexus of highly vexed micro-macro social relations.

2. **The Jew, the German.** Readers of *Fantom* familiar with Derrida's writings of the 1980s will notice an emerging theme of what he later calls "the Jew, the German" in the lecture courses *The Theological-Political* (1986–87) and *Kant, the Jew, the German* (1987–88). Whether this theme sprang up spontaneously in *Fantom* or whether it was preplanned in the sense of imagining a lengthy study on the topic of Jewish intellectuals is unclear. Certainly, the essays "Shibboleth" (1986) on Paul Celan, "Force of Law" (1989) on Walter Benjamin, and "At This Very Moment in This Work Here I Am" (1987) on Emmanuel Levinas relate to this trajectory.[13] There can be no question that by *c.* 1990 a sizable project emerges in print and in lecture that includes Franz Kafka, Walter Benjamin, Theodor Adorno, Hannah Arendt, Ludwig Wittgenstein, Paul Celan, Hermann Cohen, Gershom Scholem, Franz Rosenzweig, Baruch Spinoza, Martin Buber, and Emmanuel Levinas. *Fantom*'s consideration of Adorno, Arendt, and Wittgenstein as exilic Jewish figures exposes their own perceived national identities and vulnerabilities relative to their Germanity and Jewishness. Of central concern is the idiomaticity of the mother tongue and the writer's relation to it. Such concerns reappear in later courses.

3. **Muttersprache.** Can the thinker philosophize adequately in the absence of living within the national language into which he or she is born? For Heidegger it would be unimaginable to philosophize outside of Germany, because then he would have been cut from the idiomatic resources of the German mother tongue. But those who have been forced to emigrate for various reasons did not have the choice to remain within the mother tongue. Derrida discusses how Theodor Adorno, Hannah Arendt, and Ludwig Wittgenstein, who lived in non-German-speaking societies, thought about what it means to function as a thinker exiled from one's native tongue. Of interest is a radio speech by Adorno in which he talks about his need to have been reconnected with German language and culture, as well as a television interview with Arendt in which she expresses similar ideas about the fundamental importance of her identification with the German language as medium of expression. Of interest to Derrida is how close Arendt and Adorno are to one another with respect to expressing what approaches a crudely nationalized metaphysics of language akin to statements made by Heidegger in *Introduction to Metaphysics* (1935).

Wittgenstein, by contrast, is at war with language and tells us that he cannot find his way within it. Unlike Heidegger, Wittgenstein feels cut off from a *Denkweg*, a path of thinking proper to his philosophizing. Wittgenstein often asks whether the way in which one is proceeding is the only way or the right way, something that he views as hampered by the vicissitudes of linguistic ambiguities in the native German in which he writes. If Derrida detects traces of a nationalist metaphysics of language not unfamiliar to nationalism (if not fascism) in what Adorno and Arendt say, he sees in Wittgenstein a repudiation of metaphysics that carries the mentality of *Kampf*, an endless struggle with language that puts the Cambridge thinker at odds with himself as a Jew, which in certain marginalia has expressed itself anti-Semitically.

4. **The national versus the cosmopolitan.** This theme overarches *Fantom* and continues to be of importance in the courses that follow during the late 1980s. In terms of "the Jew, the German," it is well known that Jewish intellectuals such as Walter Benjamin have a cosmopolitan orientation, given its promulgation of social tolerance beneficial to Jews as a minority, whereas that is not the case for Heidegger, who is orientated quite nationalistically. Additionally, in *Fantom* Derrida notices a paradox that characterizes nationalist self-affirmation, namely that nationalism is justified on the grounds of cosmopolitanism. A great nation is not great unless it is cosmopolitan: capable of understanding and giving direction to other nations in a spirit of humanitarianism. Fichte in his *Addresses to the German People* is opposed to provincialism and proclaims the advent of

a new type of German who is educated and talented in ways that affiliate him and her with peoples of other nations within the common cosmopolitan cause of universal enlightenment. Fichte's nationalism presupposes that the national spirit of a particular people transcends that people in a way that crosses over into a cosmopolitan dimension whereby everyone shares humanitarian interests, principles, and ideals. However, this is the privilege of one who happens to be German in terms of thought, someone whose surpassing of German national identity establishes it. Derrida is especially interested in a statement by Fichte in which he says someone who has never set foot inside of German territory could be German on account of how that person thinks.

Relative to the nationalism-cosmopolitanism theme, Derrida will consider French socialist thinkers of the early nineteenth century in relation to remarks made by Marx and Engels in *The German Ideology*. Marx and Engels, of course, are deeply skeptical of nationalism as well as cosmopolitanism. Also, Derrida will discuss Alexis de Tocqueville's cosmopolitanism in relation to his sojourn in America where he discovers that the Americans were always already French insofar as they are natural Cartesians. This relates to Derrida's remark elsewhere in the mid-1980s that "America *is* deconstruction." The paradox of nationalism-cosmopolitanism first noticed by Tocqueville appears to be still active in the late twentieth century in terms of the question, how can Americans be more French than the French without knowing it? Here a curious exchange of identities is at stake that speaks to "spirit," the "mentality" of a people.

In what I consider part two of *Fantom* (the eight lectures on Heidegger), Derrida examines Heidegger's "Die Sprache im Gedicht" ("Language in the Poem") from *Unterwegs zur Sprache* (*On the Way to Language*) wherein the nationalism-cosmopolitanism distinction has been subsumed by rhetoric invoking Europe as evening land (*Abendland*). This land is presided over by an exilic figure. This can be taken as a deconstruction of the nationalism-cosmopolitanism distinction, though precisely what this would mean in terms of a new way of thinking is not self-evident, which, of course, is what Derrida wants to explore and conceptualize. Without taking into account part one of *Fantom*, it is not readily apparent that Derrida's chief long range interest is Heidegger's implicit deconstruction of the nationalism-cosmopolitanism distinction, a deconstruction not without fascist influence.

5. Monstrosity. The theme of monstrosity emerges in lectures six and seven of *Fantom* where the question of the *monstration* of the hand is at issue in Heidegger's corpus. In *The Post Card*, Derrida had already made mention of an album of photographs of Heidegger in which the hand holding a pen is featured, a topos of the hand to which *Fantom* returns. In these photographs, the hand is supposed to represent the piety of philosophical thought, but Derrida is quite aware that this monstration is contradicted by the monstrosity of the Nazi salute that also features the hand, a monstrosity Heidegger necessarily had to participate in as a card-carrying Nazi. In *Fantom*, Derrida discusses Heidegger's various depictions of the hand and, in particular, seizes on Heidegger's distinction between the human hand and the paw of the ape, which again touches on a certain monstrosity in Heidegger's mind, that of the ape's inferior hand. Derrida does not say it explicitly, but a certain xenophobia probably interposes itself here as conceptual violence.

Above all, Derrida will be making the case that *Geschlecht* is itself a monstrous word that exceeds measure. Etymologically it carries within itself the verb *Schlagen* (to hit or beat) that reveals *Geschlecht*'s originary violence as a social determinant. *Geschlecht* as a term for sex presumes *Schlagen* as sexual hitting or banging (*Ficken*), though the *Schlag* or blow also points to domestic violence whereby gender relations are forcefully established (e.g., the battle of the sexes). One could and should think of the *Schlag*, too, in the context of racial violence, the policing of kinds as reflected in, say, apartheid.

Etymologically, it is clear that *Schlag* and *Geschlecht* are monstrous because, like any monster, they are excessive in scope and inherently express a violence that cannot be contained. *Schlag*'s iteration of *Geschlecht* and *Geschlecht*'s iteration of *Schlag* can be viewed as an insistence upon some primordial or fundamental violence both constitutive of the social relation and hostile to it. Derrida will become very attentive to Heidegger's innovation, by way of Trakl, of an account of an inceptual or latent *Schlag* whose disruption is gentle—a privative or withheld violence—given alongside a successive or manifest *Schlag* that is overtly violent and divisive. That in Heidegger these two manifestations of the *Schlag* are undecidably hinged leads to what Derrida knows is a monstrosity of logical contortions born of the kind of hermeneutical violence that Trakl's poetry encourages.

6. **Difference and Identity.** The eight lectures of the second division of *Fantom* were part of a laborious project to deconstruct difference and identity to an extent hitherto unknown in Derrida's work. The central question concerns whether *Geschlecht* is one or many and whether this either/or distinction is decidable. Does the word *Geschlecht*, which puts kinds into relation as different, function in a way that withdraws into oneness, hence refusing difference? Emphasis falls on Trakl's phrase "E I N Geschlecht," which is of concern to Heidegger in "Die Sprache im Gedicht." Is the one really just *one*? Also, difference/identity and one/

many relate to nationalism in terms of difference and cosmopolitanism in terms of identity and unity. The word *Geschlecht* in Fichte and others also concerns difference (as particularity: race, stock, kin) and identity (as universality: humankind, humanity). In the lyrics of Trakl, questions arise about whether human figures are distinct or identical. Are the brother and sister one *Geschlecht* (in the sense of sex) even if they are male and female? Moreover, in terms of *Geschlecht*'s meaning as kin, does this oneness trespass incestuousness, as Trakl's biographers might ask? There are similar issues concerning Heidegger's use of *Geist* and its adjectival variants, the seeming protons of *Geist* that are and aren't identical in ways that perform Heideggerian dis-appropriation. With respect to *Schlag*, once more, there is a twofoldedness noted above in which the inceptual gentle *Schlag* (metaphorically, a wingbeat) suggesting oneness (identity, unity) is hinged to a successive but inherently related violent blow of dissension and differentiation. Derrida will discuss that hinge as a fold or *pli* characterized by instantiations of *la différance*.

7. **Revenance.** *Fantom of the Other* names revenance. Long before Derrida wrote *Specters of Marx*, he had given specters, fantoms, ghosts, and apparitions considerable thought in "Fors" (on the crypt), in *The Post Card* (on the spectral effects of quotidian life), and in the film *Ghost Dance* (1983) (on Derrida's belief in ghosts). Revenance recalls the eternal return in Nietzsche, the return of the repressed in Freud, and of the anniversary in Hölderlin and Celan (meaningful cyclicality, commemoration, holiday). In *Specters of Marx*, the revenant appears at moments when time is out of joint, something that in *Fantom* is explored in terms of Heidegger's idioms that are out of joint vis-à-vis their historical appearances separated by momentous events. Heidegger's analysis of Trakl in the 1950s reprises Trakl's repeated mention of the word *Geschlecht* and in so doing calls up even while it mutes specters of the past, among them revenants of the National Socialist period but also the biographical history of Trakl's controversial relation with his sister on which Heidegger is silent. In the essay "Restitutions," Derrida connected a notion of restitution with revenance. This concerns the de-monstration of a Germanic *Geist* by Heidegger, a *Geist* that has become detached and must be reattached (restituted) by way of a philosophical reading of a poetic notion of *Abendland* as twilight and decease into which the poet heads. Herein Germanic *Geist* is restituted; or, as Derrida has put it (idiomatically), "ça me revient" ("it's coming back to me"), as "revenance."[14] For the philosopher, this return indicates a desire for re-appropriation—*Er-eignis*, in Heidegger's parlance—which requires a certain circularity, something that Derrida considers at some length in the final lectures on Heidegger and Trakl.

The title, *Fantom of the Other*, can be interpreted in various ways. Among them would be the perception that a fantom stalking Derrida's seminars is Martin Heidegger. Such revenance is, in fact, discussed in *The Post Card* where Derrida talks about meeting Heidegger's ghost.

> On the subject of Jewish stories: you can imagine the extent to which I am haunted by Heidegger's ghost in this city [Freiburg]. I came for him. I am trying to reconstitute all his paths, the places where he spoke ..., to interrogate him, as if he were there, about the history of the posts, to appropriate his city for myself, to sniff out, to imagine, etc. To respond to his objections, to explain to him what he does not yet understand (this morning I walked with him for two hours ...).[15]

This recollection is crucial to understanding Derrida's lecture courses in which Heidegger ghosts many of the contents that communicate themselves as allegories of how to read and debate Heidegger's philosophical texts. Throughout the earlier lectures of *Fantom* one is often acutely aware of unspoken comparisons and contrasts with Heidegger's life and work as if Heidegger were ghosting what was being said.

8. **Exile.** In *Fantom of the Other*, it is easy to track exile in the Syrian poet Adonis as well as in the Jewish figures Arendt, Adorno, and Wittgenstein. Have any of them felt entirely "at home" anywhere? The theme of home is quite marked in Heidegger who, unlike these other figures, never experienced exile, but who writes at great length about homelessness in his work on Hölderlin and Trakl. "Die Sprache im Gedicht," discussed in *Fantom*'s part two, is largely about the exile in Trakl's poetry of an anonymous figure who "goes under" and passes out of sight in the forest twilight that leads into darkness for the sake of restituting European humanity. Central to this restitution is homecoming.

In the case of the lectures on Adorno, Arendt, Adonis, and Alexis de Tocqueville in *Fantom*, Derrida also addresses leave-taking and home-coming (returning). Only in the case of Adonis is there no going back home as his poetry abandons (deconstructs?) the notion of homeland. The "it's coming back to me" or "*ça me revient*" (mentioned in "Restitutions") occurs in *Fantom* in relation to Arendt when she comes back to Germany in order to visit Heidegger, or when Adorno returns to occupy a post at the University of Frankfurt. Things "come back" to one when one returns home, at times according to a logic of revenance, the return of an attachment, the possibility of reattachment, however "out of joint," as mentioned in *Specters of Marx* and foreshadowed in *Fantom*. For those who never left, the *survivance* of Jews was seen as rather uncanny: they were there where they weren't supposed to be, which to some seemed monstrous. That is, for many Germans who had experienced twelve years under Hitler, Jews in post-war Germany seemed like the living dead; like ghosts, they were unwelcome. In the case of Adorno's return to the University of Frankfurt, he had been confronted with hostile colleagues who thought it monstrous to restitute Jews as if they were owed a "ghostly debt" (as Derrida puts it), just because they were Jews. In such a context, Derrida clarifies that exile and return as *revenance* are closely related.

Notes

1. At UC Irvine's Derrida Archive the manuscript can be found in box 18.
2. Following Derrida's passing in 2004, a translation team embarked on editing and publishing Derrida's courses (or seminars, as he preferred to call them) starting from the last course, *The Beast and the Sovereign*, with the intention of working backwards from there year by year. (The courses were published in French by Editions Galilée and then in English by University of Chicago Press.) For whatever reason, courses began appearing with Galilée from very different time periods, for example, *Heidegger: The Question of Being and History* (1964–65), trans. Geoffrey Bennington (Chicago: University of Chicago Press, 2019) and *Theory and Practice* (1976–77), trans. David Wills (Chicago: University of Chicago Press, 2019). Recently the course *La vie la mort* (1975–76) (Paris: Seuil, 2019) appeared in the *Bibliothèque Derrida* series. Even if the original master plan obtains, there is no longer reason to think it will preclude simultaneous publication of other courses in whatever order. At what point an integral publication of *Fantom of the Other* will appear is therefore unclear.
3. Jacques Derrida, *The Politics of Friendship*, trans. George Collins (London: Verso, 1997), vii. The list has been corrected, because it is very inaccurate in terms of dating the seminars; in addition, the course listed as *Nomos, Topos, Logos* (given in 1985, not 1984) is probably incorrect (unless Derrida had changed it on purpose) and should most likely be *Mythos, Logos, Topos*, which would conform to what Derrida originally wrote in the manuscript. Of course, *Questions of Responsibility* was still in progress when Derrida referenced it in *The Politics of Friendship*.
4. Derrida delivered the lecture course at the ENS, even though he was faculty at the EHESS, a point mentioned in the first lecture. For the purposes of clarity, I have adopted the nomenclature of referring to courses and lectures. Derrida himself preferred using the term "seminar," which could refer to an individual lecture or the lecture course as a whole. For a detailed discussion of Derrida's usage, see footnote

2 of the "General Introduction" to Jacques Derrida, *Heidegger: The Question of Being and History*, trans. G. Bennington (Chicago: University of Chicago Press, 2016), vii.

5   See my *The Theory Mess* (New York: Columbia University Press, 2001) for a discussion of this topic.

6   Jacques Derrida, *Of Spirit*, trans. Geoffrey Bennington and Rachel Bowlby (Chicago: University of Chicago Press, 1989), 109. Originally published as *De l'esprit* (Paris: Editions Galilée, 1987).

7   Johann Gottlieb Fichte, *Addresses to the German Nation*, trans. Gregory Moore (Cambridge: Cambridge University Press, 2008), 41. *Reden an die deutsche Nation* (Berlin: Holzinger, 2014), 47.

8   Ibid., 165–88.

9   "Onto-Theology of National-Humanism (Prolegomena to a Hypothesis)," trans. Geoffrey Bennington, *Oxford Literary Review* 14, no. 1 (1992). There is no mention in the notes to the translation that these materials come from the beginning of *Fantom of the Other*. The first two lectures are continuous in that the beginning of the second lecture finishes up remarks Derrida was making in the first lecture on Fichte. It then turns to Adorno, which is beyond the scope of the English translation.

10 Jacques Derrida, "Geschlecht II: Heidegger's Hand" originally appeared in English translation in *Deconstruction and Philosophy*, ed. John Sallis (Chicago: University of Chicago Press, 1987). The essay appeared simultaneously in French in Jacques Derrida, *Psyché* (Paris: Galilée, 1987).

11 Jacques Derrida, *Geschlecht III*, ed. Geoffrey Bennington, Katie Chenoweth, Rodrigo Therezo (Paris: Seuil, 2018). A translation of this book will appear after my study goes into print; therefore, I won't have had the opportunity to consult it.

12 David Farrell Krell, *Phantoms of the Other* (Albany: SUNY, 2015). Derrida's "Geschlecht I: Sexual Difference, Ontological Difference" appears in *Psyche*, vol. 2 (Stanford: Stanford University Press, 2008). The French text appeared in *Psyché* (1987). The English translation of Derrida's "Heidegger's Ear: Philopolemology (*Geschlecht* IV)" occurs in *Reading Heidegger: Commemorations*, ed. John Sallis (Bloomington: Indiana University Press, 1993). In French: "L'oreille de Heidegger: Philopolémologie (*Geschlecht* IV)," in *Politiques de l'amitié* (Paris: Galilée, 1994).

13 "Shibboleth," in *Midrash and Literature*, ed. G. Hartman and S. Budick (New Haven: Yale University Press, 1986); "Force of Law," in *Deconstruction and the Possibility of Justice*, ed. D. Cornell, M. Rosenfeld, D.G. Carlson (London: Routledge, 1992/89); "At This Very Moment in This Work Here I Am," in *Psyche* (Chicago: Chicago University Press, 2007/1987).

14 Jacques Derrida, *The Truth in Painting*, trans. Geoff Bennington and Ian McLeod (Chicago: Chicago University Press, 1987), 260. Originally published as *La vérité en peinture* (Paris: Flammarion, 1978).

15 Jacques Derrida, *The Post Card* (Chicago: University of Chicago Press, 1987), 189.

Part One

Nationalism, Cosmopolitanism, Exile, and Return

1

Of Philosophical Nationalism and Cosmopolitanism

Fichte, Grün, Marx, Engels

We know that during the Middle Ages and the Renaissance, educated people mainly wrote in Latin, not only in order to keep their thoughts and speculations out of public circulation where they could be misunderstood and condemned as heretical, but because the educated assumed vernacular national languages would be unsuitable for expressing advanced ideas, given that the vernacular was far too idiomatic and imprecise. Latin by contrast soared above nationalist and regional differences of linguistic expression (including untranslatable idioms) and functioned on a plane considered to be firmly established in terms of conceptual specificity (precision) and general access, given that Latin was transnational (in our own historical terms, cosmopolitan) and, as such, considered universal. Even as late as the middle of the seventeenth century, John Milton was trading barbs with intellectuals on the Continent in political tracts written in Latin in order to elevate local political justifications with respect to England on a plane that was not merely nationalist in orientation. This was extremely important to the English who did not want the Continent to contemplate invasion of their country for being what today we would call a rogue state. However, like many of his educated countrymen, Sir Thomas Browne and Robert Burton included, John Milton wrote in English for an already large reading public, anglicizing tracts whose rhetorical staging and execution were derived from Latinate tradition. Hence in Milton's corpus one can easily see a national-cosmopolitan divide concerning a certain politics of language concerning the nation-state.

In the lecture course *La Langue et le discours de la méthode* (Language and the Discourse on Method), given in 1981–82, Derrida explored the vexed set of circumstances with respect to de-Latinization that in France had started occurring under kings of the sixteenth century who were seeing relationships between language, law, and the state that privileged French over Latin for the simple reason that if French were the common currency of legal discourse, people could not exempt themselves from the law on account of being ignorant of the Latin in which it was written. From the perspective of the state, French was the more universal language.

> *In the first place*, it was the great moment of establishing the monarchy as State: a massive if not terminal or decisive progress of a French language imposed on the provinces as administrative and juridical medium. What we are trying to follow in this seminar is the constitution of the legal subject and of the philosophical subject *tout court*, starting from the imposition of a language. As you know, under François I, in 1539, the royal decree of Villers-Cotterêts ordered that legal judgments and other proceedings be 'pronounced, recorded, and delivered in the French mother tongue.'[1]

Derrida will return to issues of the mother tongue in later lectures, but here his main focus will be Descartes's *Discourse on Method* and his famous declaration that "if I write in French, which is the language of my country, rather than in Latin," this is because "I hope that those who use only their pure natural reason will better judge my opinions than those who believe only in old books." Descartes tells us that he has confidence in "those who combine good sense with scholarship, whom alone I wish to have as my judges," those who "will not be so partial to Latin as to refuse to hear my reasons because I express them in a vulgar tongue."[2]

If French is considered a natural language, which by nature would be unphilosophical, crude, confusing (in terms of its various idiomatic locutions, ellipses, etc.), or, to put it in other words, homespun, how can it be justified for the purposes of a discourse devoted to a method that considers itself to be analytical, rigorous, and precise? Does philosophy not take distance from "pure natural reason"? Derrida sees a problem with the word "natural" in that it means something different when addressing language versus reason. "We call 'natural' a particular language, a *historical* language as opposed to the artificial, formal language constructed from the ground up to become the universal language." A natural language "is native or national, but also particular and historical; it is the least common thing in the world. The natural reason Descartes speaks of is in principle universal, ahistorical, pre- or metalinguistic."[3] Natural language and natural reason are by definition opposed as particular versus universal, local versus global.

At issue, of course, is the question of language as not just natural but national, of a "politics of language" that is hardly incidental to the history of French philosophical thought. In what is clearly a seminar laying the groundwork for *Fantom of the Other*, Derrida remarks that "it is still a question of opposing a national language, which at a given moment has become the language of the State … to national idioms that are subject to the same State authority and that constitute dissipating or centrifugal forces, risks of dissociation or even subversion, even if, and this is the first contradiction, they are simultaneously encouraged."[4] This oppositionality of idiom to what the State would like to establish as an official national language, whose rules are standardized with great precision, compares with a second related opposition that concerns privileging one's national language to "other natural languages ('dead' or 'living') that … have become privileged media of philosophical or techno-scientific communication."[5] Descartes's declaration that he is writing in French for those whose natural language is French speaks to both of these oppositions, which, not by accident, become foundational to the central concerns of *Fantom of the Other* with its emphasis upon idiom and the national-cosmopolitan divide.

As Jürgen Habermas and others have noted, the promotion of national languages over Latin was instrumental to the formation of a civic public sphere of educated readers for whom notions of natural reason or common sense became the universalizing conditions for opinion making and civic-legislative debate.[6] The French *philosophes*—among them, Condillac, Constant, Diderot, Buffon, Voltaire, Rousseau, and Montesquieu—had embraced an authoritative standard of the French language as the means of communicating with those countrymen who were hungry for opinionated debate, witty personal reflection, and methodological clarity ("theory"). In Germany, Kant, Fichte, Novalis, Schleiermacher, Schlegel, Schiller, Goethe, Hölderlin, and Hegel were all writing in contemporary German. Kant, in particular, was interested in reaching a general public, which he did in numerous articles written for national edification.

At the outset of *Fantom of the Other*, Derrida returns to the question he began thinking about in the lecture course on Descartes, namely, whether or not writing philosophy in the vernacular is inherently a species of philosophical nationalism. In *Fantom* this inquiry is historically progressed to far more recent times. Although aimed mainly in the direction of Martin Heidegger, Derrida has Fichte and Kant in mind, who as German Idealist thinkers had cosmopolitan aspirations, something that contrasts implicitly with Heidegger who openly displayed a conservative provincialism that has been roundly criticized by liberal, cosmopolitan academics. From the point of view of Derrida's course, such criticism is problematic because one cannot avoid the fact that Western philosophy is riddled with philosophical nationalism and often of the most unpalatable kinds. Even writing in Latin would represent a philosophical nationalism, one attached to some notion of political and/or spiritual identification with Roman civilization, its imperialist tendencies included, that many European nations appropriated into their cultures and politics: often by way of the arts and letters, by way of imitating or appropriating aspects of Roman law, or by way of allying with an ideology of cultural superiority and imperial power and right.

At the outset of *Fantom*, in the first lecture, Derrida states that his major concern is principally of idiom, its philosophical translation, if not idiom as a national trait. Perhaps with *Language and the Discourse of Method* still in mind, Derrida tells us that he wants to investigate "the aporias of the philosophical translation of philosophical idioms."[7] Notable is that "there are *several* philosophical idioms" and that the experience of them "cannot not be lived by a philosopher, by a self-styled philosopher, by whoever claims to be a philosopher, as both a *scandal* and as the very *chance* of philosophy."[8] In other words, there is something unpredictable about idioms, both in terms of how they may crop up more or less by chance and in terms of their resistance to translatability. Hence the scandal of idiomaticity as something irrational or unaccountable and yet most fitting and logical. "A scandal: i.e. what makes philosophy trip and fall, what stops it in its tracks if the self-styled philosopher considers that philosophy is essentially universal and cosmopolitan, that national, social, idiomatic difference in general should only befall it as a provisional and non-essential accident that could be overcome."[9] From the perspective of the universalization of philosophical discourse, which is to say, of philosophy itself, idiomaticity is a scandal; however, it is also a chance or opportunity "in so far as the only possibility for a philosophy, for philosophy itself to speak itself, to be discussed, to get (itself) across, to go from the one to the other, is to pass through idioms, to transport the idiom and transport itself, translate itself via or rather in the body of idioms which are not closures or enclosings of self but allocutions, passages to the other."[10]

But, Derrida asks, what is an idiom? Not restricted to language,

> I shall be taking "idiom" in a much more indeterminate sense, that of prop(ri)e(r)ty, singular feature, in principle inimitable and inexpropriable. The *idiom* is the proper. And given this, if I say that my most proper concern in this seminar is idiomatic difference in philosophy, it is nonetheless not entirely in an accessory or absent-minded manner that I chose for its title, "Philosophical nationality and nationalism."[11]

Not just the definition of idiom in general is in question but that of "what is a national idiom in philosophy?" Hence "how does a philosophical idiom pose itself, claim its rights, appear to itself, attempt to impose itself as a national idiom?"[12] Immediately, Derrida jumps ahead into asking about what a nation is, a question that is hard to delimit, since "it is to be confused neither with the question of people, nor that of race, nor that of State" even if these topics have to be of concern to the overarching question at hand and give "rise to the most serious equivocations." Moreover, Derrida specifies that in the past and the present we have to be aware of philosophical discourses about nationality, "discourses which claim to recognize national philosophical characteristics, in oneself or in others, sometimes to praise them, sometimes to discredit them. This national idiom may or may not be linked by those who speak of it, to a given language."[13] That said, *Fantom of the Other* is, in fact, very much about idiom in the context of language, something that is most pronounced, perhaps, in lectures six to thirteen on Heidegger and *Geschlecht*. What Derrida calls his "principal concern" with "philosophical idiom or translatability, and immediately afterwards the link of that idiom to a national characteristic" is very much mediated by how this concern (or question, as Derrida also calls it) "is set out in language, in an idiom, and with certain features of the national idiom." He continues by saying that philosophical nationality and nationalism concern everyone today and that in the past they have "always occupied all philosophers."[14]

A trajectory that Derrida appears to have had an interest in opening up is that of the Anglo-American versus Continental European philosophical divides characterized most generally in terms of communications and exchanges between "territories, institutions, groups, and schools," all of which have their own idioms, if not national limits or nationalistic claims.[15] "Exchanges, meetings, so-called philosophical communication … exposes the at least supposed national differences to influences, grafts, deformations, hybridizations," all of which encounter interests in national identity and consciousness. Such exchanges amount to "a sort of state of war, a war in the course of which, as in all wars, you see the enemy everywhere, and the collaborator, the enemy within, the one who in France likes German philosophy too much, who in the USA is over-impressed by French philosophy, or in Britain by Continental philosophy."[16] Later in this course, Derrida will consider Alexis de Tocqueville's comparison of French philosophy to American philosophic method.

Paradoxically, scholarly exchanges, colloquia, activities of translation, and instruments of archivization and collection require the recognition of national boundaries of whatever sort even as such relays of exchange presume universal unboundedness. The conviction among many philosophers and academics that idioms are an infelicitous distraction is more or less underscored by the speed with which information is transmitted across national borders today, between different groups, institutions, and so on, as if national idioms weren't relevant or significant. Given the sheer number of colloquia, translations, and other intellectual exchanges, Derrida says one easily loses sight of the effects of opacity, of national limits, though paradoxically the intensification of such exchanges actually bring out national identities and differences in terms of hybridizations, transpositions, imitation, and so on. Thus intellectual exchange across borders doesn't eradicate national affirmation and assertion. Indeed, in this and subsequent courses, national self-assertion and affirmation (a core preoccupation of Heidegger's in the 1930s) will become one of Derrida's major themes. Heidegger's reading of Trakl, which Derrida will engage, instantiates it, though from a highly deconstructed point of view.[17]

Derrida notes that each national territory attempts to awaken a national philosophical fiber, to "reconstitute the right tradition, reevaluate the corpus and the national heritage"; in the case of Japan, the identification of deconstruction with "what Zen thinking, and especially that of Master Dōgen, developed centuries ago."[18] In China, post-structuralism and deconstruction align with this or that national Chinese tradition. However, these demonstrations, Derrida says, are both convincing and without any pertinence, truthful and blind to their own presuppositions.

It would be of interest, Derrida quips, to make an international chart or map of different philosophical situations, though not in order to plant little national flags, since this is how people categorize schools and thinkers. Instead one should analyze what are called trajectories of influence, implantations, rejections of transplants, the fronts, with all the institutional phenomena, academic or not, of all the *political* stakes as they have cropped up.[19] In other words, Derrida is asking about philosophy in its most cosmopolitan context as a globalized discipline, on the one hand, and as a localized set of practices, concerns, issues, on the other, in terms of which differences, some quite acute, manifest themselves as a matter of political agreement and/or contestation at times bordering on conflict, or what he calls war. Hence, what are "the philosophical and extra philosophical" conditions for the reception of "a certain French theoretical discourse" in the United States or United Kingdom versus the reception of Anglo-American thinking in, say, France? What happens when the development, transformation, and distinguishing features of thought are dissociated from their original, national tongue and stripped of their national identity, or is that even possible? How is, say, the reception of French philosophy, received in Britain vis-à-vis the United States? Consider, Derrida implores, how the intensification of international exchanges exasperate identities, among them, national identifications. Recall that *Geschlecht*, though not mentioned as yet here, means, among other things, kind, type, or genus. It does not take much imagination to realize that at issue from the outset are *types* of philosophy or theoretical approaches, which have their corollary in the rather vast literature of establishing types of peoples according to nationalist traits (hence the talk earlier about "little flags"). Consider those who think that "analytical philosophy" is somehow inherently Anglo-Saxon or American or a combination of both.

Such philosophical nationalism rests on an uncritical sort of naturalism that Derrida investigated in *Of Grammatology* in the context of Rousseau on the origin of language. In a question that is extremely germane to *Fantom*, Derrida asks in *Of Grammatology*: "How does the place of origin of a language immediately mark the difference proper to the language? What is here the privilege of the place?"[20] In *Fantom*, Fichte's addresses to the Germans speak to this privilege of place as does Heidegger's reading of Trakl. Of course, the metaphysics of an appeal to place (in Heidegger it's "deconstructed" presumably) as the source for national attributes such as character, language, and philosophical temperament is a philosopheme foundational to Western philosophical thinking. In fact, this philosopheme occurs even in academic communities that are as hostile to metaphysics as the analytical philosophers. Recall that in 1992, a certain cultural-nationalist hostility to French philosophy broke out in a decision by analytical philosophers in the United Kingdom, United States, and Australia to petition Cambridge University to not give Derrida an honorary doctorate, given that as privileged site of British philosophizing stemming from the thirteenth century, it was unthinkable to award Derrida, a Frenchman, with supposedly heretical Continental ideas and methods, an honorary PhD in *England*.[21]

In *Fantom* Derrida begins to knit together some Franco-American relations, for example, in the later lecture on Alexis de Tocqueville. But he also alludes to the reception of deconstruction by analytical philosophers, something that seems to have an afterlife in the interview given during the same year *Fantom* was delivered. In "Deconstruction in America," Derrida says that "deconstruction is first of all an American phenomenon and that it is perceived in Europe as such."[22] This introduces the paradox that someone who has been strongly identified in America as a French thinker (someone foreign to American traditions of thought) is, in fact, more American than the Americans who famously have resisted and excoriated deconstruction and who therefore improbably resemble those French intellectuals who want nothing to do with Derrida and deconstruction. Yet, who can realistically say that Derrida is not a French thinker, not only on account of being a French national, but given the incredible importance that French language and culture have in his work? If deconstruction is more American than French, this is flatly contradicted by the idiomaticity of his writings insofar as they resist translation out of French, a resistance that refuses cosmopolitanism.

What are we to make, then, of the fact that as intellectual globe-trotter Derrida had performed deconstruction across national boundaries, traditions, receptions, and idioms? Should that not have inflected, grafted, ignored, and distorted deconstruction? But in such a cosmopolitan context could complaints (even by Derrida himself) about the distortion, perversion, or the misrepresentation of deconstruction even hold up, given the vast cultural and linguistic gaps, among much else? In other words, what would it mean "to read" or "receive" Derrida (and by extension deconstruction) as a Japanese, a Moroccan, a Jordanian, a Finn, and so on? Should one's national identity matter? Can it *not* matter? Many philosophers, and logicians in particular, reject that national-cultural determinations should have anything to do with philosophy, given that philosophy is considered in essence to be a cosmopolitan or universalizing phenomenon that would override idiomaticity, untranslatability, and cultural, religious, and national differences. However, it is precisely the overriding of such differences that Derrida, an exemplar of cosmopolitan cross-trafficking, calls into question.

Fichte and National Identity

Having raised the nationalism-cosmopolitanism distinction, Derrida asks what national identity is and what the essence of a nation is, if in fact this exists.

> What is the history of the concept of national identity as such? [...] When did this start? What is specific to our present day? What difference is there between what is happening today in this regard and what happened in the Seventeenth Century (and even before the Seventeenth Century), then in the Eighteenth and Nineteenth Centuries, in the Twentieth Century before and after the two World Wars, etc?[23]

All serious philosophers, Derrida says, presume the question of national identity is inseparable from the destiny of philosophy. In later courses, such as *Mythos, Logos, Topos* (1985–86) and *The Theological-Political* (1986–87), Derrida will consider the beginnings of philosophy in terms of national identity by considering ancient Athens and parts of the Old Testament (e.g., Samuel 1:8). In *Fantom*, however, Derrida interrogates Fichte's *Addresses to the German*

People in which we read that the German nation and the German people are identical, as if all these people belonged to *ein Geschlecht* (one kind), a people of one kind or race that thought along the same lines, spoke the same language, and shared the same ancestry. The idea that a nation is the self-assertion of one people that has the right to formally establish borders and a state apparatus whose purpose is to preserve the nation and the well-being of the people who make it up is an assumption that Derrida questions insofar as Fichte's Germans are and aren't actually one *Geschlecht* or homogeneous people related by blood, kinship, and ancestry. Fichte is quite aware of this, given that he defines the Germans as a fundamentally diverse social group that is the effect of the language that has constituted them over centuries as a distinct people. That is, long before Heidegger and Claude Levi-Strauss, Fichte advanced the thesis that *Die Sprache spricht*: that man doesn't speak language but that language speaks man. It is on account of a common language that people become akin as well as kin, which over time has biologistic (i.e., ethnic-racial) consequences. As will become clear in Derrida's later courses in the 1980s, though it is already marked in *Fantom*, there is an inquiry into *ein Geschlecht* (a phrase pertinent to Fichte, but later to Trakl and Heidegger as well) vis-à-vis the Jews, many of whom had been assimilating into German society during Fichte's lifetime and some of whom spoke German as fluently and flawlessly as any of the most well-educated non-Jewish Germans. But were these Jews Germans or not? This question is taken up somewhat obliquely in *Fantom* when Derrida turns to discussion of Adorno, Arendt, and Friedrich Schlegel (with respect to his relation to his spouse Dorothea Mendelssohn) though Derrida will tackle it far more directly in years to come, for example in 1986–87 in the course *Kant, the Jew, the German*. In *Fantom of the Other* Derrida will consider Jewish figures in a way that intentionally or not lays the groundwork for later courses by discussing the Jewish intellectual's relationship to the national-cosmopolitan distinction in the context of exile. One day, in his own address to the Germans upon receiving the Adorno Prize, Derrida will cite Adorno's *Minima Moralia* relative to this point. "German words of foreign derivation are the Jews of language."[24]

In picking up his remarks on Fichte from the first lecture at a later date, Derrida mentions a group of auditors as "our German friends" who had approached him with what concerns he doesn't say, though he says publicly that it has never been his intention to reassure, appease, or calm (*apaiser*) anyone when it comes to "speaking of old demons," the word demons having been replaced and/or supplemented in the typescript by the word specters. We should remember that in 1984–85 there was a huge resurgence in Germany of a return to expressionist painting where the specters of Nazism were on full display, for example, in Georg Immendorf's *Café Deutschland* series and Anselm Kiefer's depictions of Hitler's killing fields. In fact, this had been under way already in the 1970s. Certainly for culturally informed German listeners, it would have been impossible not to contextualize Derrida's recollection of Nazi specters with those appearing in the arts in Germany during that moment. Whatever the case, Derrida himself has nothing to say about the contemporary cultural situation with respect to the past in the two Germanies—their double scenes of readings—though, like the German expressionists of that time, he had no interest in appeasing those who would prefer to keep silent about the past.

In starting out his detailed commentary on Fichte in the first lecture, Derrida remarks that "Fichte's infamous (*fameux*) *Addresses to the German Nation*, to which we shall return often and at length, wants to be both nationalistic, patriotic and cosmopolitan, universalistic. It essentializes Germanity to the point of making it an entity bearing the universal and the philosophical as such."[25] Well known is that the rhetoric of *Addresses to the German People* appealed to the National Socialists, for example, in terms of making an alliance of spirit with a people who are given a national identity. Fichte's text, therefore, recalls a certain political spectrality or revenance by means of how it was appropriated by Nazism. However, the text is important for Derrida, because contrary to what one might presuppose, Fichte wanted to combat the metaphysics of nationalist mythologizing for the sake of a universal, cosmopolitan philosophy, albeit one that relates to "*Germanité*." Fichte, according to Derrida, ostensibly repudiates spectrality (ancestral metaphysics) by means of speaking to a certain modernity, promoted by Enlightenment liberals, who imagined that what we call the national should reach a stage when it participates in and even turns into the international, hence abandoning notions of national spirit and the spiritualism (the hauntology) upon which it is based. Whereas Derrida doesn't go so far as to make the argument that Fichte was attempting to deconstruct the difference between the national and the international, Derrida is nevertheless interested in showing the vicissitudes of this division.[26] As he argues, Fichte welcomes a humanist cosmopolitanism that denies the exceptionalist metaphysical rhetorics of nationalism in order to push beyond them while nevertheless retroactively making the claim that such cosmopolitan liberalism was inherently embedded in the national character of the German people.

Paradoxically, in their most authentic and essential German character, the German people were supposedly always already cosmopolitan, a world-people with a world culture that should lead the way for others to follow on the path to globalization. Later we will see that for German socialists, this translated into the view that the German people, of all national peoples, have a collective or socialist sensibility that puts them in the international vanguard as a nation that should lead all nations to embrace a hitherto unknown dimension of fraternal internationalism. For Derrida the structural anomaly upon which exceptionalist rhetorics of international leadership rest concerns the contradiction that a certain national character—upon which one could put a label, such as German or French—is precisely what makes one most suitable as a cosmopolitan social subject who should guide people of other nationalities (hence the philosopheme of *führung*). Paradoxically, universality inheres in one's particularity, even one's national spirit.

Derrida doesn't mention it (he assumes auditors have read the text), but Fichte actively appeals to specters in the *Addresses* when he asks listeners to:

> Imagine [*Denket*] that in my voice are mingled the voices of your ancestors from the grey and distant past [*aus der grauen Vorwelt*], who with their own bodies stemmed the tide of Roman world dominion, who won with their own blood the independence of those mountains, plains and streams which under your charge have become the spoils of strangers. They call out to you: represent us, pass on our memory as honorably and blamelessly to future ages as it has come down to you, and as you have gloried in it and in your descent from us![27]

Obvious is that a metaphysics of revenance paradoxically counterpoints the enlightenment rhetoric of cosmopolitanism and appeals to humanity generally, given that a nation is being called and convoked by the specters of ancestors, the fantoms of the others. "If our race (*Geschlecht*) terminates with you [Germans], then our honor is turned to shame (*Gehet mit euch unser* Geschlecht *aus, so verwandelt sich unsere Ehre in Schimpf*)."[28] In such passages the ghosts of *German* ancestors are mingling their voices with Fichte, who like a good mystagogue has brought back spirits of the dead.[29] In the context of the George Circle a century later, such relations of voice, nation, and *Geschlecht* point to a secret and hidden Germany, a fantom nation that Fichte appeared to be calling forth in the *Addresses*.

Gregory Moore, who introduces his English translation of the Cambridge edition of Fichte's *Address*, helpfully clarifies the reason why someone might imagine a hidden, spectral Germany, given the geopolitical situation that Fichte confronted.

> When [Fichte] delivered the *Addresses*, "Germany" did not exist as anything more than a vague geographical expression. There was no unitary German state. Nor

was it by any means clear—even to the inhabitants of central Europe—whether there was such a thing as a "German nation." How would one define its properties? What did it mean to be "German"? [...] In 1808 "Germany" referred to a collection of forty-one separate territories: Prussia, Austria and the various members of the Confederation of the Rhine, who owed their allegiance, and in some cases their crowns, to France. Even this was a great simplification of the situation prevailing at the close of the eighteenth century, before the revolutionary wars and Napoleon's redrawing of the map of *Mitteleuropa* ... Hundreds of duodecimo states, free cities and ecclesiastical possessions were scattered across the landscape in bewildering profusion.[30]

A similar account is given by Robert E. Norton in his *Secret Germany* that speaks more directly to the politics of the revenant.

During the first three quarters of the nineteenth century, when the German-speaking-lands were the only ones among the other major European states not to have been formed into a single nation, there was no "Germany" except as an abstraction or a distant historical memory. For many German-speaking writers, whose national yearnings were unfulfilled by political reality, the only option had been to imagine a unity on some other plane. From Hölderlin to Schiller to Hebbel and Heine ... one encounters repeated invocations of a "hidden," "anonymous," "spiritual" Germany that would one day emerge and take its rightful place in the world.[31]

A hidden or secret Germany, then, is in essence a spectral Germany, a place that exists in a metaphysical state of concealment and withdrawal, to use Heidegger's vocabulary. In German the word *Ge-heim* (secret) contains the word "home," which can be considered one's proper or essential place, one's spiritual or metaphysical domain. In *The Black Notebooks*, which Derrida obviously couldn't have known in the 1980s, Heidegger invokes national spectrality when he says that "We will remain in the invisible front of the secret spiritual Germany." This Germany is "the secret site of what is coming," a "new grounding."[32] Such a Germany is the fantom of an other Germany, latent in what is present to hand, that is spiritual (spectral) and immanent. In Heidegger's essay on Trakl, "Die Sprache im Gedicht," what is to come is also a secret and spiritual place of a new grounding, though whether this is Germany or Europe more generally is kept in ambiguity, not that Heidegger wouldn't think of the two together. In this context, the overlapping of Germany with Europe or even the West (*das Abendland*) recalls something of the nationalism-cosmopolitanism division in Fichte whereby it is the German who is in the vanguard as cosmopolitan (i.e., Western) subject. Both Heidegger and Fichte, moreover, have in common that they bridge this national-cosmopolitan divide by means of an appeal to a rhetoric of spirit (*Geist*). In fact, Derrida makes this point explicitly in the short book that borrowed from the *Fantom* course, *Of Spirit*.

> In his *Address to the German Nation* [Fichte says that]: he who thinks and thus wishes for "spirituality" in its freedom and in its "eternal progress," is German, he is one of us [*ist unsers Geschlechts*], whatever he was born and whatever language he speaks. Conversely, he who does not think and does not wish for such a "spirituality," even if he was born German and seems to speak German, even if he has so-called linguistic competence in German, "he is non-German and foreign for us [*undeutsch und fremd für uns*]," and it is to be wished that he separate himself from us totally.[33]

Geist refers to both mind and spirit, the idea that one has to be of one mind with the Germans, and hence spiritually connected, in order to be a German, never mind one's birthplace or ethnicity. In short, it is by means of spirit that one is kin, that a Frenchman could be more German than French without having been born and raised in Germany. But if that is so, Derrida wonders, to what does the German correspond if one is speaking of spirit in the absence of place, kith, and kin? To what does the German correspond if he or she speaks "whatever language"? What would the correspondence with spirit be precisely?

To restate the central point above, Fichte establishes spirit as a chief philosopheme of philosophical nationalism whereby the national and the cosmopolitan are brought into relation even as he detaches spirit from place in such a way that the Frenchman can be more German than the German living in Germany. In asking to what spirit the German corresponds in the absence of place, kith, and kin, Derrida cites Heidegger's reading of Hölderlin whereby "*Geist* is the unconditioned absolute which determines and *gathers* every entity."[34] Inasmuch as it gathers, *Geist* is thought itself (thus, *geistig*). "As thinking the essential, it gathers—which it does by *thinking itself*, thus finding itself at home, *close up to itself* (*zu Hauss*)."[35] Such thinking is gathered by spirit into community, according to Hölderlin. Does this mean that in order to be German that one has to find oneself at home by means of a thinking that "gathers into community," whatever is meant by this? Fichte is not nearly this abstract, but in his address he too is thinking about affinity of mind (what Heidegger sometimes calls attunement [*Stimmung*]), a sense of being at home, a correspondence with community, all of which might be reductively called "thinking alike," though in some elevated sense of identification.

In both Fichte and Heidegger, then, one encounters what appears to be a *disembodied nationalism* that takes distance from the usual identitarian politics that concerns racial stock, national character, territorial homeland, cultural tradition, and language. In *Ponderings II–VI* (of the *Black Notebooks*), we can now see, in a way that Derrida could not, this rather disembodied nationalism in terms of Heidegger's many attempts to distance himself from the grotesque conceptual reductivity of everyday National Socialism by invoking what he calls a "spiritual National Socialism."³⁶ "No spiritual world arises overnight and to order," Heidegger writes. "But we must not fail to work toward the advent of such a world by creating the transition to it: therefore now: by criticizing most sharply the current circumstances." This critical rejection would comprise "an actual rebellion that does not end in slogans and abusive language."³⁷ Presumably a critical rebellion would be one that does not fall into nationalistic jingoism and physical violence even as it brings about, through proper education and contemplation, a spiritual transformation of what it means to belong or correspond that transcends *Volkstum* (ethnicity).³⁸

Nevertheless, running alongside and contrary to such disembodied nationalism is Heidegger's insistence upon considering the Germans as a people who are required historically to struggle over their essence (*Wesen*). Derrida considers this more than once in the 1980s in the context of Heidegger's *Introduction to Metaphysics* in which an instrumentalized worldview is condemned in light of German *Wesen*. For Heidegger, the Germans had a desperate need, if only they could perceive it, to confront the eclipse of being by modernity ushered in by the Soviets, the Americans, and (withheld in print at the time) the Jews (accused of the worst ills of modernity in *The Black Notebooks*). As Heidegger put it in 1939, the "transformation of the human being [he means, the *German*] from subject to the grounder and steward of Da-sein is the necessity of *Seyn* (Beyng) itself."³⁹ However, here too one can see a resistance to the kind of crude political nationalist metaphysics of the Nazis, because for Heidegger the "steward of Da-sein" is the antithesis to the Cartesian subject as egotistical self. What elsewhere Heidegger calls "critical rebellion" is a thinking of Being by way of withdrawing selfhood as a precondition for such meditation. "The goal is always meditation—the self-transposing of humanity into the domain of the truth of *Seyn* [the endlessly deferred trait of what is to be, the step back from being as being-present]."⁴⁰ That this transformation repudiates racism is key, in this particular context, given that for Heidegger the Cartesian subject, which Heidegger invokes as *subjectum*, is objectionable insofar as it is merely something "present at hand." Unacceptable would be "if this [*subjectum*] that is present-at-hand is understood 'biologically,' and if the biological is 'concentrated' only on blood as what is genuinely present-at-hand, and if this ... becomes the genuine bearer of heredity and of 'history.'"⁴¹

Here, as in Fichte, racism has to be rejected as the ground for deciding the fate of the German people vis-à-vis its Being, since this is a matter of what we today would call "biopower," which from the Heideggerian perspective is a brutal technological means of interfering with being without any ability to think or know what being is apart from objects to be prejudicially discriminated among and acted upon.

The point of briefly supplementing *Fantom* by way of the *Black Notebooks* is to show the accuracy of Derrida's analysis (his evidence is taken from Heidegger's "Letter on Humanism") whereby the makeup of philosophical nationalism includes anti-nationalist convictions, which in the case of Heidegger bears on questions of ontology (or political ontology, if one prefers). In Fichte's *Addresses* this bears on questions of European enlightenment and cosmopolitanism. In the course *The Theological-Political*, Derrida will analyze Spinoza's theology from a similar point of view wherein Spinoza's analysis of the ancient nation of Israel is focalized from an anti-nationalist point of view, given that in Spinoza's estimation God in the *Old Testament* is conflicted about establishing/destroying the nation of Israel.

Problematic for Derrida with respect to nationalism-cosmopolitanism is that wherever one looks, one finds that the logic of philosophical nationalism requires the invocation of philosophemes that serve to establish the essence of a national people while making claims for that people's universal humanity and hence brotherhood with other peoples. As we have noticed, Fichte had found such a philosopheme in the word spirit (*Geist*), a word that as Derrida explains in *Of Spirit* Heidegger would repudiate in *Being and Time* and then re-appropriate in later writings. As a direct offshoot of *Fantom*'s concern with nationalism-cosmopolitanism, *Of Spirit* explores the philosopheme of *Geist* as a German national idiom (on the order of *Geschlecht*) that awkwardly negotiates the particular with the universal, the national with the anti-national, the internal with the external, the native with the exile. However, if spirit is a chief philosopheme of asserting and negating national circumscription, so are the philosophemes of fraternity (of which Hannah Arendt is critical), and language (insofar as a national language is at once deemed local and global, particular and universal). Notions such as civilization, Enlightenment, humanity, rights, culture, and the West may well function similarly.

In order to point out the extent to which *Geist* (spirit) both particularizes and universalizes, Derrida quotes Fichte.

> Those who believe in spirituality and in the freedom of this spirituality, who desire the eternal progress of this spirituality through freedom—wherever they

were born and whichever language they speak—are of our race (*Geschlecht*), they belong to us and they will join with us.[42]

Here the word *Geschlecht* doesn't refer to race in any concrete or physical sense, but to kind or type in an abstract, metaphysical sense, given what is called "the freedom of spirituality (*Geistigkeit*)." Along these lines Fichte will say, "German philosophy raises itself truly and by the act of its thinking ... to the immutable 'more than all infinity' and finds true being in this alone."[43] German philosophy can do so only because of its *Geistlichkeit*, its spirituality, to which all philosophically inclined people are going to be necessarily drawn, hence this philosophy's inherent or essential universalism and cosmopolitanism. In this context, both *Geistlichkeit* and *Geschlecht* function as philosophemes that negotiate identity and difference in such a way that mere nationalism, as an isolationism, is overcome in terms of fraternity, universal enlightenment, and a notion of humanity. Of course, the fact that *Geist* and especially *Geschlecht* are specific German idioms that do not translate altogether well reveals the extent to which such philosophemes, however altruistically motivated, resist denationalization. *Geist* remains a shared mentality among locals, the *Einheimische*, a mentality that can't be shared globally. Although Fichte may attempt to open up the word *Geschlecht* so that it refers to all kinds of people who think in a way compatible with a German outlook, it nevertheless refuses to give up its more restricted denotations to race, sex, gender, kin, generation, and kith (friends and neighbors). Identitarianism is always already asserting itself even in instances, as in Fichte's addresses, where attempts are being made to transcend and leave it behind.

Derrida, for his part, stresses that Fichte's "nationalism is essentialist and archeo-teleological enough not to concern any German naturality or factuality—at least not in principle, and philosophically speaking, and that by that very fact, on the other hand, nationalist affirmation is thoroughly philosophical; it becomes merged with the evaluating, hierarchizing evaluation of the best, true philosophy, with the philosophical principle and the philosophical *telos* as such."[44] A nationalism such as this, Derrida remarks, isn't *a* philosophy but *philosophy itself*. These statements pertain to the last paragraphs of Lecture seven of the *Addresses*.

Derrida doesn't say so, but Fichte appeals to a Pauline distinction between the living and the dead, the spirit and the letter. Those who believe in spirituality, as cited in Fichte above, are of our kind or race. Those who believe in stagnation and who go round and round in circles, "who even set a dead nature at the helm of world government ... are un-German and strangers to us, and the sooner they completely sever their ties with us the better."⁴⁵ Slightly earlier, Fichte condemned those who "resign themselves to being secondary and derivative," who are merely "an appendage to life" and who are "an echo resounding from the cliff-face, an echo of a voice that has already fallen silent; they are, viewed as a people, outside the original people and strangers and foreigners unto it."⁴⁶ From a Hitlerian point of view, those who are derivative and are aware of it, moreover, are to be identified with the Jews who in *Mein Kampf* are excoriated for being unoriginal and as such inauthentic, crassly imitative, parasitical, and hence dangerous to the Germans who are viewed as creative, spiritual, and modern. What Fichte identifies as stagnation, retrogression, and circularity (blind repetition) would from the National Socialist perspective characterize the Jews whose religion represents an adherence to the past and what is archaic. This way of reading Fichte is left unremarked by Derrida, who doesn't identify dead philosophy with any social body but merely cites Fichte in the abstract as talking about a dead man who "has nonetheless to be diverted, prevented from causing harm." Derrida continues that according to Fichte "we must prevent the doleful return of the dead who can still—for the dead still have some power—*verdrehen die Worte*, falsify words, divert them from their meaning, twist them, pervert them, corrupt them in the shadow, in the shadow of death, which is shadow of nothing, the shadow of the shadow of a shadow, as Fichte calls it."⁴⁷ Here reference to the dead is ambiguous if one considers it from a Pauline point of view, because in that context the dead are not those who are literally dead (though that might well cross our minds) but those who are spiritually unenlightened and, as Fichte points out, as well, uneducated or, if not quite that, not sufficiently or properly educated. Such people can twist words around because they have no proper understanding of them and cannot be led into the light. Literal death, however, seems to be meant as well when Fichte writes that "all stable existence that does not appear as spiritual life is only an empty shadow cast from the domain of sight, a shadow multiply mediated by nothingness."⁴⁸ Rather than citing this passage, Derrida seizes upon Fichte's association of death with a philosophy of nature. "The philosophy of Being as philosophy of nature (in opposition to the philosophy of spirit and therefore life) is a philosophy of death, and therefore, as philosophy of nature, a denaturation of life." However, Derrida wonders what would transpire in the gap between life and death. "Between life and death, nationalism has as its own proper space the experience of haunting. There is no nationalism without some ghost."⁴⁹ Derrida doesn't elaborate, turning instead to a consideration of language in the *Addresses* that for Fichte implicitly must hold open a space for hauntology. "One may speak this essential German, this philosophical, philosophy-of-life German without speaking what is commonly called the German language; and conversely a German linguistic subject may not speak this essential German and speak, in German, a philosophy of death that is essentially foreign to the essential German."[50] That is, even if one isn't speaking German per se, one may well be speaking it spiritually or in spirit—in a way that is *geistlich* (spiritual but also ghostly). Conversely, the German speaker may well be speaking the language properly and yet be speaking something alien or foreign that is dead (as if the German were haunted or possessed by something dead). Derrida notes that for Fichte, "Germanity is not even linguistic … for this essence of the national language is defined by philosophy, as philosophy of spirit and life."[51] This, we are told, gives the word "German" a cosmopolitan meaning.

Derrida concludes this section of the first lecture in *Fantom* by saying that in Fichte:

> The equivocality of the signs, the heritages, the historical junctions, depends, among other things, on the following fact, which has not escaped you: this essentially philosophical nationalism (as I believe every nationalism is philosophical, and this is the main point I wanted to emphasize at the outset) claims to be totally foreign to any naturalism, biologism, racism, or even ethnocentrism—it does not even want to be a political nationalism, a doctrine of the Nation-State. It is, further, a cosmopolitanism, often associated with a democratic and republican politics, a progressivism, etc. But you can see quite clearly that everything that ought thus to withdraw it from reappropriation into a Nazi heritage (which is biologistic, racist, etc.) remains in essence equivocal. It is in the name of a philosophy of life (even if it is a spiritual life) that it sets itself apart from naturalizing biologism. And it is perhaps of the essence of every nationalism to be philosophical, to present itself as a universal philosophy … to sublate its philosophy of life into a philosophy of the life and of the spirit—and as for cosmopolitanism, this is a fearfully ambiguous value: it can be annexionist and expansionist, and combat in the name of nationalism the enemies within, the false Germans.

Reference to false Germans alludes to the Jews who "even though they speak German, are Germans living on the German soil, are essentially less authentically German than certain 'foreigners' who, etc."[52] Unremarked, however, is the overlap in Fichte of a Pauline conception of spiritual life and death that is onto-theologically critical of the Jews, a Christian onto-theology that F. Schlegel will operationalize in his remarks to Dorothea, discussed by Derrida in lecture five, and that in the lectures on "Die Sprache im Gedicht" will be shown to be rejected by Heidegger. However, we shouldn't lose sight of the fact that in this first lecture, spirit is being posited as a bridge between the national and the cosmopolitan, one that equivocates considerably and, as Derrida puts it, dangerously. This equivocation between the national and the cosmopolitan is apparently the pragmatic function of spirit as a philosopheme, one that is everywhere assumed by Derrida rather than stated by way of categorical reification.

Nationalism, Cosmopolitanism, and *The German Ideology*

Having explored Fichte, Derrida announces that he will situate "two other indices" that punctuate this history. "I shall not speak of Nietzsche to whom we shall also devote long developments, for he was inexhaustible on this subject. I shall speak of Marx and Adorno."[53] In fact, these long developments on Nietzsche will not transpire in *Fantom*. Regarding Marx, Derrida says that he was "one of the first, perhaps *the* first, to suspect lucidly what I have just called national-philosophism: i.e. the claim laid by one country or nation to the privilege of 'representing,' 'embodying,' 'identifying with' the universal essence of man, the thought of which is supposedly produced in some way in the philosophy of that people or that nation."[54] In the second lecture of *Fantom*, Derrida takes forward the thesis on *esprit* (or *Geist*) as vexed national-international borderline by pointing out that for socialists of the early nineteenth century, of whom Marx is sarcastically skeptical, *esprit* concerns that to which a national philosophizing is raised: the general spirit of mankind or humanity. "Marx ironizes Karl Grün," Derrida says, on account of such a spiritual humanism. Problematic is that if spirit takes to the side of man or humanity writ large in order to transcend a national philosophy, it nevertheless functions to smuggle that national philosophy paradoxically under the cover of cosmopolitanism. Marx, as Derrida indicates above, was alert to this phenomenon, which he details in *The German Ideology*. Notable, of course, is that this is one of the places in Derrida's work where he and Marx closely converge.

Derrida, who wants to cover considerable ground at the risk of being quite cursory at times, does not fill his auditors in on much of the background required to fully appreciate his remarks on Marx and Karl Grün, though he gives everyone a general reference point when he tells them that "Marx denounces the alliance between this [socialist] humanism [of Grün], this humanist teleology and a philosophical nationalism which confers on German philosophy a mission in which it cannot be replaced, the mission of thinking and realizing the essence of man."[55]

An attentive reader of the course has to ask, no doubt, whether Heidegger's writings on *Dasein* can be entirely excluded from this critique, since it should be obvious that to some extent "*Dasein-analyse*" is also a manner of "thinking and realizing the essence of man" that in *Being and Time* could be considered universalizing, whereas in the writings on metaphysics and Friedrich Hölderlin this is narrowed to a meditation on *German Dasein*.

Derrida expects one to know that the main thesis of Marx and Engels' *The German Ideology* is that German thinkers are idealists who begin philosophizing by imagining the essence of man and positing various historical fantasies that will account for man's development. In contrast, *The German Ideology* avoids a consideration of man as a being thrown into the world with an inherent capacity for hermeneutical cogitation; rather, it posits man as the consequence of forces of production with an a priori material history. Hence there is no "man" as such that preexists in some trans-historical sense as a given with inherent, unique properties that are identical to themselves, no transcendental "human condition" as such. As Marx and Engels put it, man doesn't simply *have life*; rather, *he has to live*. This means physically apprehending the world, for example, with one's hands in order to bring about the conditions for feeding oneself and others. If one sees that fish are plentiful in the river, one does not withdraw into fascination, one catches the fish by hand or by means of a tool. In cooperating with others in order to catch or gather food, one enters into a social relationship based on *material* production: as in catching, preparing, distributing food. Whatever we call man is defined retroactively in the context of such material/social production, however simple or advanced. Language too isn't a thing in itself, but what Marx and Engels call "practical consciousness" that exists largely *for* other men. According to Marx and Engels, the ideas and concepts of human beings are "the direct efflux of their *material* behavior," not disembodied contemplation.[56]

In mocking the German socialists, Marx says that they "detach the consciousness of certain historically conditioned spheres of life ... and evaluate [such consciousness] in terms of true, absolute, i.e., German philosophical consciousness."[57] Because ideas are divorced from material, productive existence, these idealists traffic in an "ology" of ideas (hence idea-ology) that Marx calls fantastical and spectral. That is, they traffic in "some fantastic relationship with the help of the 'absolute.'"[58] He could just as easily have substituted the word "spirit" for "absolute," in this case, because words such as "spirit" and "absolute" pertain to an idealist mode of thinking that by its very nature transcends the limits of anything concrete and thereby can traffic in universals that depoliticize and consequently denationalize human relations for the sake of establishing humanity as a supervening category, one that elevates itself above ethnic, racial, and national identities.

Relevant to Derrida's interest in the national versus the cosmopolitan is Marx's critique of the socialism of his day as a hybrid and as a translation, both nationally and philosophically. "This translation of French ideas into the language of the German ideologists and this arbitrarily constructed relationship between communism and German ideology, then, constitute so-called 'true socialism,' which is loudly proclaimed, in the terms used by the Tories for the English constitution, to be 'the pride of the nation and the envy of all neighboring nations.'"[59] There is a transfiguration, Marx says, of French and English understandings of proletarian communism "within the heaven of the German mind and ... the German sentiment."[60] This speaks not just to Derrida's concern with nationalism and cosmopolitanism, but of a cosmopolitanism that is affirmed and celebrated by means of a certain national chauvinism that Marx identifies not with politics but with philosophy (e.g., German *ideology*) whose *philosophemes* include "the thinking mind," "man," "free activity," "pleasure," "social instinct," "the scientific," and "humanism," among various other expressions scattered throughout the writings of Karl Grün, Moses Hess, Étienne Cabet, Ludwig Feuerbach, Hermann Semmig, Max Stirner, and Bruno Bauer.

For Derrida the filiation of these thinkers with Fichte's *Addresses to the German People* is very noticeable, not that Fichte could be construed as a socialist thinker, merely an idealist one who shares the vision of the advent of a new sort of man, one that is both decidedly German in his particularity and yet has a universal if not universalizing dimension. Derrida, of course, is very aware of the deconstructive dimensions of an undecidability that concerns the status of this so-called man, of this paradoxical "nationality of 'man'"[61] that during the Enlightenment period has been arriving on the European scene and who will be followed by other such human advents, Nietzsche's infamous *Übermensch*, among them. Constitutive of the nationality of man is that of human essence which, of course, concerns spirit.

When Marx encounters the intertwining of nationalism with cosmopolitanism on the basis of an appeal to *Geist* as mentality or philosophical aptitude, he finds it ludicrous. Sarcastically, Marx paraphrases Hermann Semmig as follows: "It is true that socialism is French in origin, but the French socialists were '*essentially*' Germans [from a mental (*geistig*) point of view], for which reason the *real* Frenchmen 'did not understand' them."[62] To Marx, this is nonsensical. He mockingly quotes Semmig as follows:

> *Communism* is *French*, *socialism* is *German*; the French are lucky to possess so apt a social instinct, which will serve them one day as a substitute for *scientific investigation*. This result has been determined by the course of development of the two nations; the French arrived at *communism* by way of *politics* ... the Germans arrived at socialism (namely, true socialism) by way of *metaphysics*, which eventually changed into *anthropology*. Ultimately both are resolved in *humanism*.[63]

Rather immediately, Marx seizes on not the peculiarities of national identification and de-identification but Semmig's resolving of communism and socialism into humanism, which Marx views as a Hegelian tactic and, as such, regressive and predictable, given the context of German culture that Marx deems stagnant. "[This] tendency ... was bound to occur in a country so stagnant as Germany," Marx writes, the word "stagnation" being a familiar term associated with the rhetoric of nationalism in the first half of the nineteenth century.[64] Fichte, in his *Addresses*, made the distinction between a living and dead Germany, a Germany of the letter versus one of the spirit, in order to appeal to a liberation from stagnation. The so-called true socialists that Marx mocks are, in fact, closer to Fichte than not in terms of their aspirations for a new man whose purpose is to break with old Germany, the Germany that is not even yet a nation but a group of principalities. Marx, who sees things upside down, takes the view that it is the advent of this new person, so near and dear to the socialists and their German idealist forefathers, Fichte among them, that represents impasse and stultification. What stands in the way of Communism, as Marx and Engels theorize, is the humanist conception of man that represents the class interests of the bourgeoisie, which is why Marx accuses the socialists of being what he calls petty bourgeois.

Derrida doesn't inquire into stagnation, but he notes a string of philosophemes related to it by means of antithesis: movement, development, direction, progress, telos, and futurity (all of which become significant later in analyzing Heidegger on Trakl). Closely related are change, overturning, and revolution, as well as biologically inspired notions related to the concept of life: vitality and rebirth. When Marx addresses this vocabulary in *The German Ideology*, he accuses the sociologists of being men of letters whose vocabulary reflects a "literary sociology," something Derrida calls "purely theoretical writing" detached from social-political experience.[65] The socialists, Marx specifies, are bourgeois fops pretending to be men of action and social change fighting for a better world, one that would be more humanitarian and liberal. The implication is that *literary sociology* is instrumental for cosmopolitanism. For the socialists, it is by way of a literary sensibility that cultural borders are crossed and a narrow-minded nationalism is overcome.

Marx's observation that the French socialists are "essentially Germans," which is why real Frenchmen cannot comprehend them, introduces a logic that inverts identifications while keeping everyone in place. By means of a certain twist, one is and isn't French, is and isn't German, even if, at the same time, one is clearly French and not German. There is, of course, a simpler way to understand this, which is by acknowledging that the German socialists were merely saying to the French socialists, "you're really one of us, you just don't know it yet." But this merely trivializes what is really at stake, a denial of national difference in the midst of its being affirmed, the appeal to a de-nationalization that serves nationalization's interests. If denationalization advances humanism, the declaration of universal rights, and so on, it does so in the interests of a metaphysical national spirit or identity that is assuming a hegemonic leadership role internationally.

In Marx and Engels, nothing is said about race, stock, or gender, and even nation is downplayed, because Marx and Engels are speaking in terms of "world history," or internationalism, by means of which individuals are liberated from the various national and local barriers. Presumably this extricates them from the paradoxes of nationalism-cosmopolitanism which are rooted in hegemonic thinking, for example, the Fichtean idea that the German is inherently cosmopolitan and an ideal representative of humanity. In general, German idealism's positing of "man" as the origin of all philosophical speculation— Fichte's wish to educate and spiritualize German man, to begin by invoking him as ancestral and somehow inherently superior, however much a diamond in the rough—and the idealist's invocation of what Marx and Engels call specters, concepts, bonds, higher being, and scruple are to be considered mere spiritual expressions typical of thinkers who are the product of a division of labor that relegates them to the metaphysics of mental productions (critique, philosophy, culture) in the absence of any connection with material productive forces, say, the mechanical production of cloth or nails.

Marx argues that Karl Grün's intimacy with "human essence" frees him from knowing anything about what could arise from the economic position and the political constellation of a country. Following Marx, Derrida notes that influenced by Moses Hess, Grün merely lines up French with German thought. Hess, after all, led the way by juxtaposing Saint-Simon with Schelling, Fourier with Hegel, Proudhon with Feuerbach. In socialists such as Hermann Semming and Grün, Marx says, "we have had yet further evidence of the narrowly national outlook which underlies the alleged universalism and cosmopolitanism of the Germans." Quoting Heinrich Heine, Marx writes: "The land belongs to the Russians and French,/The English own the sea./But we [Germans] in the airy realm of dreams/Hold sovereign mastery." Marx comments:

> With infinite self-confidence the Germans confront the other peoples with this airy realm of dreams, the realm of the "essence of man," claiming that it is the consummation and the goal of all world history; in every sphere they regard their dreamy fantasies as a final verdict on the actions of other nations.[66]

This typifies the German ideology, which in Derrida's view relates to an interrogation of national philosophemes that assert the privilege of philosophically representing, incarnating, and identifying the universal essence of man.

For Derrida, it is crucial to underscore that nationalism is to be understood as *philosophical* and "as a thing of our modernity."[67] If Grün is to be of interest, it is in the sense that he mediates the realization that

> If Germany has been, alone in this perhaps, the place (in what sense of place, that's what remains to be determined) of emergence of this nationalism, this is perhaps because in a certain way, at the center of Europe (this is a theme which will return), it will have marked a curious national void, a strange a-nationality. We shall come across this motif later, right up to Heidegger, that of an empty milieu, a central void, a between that, against the background of abyss and non-nationality, calls up the most powerful national-philosophical affirmation in the course of this unique sequence that goes from the eighteenth to the twentieth centuries.[68]

In the lectures on Heidegger's "Die Sprache im Gedicht," emphasis will fall upon Heidegger's remarks on *Ort* or place somewhere at the center of Europe that is at once national and a-national, Germanic and Occidental, a place between living and dying, a sort of empty milieu that is haunted by specters of decease and emergence.

Relative to Marx, Derrida will say in the lecture we are considering:

> It is thus in the name of a socialism doubled by a humanism, in the name of an apolitical people which is not a people that the national-philosophical assertion as cosmopolitanism states its paradoxes which are also, as we shall see, paradigms for the future, in spite of the basically rather caricatural character they take on here. We shall find the recurrent effects of this on the most opposite sides, in Heidegger as well as in Adorno.[69]

In other words, we can expect the oddity of Heidegger being far more subversive philosophically with respect to metaphysical-nationalist ideology, despite his political and social allegiances, about which so much has been written; whereas, in the case of Adorno, who was so critical of nationalism and nationalistic behavior, one will find him to be surprisingly disappointing from a philosophical point of view, as Derrida will demonstrate in lecture two.

However, concerning Adorno, a final point needs to be established that may escape notice. In the second lecture of *Fantom*, mention is made of Adorno's *The Jargon of Authenticity*, which is a sort of fantom text for Derrida, given that it is an updated Frankfurt School version of Marx and Engels' *The German Ideology*. When Adorno writes, "the empty phrase, Man, distorts man's relation to his society as well as the content of what is thought in the concept of Man," he is in essence addressing Marx and Engels' conception of a German ideology insofar as it is predicated on man as grounding concept. Immediately, Adorno even addresses spirit, that word of so much interest to Derrida, when he writes, "The phrase [the word Man] does not bother about the real division of the subject into separated functions that cannot be undone by the voice of mere spirit."[70] Here "spirit" refers to the authenticity that existential philosophical jargon conveys, both in its Nazified form as *Lebensphilosophie* and in its cleaned-up versions, which one could find in Jaspers, Sartre, and (with considerable reservations) Heidegger. Adorno accuses the inheritors of Kierkegaardian thinking of developing a style of automated language that is based on the oracular theatrics of repeatedly declaiming empty phrases that sound good in the absence of any conceptual development. This mirrors Marx's criticisms of Grün and fellow "literary" socialists who traffic in empty rhetoric devoid of conceptual rigor. According to Adorno, invocation of "Man" in philosophy points to an empty and banal profundity whose function is to make social subjects forget how they are socially mediated in ways that Adorno considers inhuman (bureaucratic). Like Marx and Engels, Adorno is sarcastically critical of "the ideology of universal humanity," Fuerbach's anthropologism, and the writings of the young Hegelians, because, again, these deflect social-economic mediations that are irreparably violent, material, and alienating. In fact, *The Jargon of Authenticity* devotes many pages to the critique of Man as a concept in twentieth-century German thinking and, not too surprisingly, savages Heidegger's work for rhetorically presenting itself as something other than the crude anthropology and *Lebensphilosophie* that Adorno believes it is. According to the argument in *Jargon*, substituting an abstraction such as *Dasein* for the word "Man" is merely sleight of hand. Just as "the word 'Man' sounds all the more irrefutable and persuasive the more it seals itself off against its theological origin," so, Adorno suggests, the word "Being" in Heidegger sounds all the more authentic, irrefutable, and modern the more it refutes metaphysics and theology.[71] From Adorno's vantagepoint, it is not, as in Fichte, the conception of "spirit" (*Geist, esprit*) that enables the philosopher to transcend national boundaries in order to position himself or herself internationally as champion of humanity, but rather the refutation of spirit, metaphysics, and theology that dons international and/ or cosmopolitan credentials upon thinkers who share a conception of man or humanity that has been purified of the stench of religion. For Adorno talk of spirit is merely the jargonized opiate of secularism and sophisticated atheism whereby Man's substance is viewed as "powerlessness and nothingness." Adorno writes, "Ideology [that is, its jargon] can grasp onto the fact that the growing powerlessness of the subject, its secularization, was at the same time a loss of world and concreteness."[72] Derrida will focus on loss of world when he later turns to Hannah Arendt. But he also will focus on statements where Adorno contradicts *The Jargon of Authenticity*, not that he had the time to develop this explicitly, hence leaving things up to his audience to put together for themselves.

Notes

1   "Transfer Ex Cathedra: Language and Institutions of Philosophy," in *The Right to Philosophy II*, 2 vols. trans. Jan Plug et al. (Stanford: Stanford University Press, 2004), 6. Originally published as *Du doit à la philosophie* (Paris: Gallilée, 1990). "Transfer" is derived from lecture in the course *La Langue et le discours de la méthode* (1981–82). Part of this text ("If There Is Cause to Translate I: Philosophy in Its National Language [Toward a 'licterature en françois'"]) was delivered at the Fifth International Summer Institute for Semiotic and Structural Studies in the summer of 1984 at Victoria College, the University of Toronto. *Fantom* was to begin in the late fall of that year.
2   Ibid., 1.
3   Ibid., 2.
4   Ibid., 5.
5   Ibid.
6   Jurgen Habermas, *The Structural Transformation of the Public Sphere* (Cambridge: MIT, 1989).
7   Lecture one of *Fantom of the Other* has been translated by Geoffrey Bennington as "Onto-Theology of National-Humanism (Prolegomena to a Hypothesis)" in *Oxford Literary Review* 14:1 (1992). The quotation above occurs on page 3. Bennington is not listed in the article as the translator, but he acknowledges it on his university website.

8   Ibid.
9   Ibid.
10 Ibid., 4.
11 Ibid., 4. Bennington translates the rubric of Derrida's current and following seminars as "philosophical nationality and nationalism," whereas George Collins in *The Politics of Friendship* has translated it as *Nationality and Philosophical Nationalism*. Derrida's original reads "Nationalité et nationalisme philosophiques."
12 Ibid.
13 Ibid., 5.
14 Ibid.
15 Ibid. In the lecture course of 1986–87, *Mythos, Topos, Logos*, Derrida mentions John Rajchman and Cornel West's *Post-Analytic Philosophy* (New York: Columbia, 1985) in the context of philosophical nationalisms and their differences. The remarks appear to be the beginning of what could have been an extended discussion, which may, in fact, exist elsewhere, given that this lecture course is incomplete in the archive at UC Irvine. Rajchman and West's book is an anthology that included essays by Richard Rorty, Hilary Putnam, Thomas Nagel, Harold Bloom, John Rawls, Ian Hacking, and others.
16 "Onto-Theology," 6.
17 In fact, as late as 2000–02, Derrida gave the two-year long course *Death Penalty* in which he explored capital punishment in terms of a national self-assertion of justice, and in the following two-year long course, *The Beast and the Sovereign*, sovereignty was predictably associated with national self-assertion, as well.
18 Ibid., 6.
19 Ibid., 6–7.
20 Jacques Derrida, *Of Grammatology*, trans. G.C. Spivak (Baltimore: Johns Hopkins, 1976), 218.
21 See Jacques Derrida, "Honoris Causa," in *Points: Interviews 1974–94* (Stanford: Stanford University Press, 1995). In 1992 Cambridge wanted to award Derrida an honorary doctorate, but complainants in various philosophy departments around the world protested and the degree had to be put to a vote.
22 Jacques Derrida, "Deconstruction in America," *Journal of the Society for Critical Exchange* 17 (Winter 1985), 3. It is odd that this important interview was never republished in a more prominent venue.
23 "Onto-Theology of National-Humanism," 7, 9. In these pages, Derrida raises general questions about (1) what is national identity and the use of the word nationality, (2) the various knowledges or disciplines that address such questions besides philosophy (sociology, linguistics, the techno-economic, the historico-political) and their situatedness relative to one another and to their historical moments, and (3) the acceleration of communication and exasperation of identities

and the recognition that national identity is "never posited as an empirical, natural character, of the type," 10.
24 "Fichus: Frankfort Address," in *Paper Machine* (Stanford: Stanford University Press, 2005), 171.
25 "Onto-Theology," 11. Translation slightly modified.
26 In later courses this will relate to the Jew and the German, the Jew supposedly being rootless, urban, cosmopolitan, and "cultured," and therefore not particularly patriotic (for the Jew has no Fatherland, at least not in Europe), whereas the German is thought to be essentially connected to the land and has inherited the German language and German traditions from previously landed generations.
27 J.G. Fichte, *Addresses to the German Nation*, trans. G. Moore (Cambridge: Cambridge University Press, 2008), 193. Fichte, *Reden an die deutsche Nation* (Berlin: Holzinger, 2014), 171.
28 Ibid.
29 Ibid., 193.
30 Fichte, *Addresses*, xii.
31 Robert Norton, *Secret Germany: Stefan Georg and His Circle* (Ithaca: Cornell University Press, 2002), 435.
32 Martin Heidegger, *Ponderings II–VI: Black Notebooks 1931–38*, trans. Richard Rojcewicz (Bloomington: Indiana University Press, 2016), 114. Martin Heidegger, *Gesamtausgabe 94: Überlegungen II–VI (Schwarze Hefte 1931–38)*, ed. Peter Trawny (Frankfurt am Main: Vittorio Klostermann, 2014), 155.
33 *Of Spirit*, trans. G. Bennington and R. Bowlby (Chicago: University of Chicago Press, 1989), 70.
34 Ibid., 76.
35 Ibid.
36 *Ponderings II–VI*, 99.
37 Ibid., 107.
38 Martin Heidegger, *Ponderings VII–XI: Black Notebooks 1938–39*, trans. Richard Rojcewicz (Bloomington: Indiana University Press, 2017), 24. *Gesamtausgabe 95: Überlegungen VIII–XI (Schwarze Hefte 1938–39)*, ed. Peter Trawny (Frankfurt am Main: Vittorio Klostermann, 2014), 30.
39 Ibid., 19. Translation slightly modified.
40 Ibid.
41 Ibid., 17.
42 Fichte, 97/86. "Was an Geistigkeit und Freiheit dieser Geistigkeit glaubt, und die ewige Fortbildung dieser Geistigkeit durch Freiheit will, das, wo es auch geboren sey und in welcher Sprache es rede, ist unsers Geschlechts, es gehört uns an und es wird sich zu uns thun."
43 Ibid.

44 "Onto-Theology," 13.
45 Fichte, 97/86.
46 Ibid.
47 "Onto-Theology," 14–15.
48 Fichte, 98/87.
49 "Onto-Theology," 15.
50 Ibid.
51 Ibid. 15.
52 Ibid., 16. "… who, etc." is an intentional break.
53 Ibid., 17.
54 Ibid.
55 Ibid., 17–18.
56 Karl Marx and Friedrich Engels, *The German Ideology* (Amherst: Prometheus Books, 1998), 42. Italics mine.
57 Ibid., 482.
58 Ibid.
59 Ibid.
60 Ibid.
61 "Onto-Theology," 19. The phrase is Marx's as cited by Derrida who calls it "a very fine expression" that expresses itself as a nationalism of man as opposed to a nationalism of nation, not that the two can be simply divorced, as Marx notices.
62 *The German Ideology*, 484.
63 Ibid. Italics added.
64 Ibid., 483.
65 "Onto-Theology," 21.
66 *The German Ideology*, 496.
67 "Onto-Theology," 22.
68 Ibid.
69 Ibid.
70 Theodor Adorno, *The Jargon of Authenticity*, trans. Knut Tarnowski and Frederic Will (Evanston: Northwestern University Press, 1973), p. 67.
71 Ibid., 63.
72 Ibid., 72.

2

What Is German? Adorno's Homecoming

From Derrida's point of view, there is a connection to be made between Fichte and Theodor Adorno, not only because on various occasions Adorno had addressed the German nation, but because, like Fichte, Adorno thought of the Germans as an inherently selfless and philosophical people who are in a position to educate and lead others. Also of importance for Derrida is that Adorno and Heidegger share the conviction that the German language is singularly philosophical in a manner superior to, say, English or French. Adorno shares in the nationalist paradox that the more authentically German one is, the more universal one is, a view that carries within it an imperialist assumption about cultural domination already quite marked in Fichte but that also includes figures such as Napoleon who was hardly blind to the imperialist dimensions of French cultural and linguistic influence in Europe.

Also of significance for Derrida is the question of a philosopher's relation to his or her academic institution. Fichte, Heidegger, and Adorno were philosophers who famously held academic positions, hence their nationalist philosophical considerations were mediated by the university as an inherently international or cosmopolitan institution where students and professors of different national backgrounds have the responsibility to work together in the name of universal principles concerning reason, knowledge, and truth. But why, in Adorno's case, was he so eager to return to the University of Frankfurt, given its identity as a *German* university? In lectures two and three of *Fantom*, discussion of Adorno is undertaken.[1]

Adorno's Homecoming

Of interest to Derrida with respect to Adorno, but also Hannah Arendt, were their public addresses to the German people. Adorno's address, entitled "On the Question 'What Is German'?" took place as a radio broadcast on *Deutschlandfunk*

(May 9, 1965) and has since become available in print. Hardly surprising is Derrida's recognition that "What Is German?" is immediately put into question by Adorno himself. "I cannot answer this question directly," Adorno says, for "first it is necessary to reflect upon the question itself," given that people invest this question with what they would like to think being German is. "The ideal must defer to the idealization. In its sheer form the question already profanes the irrevocable experiences of the last decades. It creates an autonomous collective entity, 'German,' whose characteristics are then to be determined."[2] Such an approach, Derrida says, is most necessary, political, and vigilant.

Derrida notes that although the question of what is German can't be responded to directly, it can be analyzed, however, first of all, by means of challenging its supposition, which concerns fantasized, idealized definitions of what is German, as well as the historicized tendency to imagine an autonomous collective German entity that one defines in terms of essentialized characteristics. At issue, of course, is what today we would call identity politics. As Adorno puts it:

> The formation of national collectives, however, common in the detestable jargon of war that speaks of the Russian, the American, surely also of the German, obeys a reifying consciousness that is no longer really capable of experience. It confines itself within precisely those stereotypes that thinking should dissolve. It is uncertain whether something like the German as a person or German as a quality, or anything similar in other nations, exists at all.[3]

The idea of a reified German self is fundamentally unthinking and uncritical and as such a reductive and crass type of "German ideology" in Marx and Engels' sense. Adorno's repudiation of such a reified nationalist subject also conforms with Fichte's idea that the education of a German social subject should lead to selfless freedom of inquiry—in short, critical thought that isn't circumscribed by a limited notion of what it is to be German. Fichte thinks of this as "spiritual development," by which he means, in large part, the kind of mental training that avoids simplistic formulations and prefabricated concepts.

In his address, Adorno will also have recourse to speaking about spirit, about what is best that resists the formation of stereotypes that fall into a collective narcissism. Derrida seizes upon the Fichtean notion of "the true and the better" that Adorno takes up: "The True and the Better in every people is surely that which does *not* integrate itself into the collective subject and if possible resists it."[4] Problematic is that the nationalist social subject is generally thought of as a collective subject, one that in Adorno's view leads to psychological splitting wherein selves are good, whereas foreigners, strangers, and aliens are bad. Derrida notes that the dualism of friend/enemy, self/other, familiar/alien is, in fact, quite marked in Fichte's addresses, though at points Fichte goes out of his way to eradicate such division, for example, by arguing that someone born outside of Germany may be more German than someone within Germany's borders, given a certain mentality or spirit. This confirms Derrida's thesis that dualisms pertaining to the national-cosmopolitan division are always being maintained and exceeded.

Adorno, for his part, touches on the dual as a philosopheme of nationalism that forms the basis for state violence. "Yet after the most abominable atrocities perpetrated under National Socialism by an ideology of the primacy of the collective subject at the cost of any and all individuality, there is doubled reason in Germany to guard against relapsing into the cultivation of self-idolatrous stereotypes." Nazism was perhaps the apogee of the German ideology if not its most pernicious expression insofar as it glorified a reified, archaic conception of the pre-individual social subject in terms of "a tribal consciousness, to which one can appeal with all the greater psychological effectiveness the less such consciousness actually exists."[5] Again, Fichte was careful not to embrace such a tribal consciousness, for his project was to educate and thereby form a *German* social subject by means of "mental activity" (active reflection, "pleasure in knowledge"). In the context of education, Fichte was a proponent of selfless critical thought, of a nationalism that didn't invest itself in mindless collective identification with certain groups imagined to be most authentically German on account of some biologistic circumstance.

That nationalism is an imaginary construction is of crucial interest to Derrida in *Fantom*, which is why he points to Adorno's statement that "relapsing into the cultivation of self-idolatrous stereotypes" is among those "tendencies" that "have emerged in recent years."

> They [the stereotypes] are conjured up by the political questions of reunification, of the *Oder-Neiße* Line, also by several claims raised by the refugees; a further pretext is offered by a completely imagined international ostracism of the German, or a no less fictive lack of that national self-esteem that so many would like to incite again. Imperceptibly an atmosphere is slowly taking shape that disapproves of the one thing most necessary: critical self-reflection.[6]

Derrida comments that Adorno is speaking of a certain "a-nationality" that translates into hypernationalism, regression to a pre-individual archaic self, or a primitive tribal conscience. At issue for Adorno was the post–Second World War division of Germany into the Federal Republic of West Germany and the German Democratic Republic (East Germany). In this context, the pre-individual archaic self avoids having to acknowledge that there are, in fact, two Germanies.

This raises a point with respect to Derrida's mention of his "German friends" noted in the previous chapter concerning the theme of historical fantoms, given that haunting this and future courses is the nationalist specter of de-unification, of there being an aporia concerning unity as a national possibility. Once again it has to be noted that Derrida could have (and probably should have) asked in 1984 whether one can decide if there really are two Germanies or if in fact there is only one German nation and one German people who are just physically separated by means of the artificial political line implemented by the Allies after the end of the Second World War. When President Kennedy famously proclaimed "Ich bin ein Berliner," was he speaking to just half of Berlin or not? Recall that when Germany was reunified on November 9, 1988, the Germans on both sides of the *Oder-Neiße* Line behaved as if that line had never legitimately existed and as if the Berlin wall had been simply a fantastical political monstrosity that for all its physical presence did nothing to split the German people from the point of view of the German spirit (people's heartfelt emotions, their mentality, their sense of connectedness, etc.). This would have struck Fichte as entirely natural, but Derrida, oddly enough, overlooks spirit from the perspective of a divided Germany in what was still the post-war period before unification. Heidegger, too, it has to be said, avoids this subject as well, though in many of his writings the twofold is thematized. In "Geschlecht II," Derrida even puts emphasis on the two versus the one—in terms of Heidegger's figure of the hand(s), the division of *Dichtung/Gedicht*, and in terms of *Geschlecht* as gender. Why nationhood in terms of the two Germanies was ignored is odd, given the effraction of nationhood in this case that, as has already been mentioned, was thematized by German artists of the time. Consider, for example, Georg Immendorf's representations of German nationhood in the context of National Socialist Germany versus the post-war partitioning that created an East and West Germany and how Immendorf's Café Deutschland series was predicated on a double scene of political deconstruction undertaken at the time Derrida delivered *Fantom*.

Addressing unification, Adorno himself said:

> Historically German unification was belated, precarious, and unstable; one tends, simply so as to feel like a nation at all, to overplay the national consciousness and irritably avenge every deviation from it. In this situation it is easy to regress to archaic conditions of pre-individualistic disposition, a tribal consciousness, to which one can appeal with all the greater psychological effectiveness the less such consciousness actually exists.[7]

Derrida simply asks, "So what does Adorno do? He speaks of '*la bonne tradition allemande*,'" of a tradition the Germans should reclaim if they want to act like adults. Derrida then asks, what precisely is this good German tradition that Adorno refers us to? Adorno tells us: "To escape these regressive tendencies, to come of age, to look one's own historical and societal situation and the international situation straight in the eye, is incumbent upon precisely those people who invoke the German tradition, that of Kant."[8]

Kant versus Fichte

Derrida notes that Fichte is excluded by Adorno. In his place, Kant is considered the chief observer of the German tradition. Kant represents the critical tradition which, as Adorno says, is predicated upon the concepts of autonomy, self-responsibility, and individual reasoning as opposed to "those blind dependencies, which include the unreflected supremacy of the national."[9] The "universal of reason" is realized in the individual person as opposed to "collective obedience and self-idolatry."[10] With respect to idolatry, Kant, Beethoven, and Goethe are not to be considered "German property" or "brand names" that the German simply possesses, since that is just blind cultural dependency upon fetishized objects that would typify nationalist thinking; rather, such figures belong to a tradition of *critical thinking* that in the context of Adorno's negative dialectics (also unremarked in Derrida's text, but no doubt presupposed) is aggressively anti-identitarian.

Derrida tells his listeners that Adorno's orientation to nationalism concerns the psycho-political, which is why Adorno approves of Kant who rejects the psychology of ethnic identification. Kant's practical reason and autonomy of self are philosophically allergic to fascist nationalism and therefore rebel against it. According to Adorno, working against reason and autonomy was Germany's lack of sufficient "bourgeoisification" which "allowed a reserve of untapped natural forces to accumulate."[11] Hence "the unwavering radicalism of spirit" wasn't put in sufficient check, something that in the twentieth century was fundamental to Hitler's rise to power in terms of "the pathos of the absolute."[12]

Derrida, who is unconvinced by Adorno's faith in Kant, focuses upon part two of Kant's *Anthropology from a Pragmatic Point of View* which is devoted to discussing character: that of the person, of the sexes, of peoples, and of species. Derrida cautions everyone to read "The Character of the Peoples," which opens as follows:

> By the word *people* [*populus*] is meant a *multitude* of human beings united in a region, in so far as they constitute a *whole*. This multitude, or even the part of it that recognizes itself as united into a civil whole through common ancestry, is called a *nation* [*gens*]. The part that exempts itself from these laws (the unruly crowd within the people) is called a *rabble* [*vulgus*].[13]

Derrida explains that if a people is just a mass of individuals living together in a specific territory, this people has an origin in terms of a stock and over time forms a civil whole or bourgeoisie that is foundational for the formation of a nation. The nation is not natural because it has civil constitution and complex organization. The nation is something separate from just a natural population of individuals living here and there. Yet the nation preserves a certain relation to this indigenous population in terms of what is pre-political. In terms of shared fantasy, the nation alludes to its birth, to its natural law of birth, even if a nation isn't natural. The nation represents a break from naturalism, because it is to be considered in terms of a historical dimension linked to what is a political and teleological project. And yet, the break with the natural condition of the people in their habitat isn't absolute, since despite the development of civil law and government, the nation ambiguously adheres to an identity with the natural, the pre-political, and the prehistorical—to a primitivism, however fantasmatic. Here, again, the phrase *Fantom of the Other* takes on a somewhat different meaning.

Derrida follows Kant in turning to Hume, who says that a nation can have no specific character. For him the nation has the privilege of being representative of humanity, for the essence of humanity is reflected in it. The vocation of a nation, as embodied in its laws, is to speak the universal essence of man. However much people may wish to embody a national character, the nation itself is without character. Derrida notes that Hume's appeal to the national citizen as universal social subject strikes Kant as an assertion of privilege and superiority. Was Hume proposing a nationalism without nationalism? And is the universal character of which Hume speaks not representative of some sort of character, nevertheless? For example, the cosmopolitan socialist character of whom Marx and Engels were so critical? Rather in line with the sort of thinking one finds in Karl Grün, there is a tendency to accuse an other of nationalism by way of making a plea for the superiority of one's own nation, which is deemed to be non-nationalist. Derrida says that once more we can see a paradoxical logic at work insofar as one accuses the other of nationalism in making a plea for one's own nation as non-nationalist, cosmopolitan, hospitable, a nation to which nothing human is foreign.

Derrida has greatly amplified what in Kant is a far less wide-ranging discussion that devolves into Kant accusing Hume of "arrogant rudeness" and "obstinate behavior" which Kant thinks is typical of the English who because of their island nation naturally stand apart from the Continent out of "supposed self-sufficiency, where one believes that one has no need of anybody else and so can be excused from kindness toward other people."[14] Derrida underscores that Kant sees in the English a *Handels Sprache* or mercantile language as fundamental, given that historically the island nation shaped the population in this manner, given that islands rely heavily upon trade which shapes speech and behavior. As Derrida puts it, Kant specifies that the affectations of British character reveal a people suspicious of all foreigners, which is why Hume, for example, extols a constitution that associates civil liberty internally alongside power projected externally. The French by contrast privilege conversation which tends toward the frivolous and the feminine; therefore, the French cannot be properly philosophical, especially when one considers the conversational idioms of the French that will not translate across languages. Kant lists words and plays of words in French that cannot be translated, though he says nothing about German idioms in this respect.

Like Fichte, Kant thinks that a national people are very much shaped in terms of a common character by means of language which reflects a population's history of adaptation, whereas Hume would represent the cosmopolitan route of arguing for the nation as the means for promoting universal humanity through the rule of law. The idea that all men are created equal, which is a principle to be embodied in civil laws, contrasts with the Fichtean/Kantian reliance upon a people's relation with language as the basis for ascertaining national characterological differences that imply an inequality among peoples.

In the *Anthropology*, Kant specifies that a people have a "natural aptitude" reflected in the formation of language that is "derived from the *innate character* of the original people of their [the people's] ancestry."[15] Fichte, by contrast, puts far less emphasis on anything innate, since it is too far removed from the present to know anything about. Instead, one would have to look at the evolution of the German language and how German speakers were affected by it. Adorno, who says nothing of Kant's *Anthropology*, contrasts the "pure will of the Germans with an allegedly petty mercantile spirit, that of the Anglo-Saxons in particular."[16] The Germans, far from being instrumentally oriented in terms of engaging things for some purpose other than in the interest of the things themselves, have an interest "to do something for its own sake."[17] The Germans, for whom the exchange relations common to capitalism had not quite become dominant in even Richard

Wagner's day, could imagine, as Wagner did, intellectual production as "a being-in-itself, not merely a being for-something-else or for-others, nor as an object of exchange."[18] Derrida points out that Adorno does, however, recall Kant's voluminous writings on duty when he notes the German character is not that of "the entrepreneur operating according to the laws of the market but rather the civil servant fulfilling his duty to the authorities …. In Fichte's doctrine of action as an end-in-itself it found its most rigorous theoretical expression."[19] Adorno, in other words, is as heavily involved in characterology as was Kant in the *Anthropology*, which speaks to Derrida's suspicion that philosophical nationalism, since this is what is under discussion, cannot do without the very regressive tendencies that even the most anti-identitarian philosopher would condemn, even while engaging in them.

Hence Adorno writes apropos of his criticisms: "This is not to say that the stereotypes [of the Germans] are devoid of any and all truth. Recall the most famous formulation of German collective narcissism."[20] For Derrida all of this comes preliminary to his major interest in Adorno's address to the Germans, given that on Derrida's mind is the exploration of relations of exile and language.

Exile, Language, Return

Adorno, of course, was a Jew in exile in America for some years and, despite everything that had transpired in Germany during the National Socialist period, returned to Germany after the war in order to accept a post at the University of Frankfurt. Much later in *Fantom* Derrida will discuss *Heimkehr* in Heidegger's work on Trakl with an eye on Hölderlin as well. That is, the theme of return is a very major thread running through the course. With respect to Adorno, uppermost on Derrida's mind is the simple question of what motivated him to return. That prompts Derrida to look closely at Adorno's text. Lacking at that time, however, was biographical context provided in later years by Stefan Müller-Doohm's biography of Adorno in which we learn that the return to Germany by Adorno, and also his friend Max Horkheimer, was motivated not by language chiefly, but by their desire to become culturally and politically influential.

> Adorno spent the last twenty years of his life mostly in Germany—he died a few weeks before his sixty-sixth birthday. There he not only enjoyed an incomparably influential life as an academic, but also helped to shape the direction of the Federal Republic in its efforts to discover its own cultural and political identity and to help the post-war generation in its attempts at self-clarification. As a

representative of the "Frankfurt School," he made a significant contribution to "the intellectual foundations of the Federal Republic" which formed the kernel of the political and cultural self-image of the nation twenty years after the establishment of the institutions of the German state. It may be said, therefore, that he helped to bring about the consistent policy of integration in the West, the process of democratization and, above all, the beginning of a political debate about the German past. Adorno was among those who shaped the political culture of Germany .... What was admired about [Adorno's] frequent appearances on radio and television and other cultural venues was his instinctive insistence on thinking.[21]

In "On the Question 'What Is German?'" Adorno gives the following account of what motivated him as an emigrant to return to Germany.

> It is perhaps better if I somewhat reduce the question of what is German and formulate it more modestly: what motivated me, as an emigrant, someone who had been driven out in disgrace, and after what had been perpetrated by the Germans on millions of innocent people, nonetheless to come back. By trying to convey some of the things I myself have experienced and observed, I believe I can best work against the formation of stereotypes.[22]

Is it because the émigré has lost his or her nationality that constructing stereotypes would be inadequate? Or is the émigré stereotypical, nevertheless?

> It is an ancient tradition that such people who were capriciously and blindly banished from their homeland by tyranny come back after its fall. Someone who hates the thought of starting a new life will follow this tradition almost naturally, without long deliberation. Moreover, to someone who thinks in terms of society, and who understands fascism socio-economically, the thesis that blames the German people [*Volk*] is really quite foreign. At no moment during my emigration did I relinquish the hope of coming back.[23]

Does the word "tradition" substitute for stereotype? After all, Adorno is comparing himself with refugees driven out of their homelands by tyrannies who naturally tend to return home in peace when historical conditions enable them to do so. This is followed by a remark on German society that Derrida will take up: that one cannot blame the German people when one understands that fascism was a socio-economic order. For a sociologist such as Adorno, blaming the German people would be "quite foreign"; therefore, he had no reason to relinquish the hope of return. In fact, Müller-Doohm reports that Horkheimer and Adorno did blame the German people and that once back in Germany they had trepidation about the return of anti-Semitism and the embrace of nationalism. Adorno's final point in his address concerning his return is perhaps closer to what actually transpired in terms of transitioning from a marginal intellectual in America to a dominant cultural figure in Germany. "That in my voluntary decision I harbored the feeling of being able to do some good in Germany, to work against the obduration, the repetition of the disaster, is only another aspect of that spontaneous identification (with what was familiar)."[24]

In fact, as Derrida realizes, returning was an experience of uncanny unfamiliarity. In "Im Flug erhascht" ("Caught in Flight"), Adorno mentions that the fascist dictatorship couldn't fit into the continuity of an émigré's life. If such a person returns, "he will have aged and yet remained as young as he was at the time of his banishment, a little like the way in which the dead retain the age they had when you last knew them."[25] One can't pick up where one left off. This speaks to remarks in the thirteenth lecture of *Fantom* about the thinker going into and coming out of eclipse and that when the thinker returns he or she never returns as the same. In *Specters of Marx*, Derrida would refer to this kind of experience as time being out of joint, which is the foundation upon which spectral returning is based. In "Im Flug erhascht" Adorno is contemplating familiarity in the exile's return as a spectral interplay that is multidimensional and riddled with holes: that is, the past returns within the present despite the fact that the past is riddled with gaps—all the fantasmic things that the returning émigré wasn't there to experience and has to fill in imaginatively.

Derrida doesn't probe all these issues, given that he is moving quickly, but he does seize on something Müller-Doohm will mention in his biography of Adorno, namely that for Adorno the return to Germany wasn't just a matter of homesickness, though, as Adorno admitted, he had such sentiments; rather, a very major personal reason for wanting to return was on account of the German language, because "it has a special affinity with philosophy."[26] The remark on language is crucial from Derrida's perspective, given how central language is to the history of philosophical nationalism, judging from Fichte, Kant, Heidegger, and now Adorno, though, as we will see, it will be no less important for Hannah Arendt. Also, it is the overlap of Adorno with Heidegger that is most immediately conspicuous, since both agreed on the conviction that German has a special relation with philosophy. This is hardly a cosmopolitan point of view.

Derrida, who is largely recapitulating Adorno, cites a passage in which Adorno speaks of returning to Germany as a way to "regain childhood." "For that reason I feel justified in speaking of the strength of the motives that drew me home."[27] Home, of course, is a Heideggerian philosopheme with nationalist significance concerning one's "being at home" that in Adorno's context involves one's being at home in language. Of special interest to Derrida is a lengthy passage in which Adorno complains of being told by a publisher (presumably in America) that his *Philosophy of New Music* was "badly organized." Also, in forwarding the galleys of a lecture written in English to be published by a journal of the Psychoanalytical Society of San Francisco, Adorno saw that the editors "had not been satisfied with improving the stylistic deficiencies of an emigrant writer. The entire text had been disfigured beyond recognition, the fundamental intentions could not be recovered."[28] Central to Adorno's concerns is the question of translation and the fact that his thinking is idiomatically alien to English and therefore can't be well captured outside of German. As Adorno put it, writing in German in Germany would not "impair my work."

Derrida relates that Adorno went back to Germany on account of the issue of translation, a key problematic in *Fantom*. Derrida stresses that Adorno went back when he realized that translation wasn't possible, that his *idiom*, within language, couldn't be translated or transferred over into any other idiom.[29] Adorno went back when he had understood this in his bones (as we would say in English). He made the decision to repatriate—whatever it would cost him. Derrida continues by saying that the issue of translation broaches the enigmatic center of the course's problematic that is "*l'idiome de l'idiome*." In this we confront "*l'essence de la nationalité*" as detached from its supposed nationalist, racist, and even political impurities, which is to say, the essence of nationality as philosophy. Here, of course, Derrida is underlining the central theme of *Fantom of the Other*, upon which he expands enormously in the context of Heidegger on Trakl in the later lectures on *Geschlecht*.

Derrida calls Adorno's text a narrative of impossible translation and presents the major issues, which we have previewed, as follows: first, Adorno refuses the thesis of the culpability of the German people. He refuses it as a sociologist. "As someone who thinks in terms of society, and who understands fascism socio-economically, the thesis that blames the German people is really quite foreign."[30] Second, Adorno recognizes a desire to return at every moment, that it is an identification with the familiar, and with childhood. This is the desire to re-find childhood, a non-regressive desire. Derrida asks his audience to recall that "in the passages we analyzed already," Adorno accuses childhood in the context of saying nationalisms are puerile and archaicizing. Hence there is a bad childhood, which is that of "*l'enfance nationaliste*," the archaic fantasies of origins, though there is also a good childhood, the one Adorno mentions when he says he wishes to return to himself. In this return, he preserves the desire to do something good for his country, that is, the country of his childhood. Third,

Derrida says, Adorno dissociates the nationalism of citizenship from rootedness in a territory. To Derrida it is interesting that Adorno suggests a nationalist will be nationalist anywhere. For Adorno this is a matter of personality: an insistence upon conformity. This means that a German can be an American nationalist if he or she happens to live in America. One can be anti-cosmopolitan anywhere. Derrida seizes on the paradox of a nationalism without attachment to any particular nationality. If there is a place where that idea becomes possible for anyone to imagine, Derrida says, it would be in the United States where recent immigrants can be passionate nationalists.[31] Fourth, Adorno accepts distinctions between culture and civilization, spirit and techne, though not if they are a reflection of prejudice.

> In Germany, arrogance toward America is inappropriate ... One need not deny the distinction between a so-called culture of spirit and a technological culture in order to rise above a stubborn contraposition of the two. A utilitarian [that is, American] view of life that, impervious to the incessantly increasing contradictions, believes that everything is for the best just as long as it merely functions, is just as blind as the faith in a culture of spirit [which is German] that, by virtue of its ideal of self-sufficient purity, renounces the realization of its contents and abandons reality to power and its blindness.[32]

Whereas Adorno is critical of the spirit/techne distinction, which characterizes the thinking of someone such as Heidegger, Adorno's account of why he returned to Germany suggests belief in precisely such a distinction whereby America is aligned with technicity and Germany with the spirit of the mother tongue. The context for this is Adorno's vicissitudes with English publishers recounted above, given that it speaks to the technological dimension of American life.

> I was perfectly aware that the autonomy I championed as the unconditional right of the author to determine the integral form of his production had ... something regressive about it in relation to the highly rationalized commercial exploitation even of spiritual creations. What was being demanded of me [in America] was nothing other than the logically consistent application of the laws of highly advanced economic concentration to scholarly and literary products.[33]

In short, thought had become industrialized by means of the copy-editing process, which demanded the conformity of language to commonplace standards. In conflict are "autonomous creations of spirit" and "products for the marketplace," a conflict Heidegger would certainly have condemned for similar reasons, though Heidegger, it has to be said, had a publisher in Vittorio Klostermann that respected his autonomy and idiosyncrasies with a certain piety and respect few thinkers have enjoyed. Derrida takes notice of Adorno's remark that these publishing issues were simply "bagatelles" in comparison with the Holocaust, but that they nevertheless concern a fight against "techno-capitalism" that in its own way is as important as the fight against fascism.

Derrida points out that in order to take a stand against such techno-capitalism a certain turn toward nationalism and national identity had to be taken, one that has elements in common with a fascist mentality of the recent past. As anti-nationalist, Adorno took what he calls "the chance for the German spirit ('*les chances de l'esprit Allemande*' in Derrida's script) – with all the dangers of a reawakening nationalism that implies."[34] Such dangers have to be risked for the sake of defeating the standardizing laws of the marketplace which seek to regulate and determine intellectual production. Do Adorno and Heidegger converge here? Derrida implies that they do. Later in the course, Derrida will discuss *What is Called Thinking?* in which the hand and the pen is preferred to the typewriter, which is a sort of diatribe against techne's relation to writing.

Key to Derrida's discussion of Adorno is the fact that Adorno knows he is risking what he calls the "dangers of a reawakening nationalism" and that these dangers are detectable throughout the radio address, particularly with respect to language. The Achilles heel, of course, is language's idiomaticity, that it is in terms of idioms, linguistically but also culturally, that a certain philosophical nationalism cannot be avoided. Müller-Doohm, in addressing cultural idiom, mentions that Adorno and Horkheimer felt the return to Frankfurt was most felicitous on account of the superiority of everyday German cultural practices—e.g., café culture. In such an environment they agreed that they "could think." As to the German language, Adorno needed to be immersed in it,

> not only because one can never express one's intention so exactly, with all the nuances and the rhythm of the train of thought in the newly acquired language as in one's own. Rather, the German language also apparently has a special elective affinity with philosophy and particularly with its speculative element that in the West is so easily suspected of being dangerously unclear, and by no means completely without justification .... The German language has become capable of expressing something in the phenomena that is not exhausted in their mere thus-ness, their positivity, and givenness.[35]

And he insists, as Derrida noted, that a specific quality of German is "the prohibitive difficulty of translating into another language philosophical texts of supreme difficulty such as Hegel's *Phenomonlogy of Spirit* or his *Science of Logic*."[36] German is not a language of fixed meanings, but contains a "power of expression" that is *exceptional* to German. That the mode of linguistic "presentation is essential to philosophy," means that, as Ulrich Sonnemann says (and Derrida quotes), "there has never been a great philosopher who was not also a great writer."[37] One simply cannot underestimate the importance of the language in which one writes.

Again, Adorno knows full well the nationalism that he is invoking, which is why he insists at the end of the address that German is prone to "metaphysical excess," which the émigré must resist by rigorously reattaching his or her "native language with unflagging vigilance against any fraud it promotes," the metaphysical excess that falsely "guarantees the truth of the metaphysics it suggests." As Adorno puts it, "the metaphysical character of language is no privilege. One must not borrow from it the idea of a profundity that becomes suspect the moment it stoops to self-praise."[38] Notions of depth, profundity, of German soul are all suspect effects of a language that says more than it denotes and that is freighted with metaphysical/spiritual excesses that lay claim to truth and authenticity. The German national psyche, Adorno says, has been culturally predisposed to accept such a jargon of authenticity because it more or less rolls off the tongue in a seductive and easy manner. It is for this reason, Adorno says, that *The Jargon of Authenticity* was written.

Derrida's lecture on Adorno ends by stressing the paradox that appears endemic to philosophical nationalism: that two gestures have to be made at once, which in Adorno's case concerns (1) the assertion of the metaphysical excesses and privileges of the German language and (2) adherence to the critical vigilance of Immanuel Kant whereby a tradition of reason is being upheld according to which individuals are held responsible to uphold the exercise of free judgment in the pursuit of truth. Like Fichte, Adorno knows that, as Derrida puts it, to be truly German one can't ask what it means to be truly German; rather, one has to imagine the concept of Germanness in terms of humanity. Derrida says that this is the gesture of cosmopolitan nationalism that his course has previously referenced, a gesture of nationalism in which it is the nationality of mankind that one finds in nationality. It is always in the name of "a national humanism" that one critiques nationalism, the point being that with respect to nationalism there are always the two levels of the particular and the general that are in play. In making this point, Derrida alludes to another essay by Adorno, "Education After Auschwitz," in which Adorno says that the revival of nationalism "is so evil because, in the age of international communication and supranational blocs, nationalism cannot really believe in itself anymore and must exaggerate itself to the extreme in order to persuade itself and others that it is still substantial." Moreover, "so-called national revival movements in an age in which nationalism is obsolete are obviously especially susceptible to sadistic practices."[39] According to Adorno, in the 1950s one could not any longer assume the nationalist alibi of being on the side of humanity, because nationalism was so bankrupt as a social concept that it required demonization and persecution in order to appear valid. What Adorno calls "the archaic tendency toward violence" is very much on Derrida's mind too and will continue to be so in subsequent courses, among them, *Eating the Other (Rhetorics of Cannibalism)* (1990). In fact, like Adorno, Derrida suspects that conceptions of social bonding are based on extremely shallow authoritarian foundations, given that, as Adorno observes, everyone knows such bonds have been unbound by external "interchangeable authorities" of an "administered world" whose norms people follow in the absence of any compelling social relation. Contrary to common sense perception, nationalism doesn't establish social bonds; rather, it exposes their absence. According to Adorno, "Genocide has its roots in this resurrection of aggressive nationalism that has developed in many countries since the end of the nineteenth century."[40] That is to say, "society, while it integrates itself ever more, at the same time incubates tendencies toward disintegration."[41] That society's love for humanity might be the big lie of a genocidal drive born in the disintegration of the social relation is a rumination that Derrida shares with Adorno.

Notes

1 In the manuscript I consulted at UC Irvine's Critical Theory Archive, Derrida's discussion of Fichte is split between the first and second lectures, and the discussion of Adorno is split, as well, between lectures two and three. Lecture four is entirely on Tocqueville.
2 Theodor Adorno, "On the Question: 'What Is German?'" in *Critical Models: Interventions and Catchwords*, trans. H.W. Pickford (New York: Columbia University Press, 1998), 205.
3 Ibid.
4 Ibid.
5 Ibid., 205–06.
6 Ibid., 206.
7 Ibid.
8 Ibid.
9 Ibid.
10 Ibid.
11 Ibid., 208.

12 Ibid., 209.
13 Immanuel Kant, *Anthropology from a Pragmatic Point of View*, ed. R.B. Louden (Cambridge: Cambridge University Press, 2006), 213.
14 Ibid., 213–14.
15 Ibid., 214. Italics mine.
16 Adorno, "On the Question 'What Is German?,'" 207.
17 Ibid.
18 Ibid.
19 Ibid.
20 Ibid.
21 Stefan Müller Doohm, *Adorno: A Biography*, trans. R. Livingstone (Cambridge: Polity, 2005), p. 325.
22 Adorno, "On the Question 'What Is German?,'" 209.
23 Ibid.
24 Ibid.
25 Adorno, *Im Flug erhascht*, published in 1954 in *Frankfurter Rundschau*, quoted Müller-Doohm, 330.
26 Quoted in Doohm, *Adorno: A Biography,* 326.
27 Adorno, "On the Question 'What Is German?,'" 210.
28 Ibid. 211.
29 This part of the Adorno analysis belongs to lecture 3.
30 "On the Question 'What Is German?'" 209.
31 Derrida seems to be glossing the following in Adorno. "Experience has taught me something remarkable. People who conform, who feel generally at one with the given environment and its relations of domination, always adapt themselves much more easily in new countries. Here a nationalist, there a nationalist," Ibid., 209.
32 Ibid., 210.
33 Ibid., 211.
34 Ibid., 212.
35 Ibid.
36 Ibid.
37 Ibid.
38 Ibid., 213.
39 Theodor Adorno, "Education after Auschwitz," in *Critical Models*, trans. H.W. Pickford (New York: Columbia University Press, 1998), 203.
40 Ibid., 192.
41 Ibid., 193.

3

Universalist Tendencies in Tocqueville, Adonis, Schlegel

Cartesian Americans: Alexis de Tocqueville

Derrida's fourth lecture of *Fantom* begins with a consideration of Alexis de Tocqueville and in so doing turns away from the Jewish motif of exile that Derrida investigated relative to Adorno, a concern to which he will return in lecture five in relation to Hannah Arendt and Ludwig Wittgenstein. At this point in *Fantom*, Derrida turns to Alexis de Tocqueville because the French historian is exemplary of a cosmopolitan thinker who spent considerable time in the United States as a visitor and not an exile. Tocqueville is actually a parallel figure to Derrida in the sense that both enthusiastically accept a Franco-American relationship, something Derrida shared with other contemporary French intellectuals too, including Michel Foucault, Jean Baudrillard, Michel Serres, and Julia Kristeva who in 1977 discovered New York as *terra incognita* for readers of *Tel Quel*. Also of significance is that discussion of Tocqueville returns to unfinished aspects of the lecture course *Language and the Discourse on Method* (1981–82) in which Descartes is discussed at length. Tocqueville too has an interest in Descartes and postulates one of the paradoxes of philosophical nationalism that fascinates Derrida, namely that "America is thus one of the countries in the world where the precepts of Descartes are least studied and most widely applied."[1] This statement forms the foundational paradox that, as noted earlier, informs deconstruction: that without having read a word of Derrida, Americans were always already thinkers and practitioners of deconstruction, just as, according to Tocqueville, Americans were Cartesians in the absence of having read any of Descartes.

> Americans do not read the works of Descartes because the state of their society diverts them from speculative study and they follow his maxims because it is this very social state which naturally disposes their minds to adopt them.[2]

Tocqueville's logic is not dissimilar from Fichte's when he says that the most German of German people may well have never set foot in Germany per se, and that therefore being German is a state of mind, or, as Fichte puts it, the spiritual condition of one's existence. Similarly, the Americans, according to Tocqueville, are inherently more Cartesian than the French, if only because their Cartesianism comes to them *naturally*. Tocqueville does not call this a spiritual condition but rather a matter of character united by the vicissitudes of environmental adaptation and subscription to a restricted number of "ready-formed beliefs," of "a few principal ideas" drawn from religion and the political philosophy of democracy.

> As for the effect which one man's intelligence can have upon another's, it is of necessity much curtailed in a country where its citizens, having become almost like each other, scrutinize each other carefully and, perceiving in not a single person in their midst any signs of undeniable greatness or superiority, constantly return to their own rationality as to the most obvious and immediate source of truth. So, it is not merely trust in any particular individual which is destroyed, but also the predilection to take the word of any man at all.[3]

Far from being allied or bonded on account of their similarity, Americans, on account of their democratic ideals, become isolated and turn inward, returning to their inherent rationality as the "source of truth." If no one is superior or greater, if all are equal, then it follows that each individual possesses an independence that liberates him or her from having to suffer the intelligence of one's neighbors. "[Americans] realize that, without help, they successfully resolve all the small problems they meet in their practical lives."[4] Does this make the world self-explanatory? "Americans have ... never felt the need to draw their philosophic method from books; they have discovered it within themselves." Similarly, "Descartes, in philosophy proper, abolished accepted formulae, destroyed the influence of tradition, and overturned the authority of the teacher."[5] According to Tocqueville, Descartes advocated attention to the things themselves, as opposed to attention to other people's teachings and opinions, which amounted to a liberation whereby the empirically minded realize that when confronted with the things themselves, everyone is equal. No matter who we are, we are all the same when confronted with changing a carriage wheel, feeding a horse, or building a barn. Such similitude is the soil upon which independence and individuality arise, according to Tocqueville, given that everyone being equals, no one has authority over anyone else. Tocqueville is hardly unaware of the disadvantages of such a view. "It is true enough that any man, accepting an opinion upon someone else's say-so, enslaves his own mind; but it is a salutary enslavement which allows him to make sound use of his freedom." Of course, this is Tocqueville's view of the educated European and Frenchman. "The independence of an individual can be more or less extensive but it could not possibly be boundless."[6]

Derrida will consider the points above in his lecture on Tocqueville, though he begins with citing the theme of method: as something egalitarian, practical, futuristic, technical, enlightening, democratic. The focus for the entire lecture is "The Americans' Philosophic Method" which comprises the opening chapter of volume 2 of *Democracy in America*. Tocqueville, Derrida says, is describing a national philosophy in terms of national character and in a manner that one might have cause to identify as Franco-centric.

Is Tocqueville writing a *"texte d'écriture très française,"* marked by an irreducible franco-centricism, not only in his tongue, but—to continue paraphrasing Derrida here—in his style and his rhetoric, which is that of an ideologue, a historian of ideas but also a political man, someone who was not only a man of science, a historian, a sociologist, an author writing about the criminal system in the United States and its application in France, on the abolition of slavery in the colonies, of essays on the politics in France before and since 1789? Tocqueville was politically active during the July Monarchy and during the Second Republic, but retired after Louis Napoleon Bonaparte's 1851 coup. His franco-centrism wasn't just readable in his writings generally, Derrida says, but in the machinery of his interpretation of America in particular: *de la méthode philosophique americaine*.

Franco-centrism, we're told, doesn't mean a blind subjectivist nationalism but the formation of a perspective that permits one to take into account how one sees and does not see within one's point of view those presuppositional limits of the position from which one speaks, such that one doesn't entirely understand one's own language, the very language without which one cannot say anything. Decades before Derrida wrote about Robinson Crusoe in *The Beast and the Sovereign*, Tocqueville was considered a bit like Defoe's castaway insofar as he has landed somewhere that is in need of naming and definition (identifying, conceptualizing, ordering, notating). If he is foreign to the phenomena he observes, the phenomena themselves are only made legible and familiar to us thanks to the expert analysis of a foreign agency that can methodically theorize the phenomena and give them coherent sense. It is by way of the outsider that the insider can be distinctly observed in terms of particulars that otherwise would be overlooked because taken for granted.

What Tocqueville sees, in fact, are inverse relations, for example, that national cohesion is based on the kind of individualism and autonomy that is the consequence of perceiving everyone as equal. The democratic structure of society therefore is in inverse relation to its national cohesion. Democracy advances to the detriment of nationality. The nation is less glorious and strong, perhaps, but the majority of its citizens enjoy more prosperity and well-being. In that sense the democratic principle is a sort of counter-nationalism, which is of central interest to Derrida. At a later point in the course Derrida will mention Hannah Arendt's similar observation made quite independently of Tocqueville, namely that America is alien to the kind of nationalism presupposed in Europe. Here, of course, we have the antinomy to Fichte's conceptions of nationalism.

As Derrida puts it, for Tocqueville the philosophy of Americans wasn't that of professional philosophers or of traditional philosophical discourses, but of the habitual political practices of everyday life that were not inherently systematic, academic, or professional and therefore lacking method. The paradox of a method without method—this will relate to Heidegger as literary reader much later in the course—is underscored by Derrida, for there is a technical, regular, organized set of practices arising out of what Tocqueville considers a natural understanding of how things are. Derrida observes that for Tocqueville no country is less philosophical than America, never mind that for him this unphilosophical tendency has a source and a method which is to be found in Descartes. Tocqueville sees Americans essentially as Franco-Saxons who are the inheritors of a Cartesianism that involves a certain oppositionality between scholarly philosophy and popular thinking. Since Americans have no philosophical school, Tocqueville claims, they have no systematic doctrine that is taught and sustained by a tradition and therefore aren't worried about the kind of intellectual concerns that divide Europe. Americans don't even know the names of major European thinkers. But, Derrida wonders, is it true that Americans were less worried about the schools of thought that divided Europe and didn't even know the names of the major thinkers? What Americans is Tocqueville talking about, and is his view not similar to Europeans who have prejudicially assumed that Americans are uncultured, even today? Such questions aside, what matters, Derrida says, is the nationalist philosophical logic of Tocqueville's gesture, what Derrida calls the national mechanism of his interpretation, the historical situation of his discourse. Derrida asks: What does that mean? And how are these judgments formed in the history of our problematic of philosophical nationalism? Rather than speak of a nation, Tocqueville speaks of Americans or inhabitants (*des habitants*) of the United States, which is to say, he refers to people in the aggregate who happen to think alike, given their commonality. This alludes to Fichte's remarks on the Germans in the *Addresses* whose commonality is rooted in the notion of *Stammvolk* or stock, something that can't be invoked in the case of the Americans, Tocqueville observes, who are all European immigrants from hither and yon. As to native peoples, Tocqueville sees them as the remnants of what must have once been a great civilization, though Derrida doesn't mention this. Still it is worth noting that the American Indian as social subject would problematize Tocqueville's notion of nature and one's adaptations to it, which in the case of native peoples is more ecologically and, some might argue, socially sound than what transpired under the settlers. However, as just noted, Derrida's attention lies elsewhere: on Tocqueville's implicit argument that American philosophy (or thinking, if one prefers) is essentially idiomatic.

Idiomaticity, in Derrida's view, is itself governed by the paradox Tocqueville has unearthed in the New World, namely that of a systematicity without system, a methodology without method, something that Derrida will re-encounter in Heidegger's treatment of Georg Trakl as discussed in future lectures. Linguistic idioms often reflect this emphasis upon a singularity or particularity that seems to be derived from some sort of system or method of thinking but, in fact, can't be explained in such terms and therefore isn't entirely translatable. In this context, one might consider analogically some of William Faulkner's fictional characters such as Abner Snopes, Thomas Sutpen, Rosa Coldfield, and Gail Hightower who are so idiomatically distinct as Southern characters that their habits and expressions defy translation into even a regional identitarianism of social comprehensibility, which, of course, is what Faulkner thinks so many of his characters have in common. "'I don't know,' Byron said, 'I reckon that's just my life.' 'And I reckon this is just my life, too,' the other said."[7] This is one of countless passing statements in Faulkner's novels (Byron Bunch visiting with Gail Hightower in *Light in August*) in which people acknowledge the gap of being apart together. This, to come back to idiomaticity, is its social embodiment as something independent, and seemingly systematic, that withholds comprehensibility. Idiomatic speech in Faulkner is often "method without method" that is taken at face value as some kind of implacable nature or circumstance fashioned by personal and collective history. Could the same be said of Heidegger's appropriation of idioms, that is part of a method without method that Derrida observes in *Unterwegs zur Sprache*? Such a performance of idiomaticity is situated in a manner that is absent in Tocqueville who is in search of commonality, not backwoods particularity and eccentricity (i.e., implacable difference often resentfully and violently on display), whether those backwoods be in Mississippi or the province of Baden.

Of interest to Derrida is that Tocqueville (who overlooks *racism*) is convinced of an absence of national prejudices among Americans, given that such prejudices are seen as childish (regressive, in Adorno's terminology). Structurally, nationalism is very puerile, in Tocqueville's view. Indeed, this judgment is upheld by a certain "natural doubt" that Americans supposedly possess. Hence Americans are thought to be skeptical of prejudices which are determined by systems of thought, for example, opinions about class, family, and the nation. The passage on Derrida's mind reads as follows:

> To escape the spirit of systems, the yoke of habit, the precepts of family, the opinions of class, and, to a certain extent, the prejudices of nation; to adopt tradition simply as information and present facts simply as a useful study in order to act differently and better; to search by oneself and in oneself alone for the reason of things; to strive for the ends without being enslaved by the means and to aim for the essence via the form: such are the main features which characterize what I shall call the American philosophic method.[8]

The treatment of tradition as information recalls Adorno's emphasis on a Kantian rational mode of indifferent analysis that has as its end the aim of acting better. Hence tradition has to be handled in a way that isn't prejudiced. This means that one cannot approach tradition with a blind faith in its authority or spirit, to use the German philosopheme.

Derrida says that he finds it telling that despite Tocqueville's awareness of the effects of the sorts of prejudices one associates with Europe—e.g., an irrational respect for tradition—Tocqueville, nevertheless, chooses to identify philosophy with nationality and methodology in a way that presupposes a connection with France in general and Descartes in particular. Indeed, the identification of American nationality with Cartesianism has nothing to do with how Americans see themselves, which relates, of course, to the observation that Descartes and the European philosophical tradition is virtually unknown in the New World. Hence, Derrida points out, Tocqueville is clearly imposing his own Eurocentric perspective onto America, imposing a European paradigm by way of denegation, that America having no interest in the concept of nation is a feature of that nation. Moreover, Derrida notes that whereas Fichte spoke of a philosophy that was proper to a people, one that stems from the depths of time, Tocqueville speaks of a philosophical method, of a sort of technics that has been historically acquired only relatively recently. This does not make up a native character of any sort in the national sense of a Fichte. Techne in America is not something given in nature but derived from the historical experience of settlement and survival, one that is divorced from heritage, stock, and the inheritance of a single common originary language. Recall, in this context, Adorno's complaints about the technics of publishing in America where standardization pays no mind to the spirit of the language (and the person) in which something is written.

Technology, Derrida continues, is deemed by Tocqueville to be part of a *second* nature, an acquired habitus, that rejects nativism and nationalism. In fact, despite what Americans might think, Tocqueville realizes this fails to avoid heritage, for example, that of a certain Cartesian mode of thinking that emerges in America like a fantom of the Other, the specter of French cultural development. However much America throws off the weight of generations, the specter of civilization as a national European formation nevertheless arrives in America as some sort of ghost in the woods without anyone realizing it. This parallels the situation in Adorno's address to the Germans wherein the spirit of the Other (the German as opposed to the Jew) steals into his discourse like a thief in the night breaking into the house of reason in order to vandalize it.

Although the major motivation for giving a seminar on Tocqueville was that of providing a counter-weight to Fichte, also on Derrida's mind was the idea of developing a Franco-American parallel to the German Jewish-American relation that had been discussed with respect to Adorno and that would be taken up later with respect to Hannah Arendt. Derrida's own personal history in terms of the Franco-American relation is directly relevant, and it is to be noted that, interestingly enough, in the interview "Deconstruction in America," given in the year *Fantom* was delivered, Derrida would define deconstruction itself as a method without method, something that aligned with Tocqueville's remarks on philosophy in America, but also with Heidegger in the final lectures of the course. Also on Derrida's agenda was an engagement with American pragmatism and analytical philosophy, which Derrida saw as Anglo-American philosophical idioms. Pragmatism, of course, is implicit in everything Tocqueville was discussing in terms of an American philosophical temperament, one that in late twentieth-century America would prove to be allergic to deconstruction.

Adonis, World Citizen

The fifth lecture of *Fantom* begins with Derrida's remarks that his theme will be emigration and that he is once more going to speak of émigrés, given the previous lecturing on Adorno dedicated to an *émigré en retour*. Of course, the discourse of Tocqueville concerned a nation made up mainly of émigrés, and related to this is Derrida's remark that the discourses of a national philosophy (typical of a Fichte) inherently address émigrés within who are outcast (*des réprouvés*), people who were forced out of their homelands. The gesture of all nationalists, Derrida says, is to constitute themselves as a nation or to restore their nationality, and if today Derrida admits that he begins a little differently, the motif of emigration, whether interior to or exterior to the nation, will be continuous nevertheless with the previous lectures.

Preliminary remarks aside, Derrida begins lecture five with an excursus on the Syrian poet Adonis who is the subject of an article Derrida glosses in *Le Monde*, "L'exilé universel," published on November 30, 1984. Derrida credits Adonis as one of the greatest living poets writing in Arabic (in later years he would be shortlisted for the Nobel Prize). Adonis interests Derrida because his is a self-given name. Of concern is the story in which Adonis poses the question of the name, of the change of name, his legitimation by the name, and access by the name to a culture that is said by Adonis to be universal. In this way Adonis is responding to the question: How does a young *paysan* called Ali Ahmad Saïd Esber choose to call himself Adonis? We are told that despite what he calls his visceral belonging the land of his birth—to his *origine paysanne*—he felt already that he had carried an "*infinité des noms*."

Derrida notes that Adonis differentiates between the earth and the name, that if he is born on natal soil, he nevertheless carries an infinity of names that to him are not linked to the land or to what Heidegger would have called *Boden*. Neither is the poet's name grounded in language or the culture into which he was born. Adonis, then, is a signifier of standing and being apart, a master signifier (as the Lacanians would say) of non-attachment. Derrida doesn't make the connection, but in the lectures on Heidegger's consideration of Trakl, the notion of *Abgeschiedenheit* or apartness (isolation, seclusion, retirement) will play a major role, given that at times the lyrics concern a wanderer who sets off to a natural place in order to retreat or withdraw. Adonis, in this sense, is conspicuously analogous to Heidegger's understanding of Trakl's figure of the stranger discussed in the eighth lecture.

The name Adonis, Derrida says, cannot be considered national, cannot be linked to the poet's birth, to a territory, or to a national identity. Derrida notes that Ali Ahmed Saïd Esber tells the journalist that he chose this name by chance. By means of qualification, Adonis says that as auto-nomination the choosing of the name exceeds all the partial explications that he might give, as if his first poetic act were this self-donation of a name, of a signature invented that is not patronymical, not patriotic, and not national. Fundamentally it is the case that this poetical act consists not in illustrating a patronymical signature but the poet's invention of his own idiomatic signature—*sa propre signature idiomatique*. This signature speaks to what Derrida at the outset was calling an émigré within who is reprobate, outcast, perhaps even damned, which is to say, someone who sets himself apart, who refuses belonging. In the case of Adonis, this setting apart concerns an emigration into cosmopolitanism in general and, eventually, to France in particular. Parricide is an early theme in Derrida's work (viz., *La dissémination*) and Adonis's self-nomination is viewed by Derrida in that light, though Derrida also notes that in substituting an idiomatic signature for a patronymical one, Adonis may well be giving something back to the father that is self-authorized.

As to the Greek myth of Adonis, Derrida relates that the poet had by chance read in a magazine the myth of Adonis and of the wild boar that he had killed. He identified with someone symbolizing love who had been destroyed by a bestial force. Under his pseudonym the poet sent a poem off that had been refused under another pseudonym. Adonis noted that the same journal printed it immediately. In taking the name Adonis, not only had the way been opened to publishing, but the poet assumed a "passage to the universal." In this way he says he exited a frozen tradition and acceded to a much greater liberty. Derrida notes that for Adonis this constituted a belonging to a cosmopolitan privilege without the loss of idiom. Adonis says that he could inscribe the Arab tradition itself in the movement of a universal culture, and that by simply the choice of a name, he transformed somewhat the stature of the poet on Arab soil. Derrida doesn't mention that Adonis had spent time in a Syrian prison in 1956 for his affiliation with a nationalist organization, something that motivated Adonis to move to Beirut where he became involved with literary publishing and the advancement of Arabic poetry. Derrida simply explains that the move to Lebanon concerned the wish to be cosmopolitan. Lebanon is cited as cosmopolis, a place where Adonis could revivify language. Paraphrasing Adonis, there is a legend told by the poet that the blood of Adonis returns to irrigate the waters of a river that runs near Beirut. In spring, this river of Adonis takes on the red color of the flowers of Adonis—the poppies that one offers on a wedding day. (*Mohn* [poppy] as blessing occurs in Trakl, as well.) *L'amour-la mort* is a *re-naissance* making up the face of the god with which Adonis sees himself, "according to a certain craziness," identified. The poet's name incarnates the myth of dying and resurrecting, of eradicating one's identity in order to be elevated to a universal plane where one reinvigorates one's maternal language. There too one finds a major correspondence with Heidegger's reading of Trakl's wanderer whose withdrawal is a prelude to resurrection. In the context of Adonis, we are told that

Lebanon, although on the road to destruction, is nevertheless the place where one can best realize and live an aspiration for universality.

Derrida remarks that a universal place recalls Fichte, that there is a universal place that paradoxically exists as unique and singular. Yet, because place cannot be both singular and universal geographically, Adonis must define this place by language, that is, by means of the name and writing. Place isn't territorial locality but the possibility of naming. Lebanon, according to Adonis, is at once a land as well as a mixture of tongues and cultures. This multiplicity of voices and idioms, Derrida says, must mix, knot, overlap, and interlace with the interiority of a unicity, of a poetic idiom that must be absolutely singular at the moment where it asserts a multiple heritage and universal access.

Derrida recognizes that for Adonis, at the time he was still living in Lebanon, there was an attachment to place as crossroads, as flow of languages, cultures, peoples that related to the entirety of the Mediterranean, including Greece, but also Turkey with its connections to Asia Minor. Because Adonis welcomes a multiplicity of heritages that stresses involvement and contact in a way that isn't institutionalized or regulated, he opens the way for idiom. Adonis writes in his natal language, Arabic; however, it is a language that idiomatically has been influenced by various cultures and modes of expression drawn from many parts of the Mediterranean in a manner that Adonis considers universal, not that he isn't writing in his personal idiom, in terms of his own signature. At issue for Derrida, then, is how the poet negotiates the divides between the national and the cosmopolitan (in this case, in terms of the Middle East per se) if not the regional and the global. This concerns relations between a philosophical and poeticist nationalism, between philosophy and poetry tied up with the question of national idiom. Derrida comments that the idiom of idiom ('*l'idiome de l'idiome*'), mentioned more than once in the course, is not separable from writing as philosophic-poetic. Of course, Derrida has not only Adonis, but Heidegger in mind, given that in Hediegger's later writings, especially, idiomaticity, poeticism, and philosophy are intertwined and lose their identity as entirely separate categories.

In "Living On: Border Lines," which was published several years before *Fantom* was given, Derrida had already been considering nationalism in relation to universalism.

> Nationalism and universalism. What this institution [the university] cannot bear is a transformation that leaves intact neither of these two complementary poles. It can bear more readily the most apparently revolutionary ideological sorts of "content," if only that content does not touch the borders of language

[*la langue*] and of all the juridico-political contracts that it guarantees. It is this "intolerable" something that concerns me here.[9]

In *Fantom*, the name Adonis signs for this intolerability, one that threatens not just the border line between nationalism and universalism but those that separate the usual distinctions between poetry, philosophy, and idiom. In "Living On: Border Lines," which is in many ways crucial for an understanding of *Fantom*, Derrida's major interest was in translation. "A text lives only if it lives *on* (*sur-vit*), and it lives *on* only if it is *at once* translatable *and* untranslatable."[10] Without an idiomaticity that doesn't entirely translate, a text won't survive. Yet, the untranslatability of idiom (that in "Living On: Borderlines" touches on Maurice Blanchot's handling of French idiom) is intolerable if only because it resists decidability. In "Des tours de Babel," Derrida addresses idiomaticity specifically. "What the multiplicity of idioms actually limits is not only a 'true' translation, a transparent and adequate interexpression, it is also a structural order, a coherence of construct. There is then (let us translate) something like an internal limit to formalization, an incompleteness of the constructure."[11] Idiom withdraws from translatability even as it promotes a structural order or coherence that dangles translatability before us.[12]

In "Living On: Border Lines," Derrida says of writing as *survivance* that it is a living-on beyond the grave that puts into question the difference of life and death.

> The same thing will be said of what I call *écriture*, mark, trace, and so on. It neither lives nor dies; it lives *on*. And it "starts" only with living on (testament, iterability, remaining [*restance*], crypt, detachment that lifts the strictures of the "living" *rectio* or direction of an "author" not drowned at the edge of his text).[13]

In terms of idiomaticity, this means that as writing, mark, or trace, the idiom lives outside or exterior to the very person to whom it is most internal and private, as remainder or remains. When Adonis writes "I scatter—am diffused—my surfaces spread and I own none of them,"[14] one suspects that the idiomatic name Adonis is part of an ek-scription of the self.[15] We know what it is to inscribe, to mark one's presence as the bearer of the mark whose function is to situate one among other bearers, or to commemorate the presence of one at a certain time and place. The inscription of the name verifies one's existence in terms of a belonging or adhering to. Ek-scription, by contrast, speaks to a writing that has neither an internal nor an external limit. It is a writing that has left the subject behind, that renounces belonging and attachment, and that exposes itself as severance: as a violence of the trace. Each word or phrase breaks and splits up the unity of language with the result that writing as ek-scription adjourns commonplace sense, identity, and world. Ek-scription disappropriates the one who writes. In *Fantom*, Adonis, the name, signs for this intolerability of being written apart, one that threatens translation and exposes idiom as fundamentally exilic. Here, once more, there is some foreshadowing of *Abgeschiedenheit* in Heidegger's writings on Trakl.

Derrida cites *Le Monde*'s interviewer who asks Adonis about staying behind in Beirut during its being bombed. What did you want to rescue from this hell?, he is asked. Adonis responds that he stayed in communion with the earth, with all those who wanted to preserve a carnal relation with place. He says he was ready to accept death, that he didn't want to flee the suffering of others. For Derrida this addresses a central question relevant to *Fantom*: whether to emigrate or not. Even those foppish French and German socialists of whom Marx makes so much fun are emigrating, if only mentally, as if one couldn't stand to remain in place. Adorno and Arendt, of course, had to emigrate. Heidegger could have emigrated out of National Socialist Germany, but chose not to leave what to him was a spiritual homeland. For Derrida, this decision to stay was as radical a decision as leaving was for the émigrés. Adonis, as it happened, both stayed *and* left. He remains where the bombs are falling *and* he emigrates to France.

Like Heidegger, Adonis privileges a relationship of a people to the earth; similarly, Adonis has taken the position that technology deforms that relation. Derrida cites Adonis's view that the industrial world is ruinous and is opposed to the regenerative desert that the poet loves. The contrast of generation with degeneration foreshadows later discussions of *Geschlecht*. Also like Heidegger, Adonis is interested in the inceptual, for example, the pre-Islamic influences within the multiplicity of archaic heritages and traditions that relate to the Middle East: Sumerian, Phoenician, Babylonian. In contrast to Heidegger, Adonis says in interview that he asserts all the Mediterranean heritages and that it makes him feel part of a universal culture of both Occident and Orient. As opposed to *Geschlecht* as asserting a specific kind, Adonis affiliates himself with human kind in general. Yet, if territory, statehood, nationality, or citizenship are obviated in favor of simply wishing to belong to humanity writ large, Adonis says that only his language and his subjectivity are proper and specific to him. Derrida is very interested in this assertion, because it agrees with Adorno and Arendt who also privilege language as their primary source of social attachment.

In short, for Adonis, Adorno, and Arendt (as we will see later), language is not just a communicative tool, as Locke imagined, but fundamental to the social relation per se. For Adonis, Arabic, however particular as a specific language, is the social relation writ large outside the frameworks of nationalism and regionalism. This is not to say that Arabic is a universal language that everyone speaks, but that it can have a non-national specificity that makes it accessible to humanity generally on account of its subjective idiomaticity, or what Derrida calls the idiom of idiom whose signature is Adonis. Still, idiomatic poetizing must give access to the universal. Here, Derrida says, one must speak of a certain crossing over of poetry/philosophy, of the co-signature of the poetical and of the philosophical. Again, the fantom of Heidegger haunts these speculations insofar as his work of the 1930s and after is heavily inflected in terms of how ontology as a universal condition is accessed poetically in, say, Parmenides, Hölderlin, and Trakl, but also in terms of Heidegger's own linguistic idiom as a philosopher, if not to say his own poems, which are not inconsiderable, though much overlooked. Derrida's point, which will be considerably amplified in the last lectures of *Fantom*, is that poetry and philosophy sign for one another in ways that concern an idiomaticity that cannot be translated, despite the fact that it is this idiomaticity that gives one access to the universal. The discussion of Adonis, apparently, was intended by Derrida to make this latter point on universality.

Schlegel's *Politiques de l'amitié*

Related to the universalizing tendency is what Derrida's auditors must have experienced as a rather odd and abrupt change of topic: Friedrich Schlegel's letter "On Philosophy. To Dorothea" which had been included in Jean-Luc-Nancy and Philippe Lacoue-Labarthe's *L'absolu littéraire: Théorie de la littérature du romantisme allemande* (1978). Derrida's remarks on Schlegel remain quite restricted, though the choice of text speaks volumes, given that among Schlegel's concerns is that of knitting philosophy and poetry together with Geschlecht (gender and genre). Quite possible is that of interest to Derrida might have been Schlegel's working of gender in a way that relates to androgyny, which is relevant to Trakl's reference to male and female as "*E i n Geschlecht*" (one kind or gender) in a poem of interest to Heidegger. Reading *Fantom* retroactively from the end, it seems Derrida may have well wondered if there is a Christianized deconstruction of the male and female relation in Schlegel that might serve as a telling intertext for consideration of the brother and sister relation in Trakl.

Derrida must have seen comments in Schlegel's letter relevant to *Fantom*'s earlier discussions of Fichte, given that Schlegel recommends Fichte to Dorothea as a model contemporary writer, not that Derrida develops this connection, which remains another sort of fantom waiting in the wings. After all, Schlegel knew Fichte and wrote extensively on him. Also conspicuous is that Schlegel's letter speaks to the theme of the Jew and the German that was undergoing development in *Fantom*. Schlegel was writing to his lover, Dorothea Mendelssohn, daughter of Moses Mendelssohn, the great Jewish philosopher of the time, and in the letter draws upon the Pauline distinction of the letter versus the spirit. In *The Rhetoric of Cultural Dialogue*, Jeffrey S. Librett brilliantly works out the complexities of this division, which undergoes proto-deconstruction when hierarchical identities are reversed, displaced, and revalued.[16] Schlegel equates himself with writing and Dorothea with the spirit, which inverts the Pauline identification of Jews with the letter and Christians with the spirit. Schlegel's thesis is that the spirit cannot be realized as spirit in the absence of mediation by the letter that is at once superior and inferior to the spirit. Conversely, the letter is dead without mediation by the spirit. Since the letter (masculine) will be identified with philosophy (writing) and the spirit (feminine) with poetry (voice), each genre (philosophy, poetry) must mediate the other in a way that dissolves their oppositionality while not relinquishing their difference. Jewish and German identities are affirmed, collapsed, and made undecidable as letter and spirit change places as if by way of a minuet, though Librett suggests quite rightly that this is only possible on account of a certain erasure of Dorothea's heritage, one she seems to have accepted by means of willingly converting to Christianity upon her marriage to Schlegel.

Derrida himself does not broach these issues and leaves them suspended. Given how relevant they are to *Fantom* and later courses, one has reason to suspect, once more, that Derrida was thinking about eventually returning to a fuller exposition of Schlegel. However, what caught Derrida's attention for the purposes of following on from Adonis is Schlegel's view that "a certain regulated exchange between individuality and universality is the actual heartbeat of the higher life and constitutes the first condition for moral well-being."[17] This sounds the theme of cosmopolitanism that is later to be contrasted with the following passage from the "Letter" to which Derrida's remarks on Schlegel crescendo.

> For where language is animated by enthusiasm there arises from the most common, simple, and understandable words and phrases, as if spontaneously, a *language within language*. Where the whole this is as if cast from the same mold, those of similar mind feel the living breath and its enchanting breeze, while those of a different mind are left undisturbed.[18]

Schlegel's insistence that "the *universe* is and remains my password" is an embrace of universality that requires an attachment to the particular—"Do you truly love if you don't find the world in your lover?"[19] It is in this context that he proposes the notion of "a language within language" that Derrida associates with the "idiom of idiom." "All studies," Schlegel writes, "even the most banal reading, may become philosophical through *the domination of the inner* over the outer form, through the development of one's understanding and thought and through the continuous relating to the infinite."[20] By domination of the inner, Schlegel is, in Derrida's terms, addressing idiom.

In speaking of Kant "who so often laments the imperfection of his presentation," Schlegel speaks of making him "accessible" in the absence of "diminishing his richness or robbing him of his wit and originality."[21] He continues: "If it were permissible to organize his works somewhat better, obviously according to his own ideas, especially with respect to sentence structure, episodes, and repetitions, they would become as accessible as, for instance, those of Lessing." However, "one does not have to take any greater liberties than the old critics did with the classical poets and I think one would then *see* that Kant, on a purely literary level as well, belongs among the classical writers *of our nation*."[22] This last remark is quite ambiguous, because on the one hand it suggests that Kant's idiom or manner of writing has to be respected, whereas on the other hand the method of "the old critics" who redacted the ancients is being summoned. To be a classical writer "of our nation," would Kant require general editing in order to make him more popular? Or would the editors, Kant's countrymen, be revealing Kant's inherent literary style, one idiomatic to him in particular that has been heard and perhaps brought out somewhat by fellow Germans?

Schlegel says that Fichte, in contrast to Kant, represents deep, infinite reflection "expressed with the popularity and clarity that you would find in his new presentation of the theory of scientific knowledge."[23] Although Fichte's "enthusiasm for popular forms of *communication*" impresses Schlegel, in the letter Schlegel acknowledges that "you [Dorothea] have no confidence in so-called popular philosophers," among them Rousseau and Voltaire who Schlegel agrees are "banal."[24] Here the popular is associated with the mediocrity of average people and the commonality of the everyday. But in the case of Fichte, who is Schlegel's countryman, one is considering "a philosopher with every fiber of his being and also, by disposition and character, the archetype and representative of the genre for our age."[25] Indeed, as Schlegel says to Dorothea, "one cannot grasp him fully without understanding his personality, not just philosophically but also historically."[26]

In short, one has to "understand Fichte himself," which Schlegel probably did, as he was a personal friend and therefore well acquainted with him. In this context, of course, understanding relates to the individual spirit or *idiom of the man*, something that enables him to become a popular thinker, first, in a nationalist sense, given that he embodies the spirit of the German people historically, but second, in a universalizing sense, for "I consider *this* kind of popularity to be a rapprochement of philosophy and *humanity* [*Annäherung der Philosophie zur* Humanität] … which reminds us that man [*der Mensch*] shall only live among men and that no matter how far his spirit [*sein Geist*] extends itself, ultimately *he must return home* [*am Ende doch dahin wieder heimkehren soll*]."[27]

Heimkehr is a figure one recognizes in Heidegger too for the nationalist gesture that it is, one that for Derrida cannot be dissociated with linguistic idiomaticity, if not the kind of regional and domestic familiarity that brings people into what seems to be a natural social relationship. Hence Schlegel's remark on Fichte that "his latest writings are friendly dialogues [*freundschaftliche Gespräche*] with the [German] reader in the candid, simple style [*treuherzigen schlichten Stil*] of a Luther."[28] Of course, Luther's importance as father of modern German is, once more, apropos of nationalist considerations close to the heart [*treuherzigen*].

The remarks above serve to contextualize Derrida's citation of Schlegel's: "For where language is animated by enthusiasm there arises from the most common, simple, and understandable words and phrases, as if spontaneously, a language within language [*Denn wo sie Enthusiasmus beseelt, da bildet sich aus den gewöhnlichsten, einfachsten und verständlichsten Worten und Redensarten wie von selbst eine Sprache in der Sprache*]."[29] Derrida seizes upon this statement in order to make the observation that in Schlegel (as in Fichte and Heidegger) "*die Sprache spricht*," language languages, and not only that, but it does so by means of an interiority or intimacy (the "within") that is idiomatically irreducible. For Schlegel the enthusiasm that animates is spirit. Much later in *Fantom*, and at more length in *Of Spirit*, Derrida will consider that in Heidegger over a century later, a spirit will burst into flame as something that crosses into the malign. For Schlegel, however, emphasis falls upon "*the infinity of the human spirit* [die Unendlichkeit des menschlichen Geistes], *the godliness of all natural things*, and the *humanness of the gods* [Menschlichkeit der Götter]."[30] For Schlegel the infinity of the human spirit concerns even the most understandable words and phrases idiomatic to a people and, as such, that people's language within language. In Heidegger emphasis falls upon a language within language that has withdrawn from common understandability and perhaps even hearing, as Derrida will explain later with respect to Trakl's *Gedicht*, an inceptual poetizing that leaves traces of what is not audible. Is it there that something evil is to be detected?

Say, the evil of an inceptual violence that will determine not *Menschlichkeit*, but *Menschengeschlecht*? Derrida gives us reason to think so.

Another passage quoted by Derrida concerns the crucial figure of crossing over, something that concerns the nationalism-cosmopolitanism binary as well as other binaries, poetry/philosophy, female/male, voice/writing, and so on.

> I know you agree with me wholeheartedly that poesy and philosophy are more than a means of filling the gaps that, despite all distractions, remain for idle people who happen to have some education; and that you agree that they are a necessary part of life, the spirit and soul of humanity. Because it seems to be nearly impossible to love poesy and philosophy equally, however, you find yourself standing at the crossroads like Hercules, or Wilhelm Meister, wondering which muse to choose and to follow.[31]

Here the German original should call our attention.

> Ich weiß es, Du stimmst mir von ganzem Herzen bei, daß die Poesie und die Philosophie mehr sei, als etwas, was die Lücken, die müßigen Menschen, welche von ungefähr ein wenig gebildet wurden, bei allen Zerstreuungen übrig bleiben, auszufüllen vermag; daß sie ein notwendiger Teil des Lebens sei, Geist und Seele der Menschheit. Da es aber kaum möglich sein dürfte, beide gleich sehr zu lieben, so wirst Du nun wie Herkules, oder Wilhelm Meister, am Scheidewege stehen, und zweifeln, welcher Muse Du den Preis geben und folgen sollst.[32]

The critical crossing over point is called the *Scheidewege*, the road or path of decision that requires a division. *Either* one chooses poetry *or* philosophy, a division Derrida is thinking of in terms of Heidegger's *Dichten und Denken*. And yet, as Derrida is quick to mention, this break is not really a break at all, given that the muses need not be separated. Hence note the following citation of Schlegel:

> It is not my intention to separate the Muses [*die Musen zu trennen*]. The thought alone would be blasphemy. Poesy and philosophy are an indivisible whole [*ein unteilbares Ganzes*]; like Castor and Pollux, they are forever linked, though rarely together. Between the two of them they share the farthest reaches of great and dignified humanity but, coming from their different directions, they meet in the middle. Here, in the innermost and most holy, the spirit is whole [*ist der Geist ganz*], and poesy and philosophy entirely melted into one [*völlig eins und verschmolzen*]. The dynamic unity of mankind cannot be rigid and unchanging; it consists of friendly exchange. [*Die lebendige Einheit des Menschen kann keine starre Unveränderlichkeit sein, sie bestehet im freundschaftlichen Wechsel.*][33]

That the place of decision and division turns out to be a place of exchange whereby opposites are displaced, reprioritized, and transvalued concerns something quite different from the antagonistic dialectics of Hegel, given the emphasis upon friendliness, of a certain politics of friendship, as Derrida would have it some years later. We should never lose sight of the fact that in Schlegel's letter foundational to the discourse is that of love between man and woman, a love crisscrossed by divisions—male/female, German/Jew, philosophy/poetry, religion/philosophy, and the popular/the academic. Essentially these divisions will relate strongly to Derrida's later handling of *Geschlecht*, a term Schlegel himself uses as follows: "*Die Geschlechtsverschiedenheit ist nur eine Äußerlichkeit des menschlichen Daseins.*" That is, sexual difference (gender) is but "an external factor of human being" (in J. Shulte Sasse's translation), if not its externalization.[34] Given Derrida's reading of Heidegger on Trakl in the lectures to come, one might well ask whether for Derrida Schlegel's statement would count as an instance of avoidance when one considers the overdeterminations of *Geschlecht*.

Notes

1 Alexis de Tocqueville, *Democracy in America and Two Essays on America*, trans. G.E. Bevan (London: Penguin Books, 2003), 494.
2 Ibid.
3 Ibid.
4 Ibid.
5 Ibid., 495.
6 Ibid., 500.
7 William Faulkner, *Light in August* (New York: Vintage, 1990), 75.
8 Tocqueville, *Democracy in America and Two Essays on America*, 493.
9 Jacques Derrida, "Living On: Borderlines," in *Deconstruction and Criticism* (New York: Seabury Press, 1979), 94–5. This text is composed of two essays, "Living On," which is on the poet Shelley's *Triumph of Life*, and a series of dated dispatches or entries entitled "Border Lines" which ran at the foot of each page separated with a borderline. The remarks on nationalism-universalism pertain to "Border Lines."
10 Ibid., 102.
11 Jacques Derrida, "Des Tours de Babel," in *Difference in Translation*, ed. J.F. Graham (Ithaca: Cornell University Press, 1985), 166.
12 See Jacques Derrida, *Parages*, ed. John P. Leavey, trans. Tom Conley et al. (Stanford: Stanford University Press, 2011). At issue is Maurice Blanchot who is the subject of all four essays in *Parages*: "Pas," "Living On: Borderlines," "Title to be Specified," and "The Law of Genre." With regard to Blanchot's French, there is a depersonalization of idiom. "They [the words: the idioms] do not speak, they are

not interior, they are, on the contrary, without intimacy, being altogether outside, what they designate engages me in this 'outside' of all speech, apparently more secret and more interior than the speech of the innermost heart ...," 70.
13 Derrida, "Living On: Borderlines," 103.
14 Adonis, *Selected Poems*, trans. Khalid Mattawa (New Haven: Yale University Press, 2010), 125.
15 On ex-scription, see my "Performativity as Ex-Scription: Adonis After Derrida," in *Performatives after Deconstruction*, ed. M. Senatore (London: Bloomsbury, 2013).
16 Jeffrey S. Librett, *The Rhetoric of Cultural Dialogue* (Stanford: Stanford University Press, 2000).
17 Friedrich Schlegel, "On Philosophy. To Dorothea," in *Theory as Practice: A Critical Anthology of Early German Romantic Writings*, ed. and trans. Jochen Schulte-Sasse et al. (Minneapolis: University of Minnesota Press, 1997), 427.
18 Ibid., 438.
19 Ibid., 427.
20 Ibid., 437. My italics.
21 Ibid., 435.
22 Ibid., 435. My italics.
23 Ibid.
24 Ibid., 434.
25 Ibid., 436.
26 Ibid.
27 Ibid.
28 Ibid.
29 Friedrich Schlegel, "Über die Philosophie An Dorothea (1799)," in *Kritische Ausgabe*, vol. 8, ed. Ernst Behler and U. Struc-Oppenberg (Munich: Ferdinand Schöningh Verlag, 1975), 60. "On Philosophy: To Dorothea," 438.
30 Schlegel, 438/60.
31 Ibid., 429.
32 Schlegel, "Über die Philosophie An Dorothea (1799)," 50–1.
33 Schlegel, 430/52 in English translation and German.
34 Ibid., 425/45.

4

World and Worldlessness: Arendt and Wittgenstein

At this point in surveying *Fantom*, one can see that Derrida has been shuttling between two major historical moments of philosophical nationalism, each of which embraces a number of figures who both overlap and diverge from one another. Fichte, Kant, Schlegel, Grün, Tocqueville, and Marx and Engels begin to fill in the first historical moment of the late eighteenth and early nineteenth centuries (Voltaire, Rousseau, Goethe, Schiller, Schelling, and Hegel loom in the background), whereas Adorno, Adonis, Arendt, Wittgenstein, and Heidegger begin to fill in the second historical moment, roughly the end of the First World War to the 1960s. In essays that Derrida was writing and publishing near the time of giving *Fantom of the Other*, he had also been focusing on Walter Benjamin and Paul Celan. In the course *The Theological-Political* (1986–87) Derrida would expand this overall grouping of twentieth-century Jewish intellectuals to include Hermann Cohen, Franz Rosenzweig, Gersholm Scholem, and, to a lesser degree, Martin Buber (his gift of his German translation of the Old Testament to the German people). As we have seen, Heidegger is present in the role of ghostly other whose thinking does and doesn't correspond with German Jewish writings, though Derrida also devoted lecture time in the late 1980s to Richard Wagner's anti-Semitic writings, Nietzsche's *Ecce Homo*, and Carl Schmitt's theory of the friend and the enemy, the latter overlapping somewhat with Derrida's reading of Buber. Taken all together, these figures make up the warp and woof of a major study that was gestating but, given Derrida's other commitments, never realized in terms of a monograph. Instead, Derrida spun off segments of this immense project as various individual pieces whose connections to one another were largely hidden to those who had not been attending the courses. Not only that, but in 1987 Derrida's controversial role in the Paul de Man Affair set off massive academic condemnation that obscured Derrida's intellectual itinerary of the mid-1980s by giving long-standing haters of deconstruction an opening whereby they could scurrilously dismiss Derrida—if not deconstruction per se—as fascist. Misunderstood in terms of Derrida's response to the war time career of de Man is that, as in *Fantom*, Derrida was interested in the contradictions and ambivalences that compromised determinate ideological or philosophical positions relative to social-political issues. The cases of Hannah Arendt and Ludwig Wittgenstein discussed below are more typical than not of this orientation.

Hannah Arendt

In turning to Hannah Arendt within the fifth lecture, Derrida largely points to various statements and positions wherein he detects something that he is not yet prepared to call Jewish anti-Semitism. This is the prelude to remarks on Wittgenstein's texts, assembled in English in the volume *Culture and Value*, that are unquestionably an expression of such Jewish self-hatred. Derrida is not interested in making a moral objection, but in examining instances wherein there are complications in the relation of the Jew and the German. Notable is that the later remarks on Wittgenstein are quite sketchy; one is simply given some very broad outlines. The discussion of Arendt is fuller, but it is more descriptive than analytical. Such discussions probably should be taken as the preliminary indications of a direction in which Derrida had taken some interest and selected some passages for consideration. Of course that was also the case in terms of his treatment of *The German Ideology* and Schlegel's "Letter."

The remarks on Arendt herself focus on two texts, the Lessing Prize address, which comprises chapter one of *Men in Dark Times* (published in France as *Vies Politiques*) and the television interview, "'What Remains? The Language Remains': A Conversation with Günter Gaus," of October 28, 1964. Clearly, the televised interview with Gaus is to be paired with Adorno's radio broadcast on "What Is German?" by way of an assumed understanding that one is operating in a comparative framework, a view that is presupposed in the lecture courses as a whole. In this sense, the phrase "fantom of the other" can be taken as a metaphor for comparative analysis wherein Adorno and Arendt ghost one another, for example, in terms of their remarks on language and their personal relation to Germany and its recent history. In the background as well are the remarks Derrida made on Adonis, particularly with respect to notions of world, which are very relevant to Derrida's discussion of Arendt.

Three main topics at issue in Derrida's consideration of Arendt are worldlessness, friendship versus fraternity, and language. Adonis, as we recall, embraced a certain worldlessness in terms of a personal liberation that went so far as to erase his given name for a pseudonym that brought him in cosmopolitan relation with all people. Of course, as the word cosmopolitan suggests, there is some sort of cosmos in play within which one's identity, however pluralized or multi-aspectual, functions in a fraternal manner. In this context, one could say that the name Adonis is synonymous with *fraternité* in its politicized sense, which has its conceptual roots in eighteenth-century France.

As Derrida points out, Arendt identifies worldlessness (*acosmie*) with fraternity, given that this is the philosopheme of a collective condition relating to those populations who wind up dispossessed and denationalized. Fraternity, for Arendt, is the universalizing Band-Aid thought up by social reformers and is applied as a principle of social justice to minorities that exist permanently outside the full protection of laws afforded a nation's legal citizens.[1] Fraternity, in other words, speaks to mutual dependency under conditions of existential threat, real and potential, wherein one has little or no ability to act politically in ways that could improve one's status. However, if fraternity has a significance beyond maintaining a semblance of the social relation, however stripped of legality, it also has the function of counteracting the dehumanization of being considered unwanted, alien, and expendable. That this function is abstract and requires good will, which in times of trouble may be in short supply, means that fraternity isn't reliable in practice. Terms such as "humanity" and "mankind" are also part of a universalizing discourse that transcends nation-states and as such transcends protection under their laws, much as invocation of "the environment" does today, despite international conferences on how to address climate change.

In the Lessing Prize address, Arendt points out that "fraternity has its natural place among the repressed and the persecuted, the exploited and humiliated, whom the eighteenth century called the unfortunates, *les malheureux*, and the nineteenth century the wretched, *les misérables*." It is through compassion, Arendt points out, that "the revolutionary-minded humanitarian of the eighteenth century sought to achieve solidarity with the unfortunate and the miserable—an effort tantamount to penetrating the very domain of brotherhood."[2] This kind of "humanitarianism," we're told, is "not transmissible and cannot be easily acquired by those who do not belong among the pariahs. Neither compassion nor actual sharing of suffering is enough."[3] Compassion is problematic, furthermore, because it only leads to an attempt at improving conditions instead of establishing justice for all. Therefore, fraternity is insufficient, because not only does its humanitarianism fall short of actually grasping the experience of "the pariah" (the dispossessed, the stateless, the alien, etc.), but because it winds up resorting to half-measures that do not include the sort of equality under the law that only legitimate citizenship can guarantee. Fraternity has the consequence of maintaining the idea that minorities can exist in perpetuity outside the nation-state's full legal protections, while residing within it, which for the dispossessed and displaced amounts to denying them "world": a place in which to live wherein one can take effective political action. In the television interview and the Lessing Prize address, it is clear that for Arendt, world corresponds to the word *polis* in Ancient Greek philosophy.

If fraternity is the denial of world or polis, friendship is its life blood, so to speak. As Arendt reminds us,

> We read in Aristotle that philia, friendship among citizens, is one of the fundamental requirements for the well-being of the City … For the Greeks the essence of friendship consisted in discourse. They held that only the constant interchange of talk united citizens in a *polis*. In discourse, the political importance of friendship, and the humanness particular to it, were made manifest.[4]

The *polis*, we're told, only becomes humane when it is "an object of discourse" among "our fellows." Again, "we humanize what is going on in the world and in ourselves by speaking of it, and in the course of speaking it we learn to be human."[5] Friendship, *philanthropia*, means "'love of man,' since it manifests itself in a readiness to share the world." The Latin word *humanitas* relates to "the political fact that in Rome people of widely different ethnic origins and descent could acquire Roman citizenship and thus enter into the discourse among cultivated Romans [and] could discuss the world and life with them."[6] Friendship, as opposed to fraternity, is therefore allied in Arendt's mind with being part of the world as a political space in which one has a voice, as we would say today.

Derrida's lecture course of 1989, *The Politics of Friendship*, may well have had some of its inception in the consideration of Arendt's acceptance speech, though readers familiar with Derrida's redaction and publication of the course may recall his emphasis falls on Carl Schmitt's friend/enemy opposition, not Arendt's opposition of friend/fraternity. In *Fantom*, Derrida remarks that Arendt's opposition of fraternity with friendship raises many troubling questions, among them, the sense derived from her remarks that she is uncomfortable with humanity in a way that isn't based on any conceptual justification but upon a personal psychological response that suggests revulsion. Derrida doesn't use as strong a word as xenophobia to describe Arendt's attitude, but something along that line is being suggested. Derrida is quite aware that her use of a word such as "pariah" to describe the Jews in various states of unbearable disenfranchisement and dispossession seems ambiguously if not objectionably focalized from the perspectives of both persecutor and persecuted.

For Derrida, who is summarizing what he considers vital points in Arendt, the following is exemplary of Arendt's distaste of social belonging.

> I have never in my life "loved" any people or collective group, either the German people, the French, the Americans, nor the working class or anything of that sort. I indeed love only my friends, and the only kind of love I know of and believe in is the love of persons. Moreover, this "love of the Jews" would appear to me, since I am myself Jewish, as something rather suspect.[7]

Why, Derrida wonders, is there this distance between Arendt and the Jews? What makes love of the Jews suspect? What about them does she find distasteful? Here Derrida opens the door for one to wonder about whether Arendt's admission of having an aversion doesn't relate to xenophobia, one that overlaps with the history of German hostilities to alien people in their midst? Derrida is interested in Arendt's remark largely because it reveals a conflict within Arendt about being both German and Jewish.

At the time *Fantom* was given, Arendt's love affair with Heidegger was not known. Since publication of the written correspondence between them, academics have not been able to avoid the topic of Arendt's conflictedness, something Derrida had noticed in a different register, not to mention that of Heidegger's unfaithfulness and his wife's reaction. In the context of Derrida's theme of the Jew and the German, it is very evident that Heidegger treats Arendt as German, not Jewish. For example, in a letter of July 24, 1925, Heidegger calls her "you saucy wood nymph," which is clearly a Germanic reference, not a Jewish one. On June 14 of the same year, Heidegger writes to Arendt, "Nothing stood between us. The simplest togetherness—without restless desire, without doubts or reservations—so completely at ease I could have shouted for joy if reverence at such a moment had not blessed me even more."[8] In comparison, Heidegger's contemporaneous letters to his wife, Elfride, are considerably more formal and stilted, filled with academic news and reports of his day-to-day activities. That something stands between husband and wife is clarified slightly in 1931 after Elfride had become aware of her husband's affairs with women. Heidegger writes: "I haven't yet learnt to see your love fully in your severity and hardness" (August 17, 1931).[9] This is a backhanded compliment to a strong-willed German woman who by that time was already a Nazi Party member. In what is Heidegger's last letter to Arendt until 1950—it was written in the winter of 1932–33—he defends himself against her complaint that people are accusing him of being an anti-Semite and lists numerous examples in order to nullify this claim. "And above all it [the controversy] cannot touch my relationship to you."[10] Telling, however, is that this remark is followed by a gap of silence for nearly twenty years, one that is renewed in 1950. In a letter of September 14, 1950, Heidegger again characterizes Arendt as un-Jewish. "The way you stand with your coat blowing in the sea breeze speaks to me in language as pure as the birth of Aphrodite."[11] That Arendt doesn't object, that she eagerly pursues the postwar relationship with Heidegger and his family (she and Elfride reconcile, much to Martin's satisfaction) is strong indication of the extent to which she happily identified as a German.

Derrida, of course, did not have access to this information in 1984. He nevertheless detects the conflictedness in Arendt's identity by noting her remark in the interview with Gaus that "I did not know from my family that I was Jewish. My mother was completely a-religious."[12] He also cites her acknowledgment that the word "Jew" was first made known to her as a child by other children who were insulting her with anti-Semitic remarks. As she grows up, she realizes "I looked Jewish. I looked different from other children. I was very conscious of that." Could she have had mixed feelings about this difference? She reports that her home was not like that of other Jewish children or German children either, for that matter. For her mother being Jewish "did not play a role for her."[13] Yet in a letter to Gershom Scholem, Arendt claims her Jewish identity. To Gaus, she says, "I myself, for example, don't believe that I have ever considered myself a German—in the sense of belonging to the people as opposed to being a citizen, if I may make that distinction."[14] In 1930 when Carl Jaspers exclaims "Of course you are German!" she responds "One can see that I am not."[15] Nevertheless, she identified herself intellectually with Ancient Greek thought, Christian theology (which she studied at university with Rudolf Bultmann), took a strong interest in Kant, attended Heidegger's lectures, and eventually wrote a dissertation under the direction of Carl Jaspers who considered her German.

Perhaps given the psychological identitarian conflicts Arendt may have experienced, friendship would have been more palatable than fraternity, given that the former allows one to be allied with individual Jews and Germans whereas the latter puts one in the category of the worldless Jew, the oppressed who are homeless and who must resort to fraternity as a matter of basic survival. That one might have reservations about belonging to such a group, given a choice, is no doubt understandable. But here again Arendt's conflictedness emerges, as Derrida notices in the following statement to Gaus. Arendt expresses the view on German television, of all places, that the end of Jewish worldlessness is not necessarily to be considered an altogether good outcome for Jews. In other words, the nation-state of Israel, while desirable for many reasons, in Arendt's view, represents a certain loss of humanity that comes with offering people a national homeland. Jewish worldlessness, she says, was very beautiful; it is a worldlessness with which she identifies.

> Yes, one pays dearly for freedom. The specifically Jewish humanity signified by their worldlessness was something very beautiful. [To Gaus:] You are too young to have ever experienced that. But it was something very beautiful, this standing outside of all social connections, the complete open-mindedness and absence of prejudice that I experienced, especially with my mother, who also exercised it in relation to the whole Jewish community. Of course, a great deal was lost with the passing of all that. One pays for liberation. I once said in my Lessing speech … that "this humanity … has never yet survived the hour of liberation, of freedom, by so much as a minute." You see, that has happened to us.[16]

By "us," Arendt is referring to herself as a Jew related to Jews as a group. Her identification as German is now absent. Derrida has cited her statement because it is conspicuously controversial in terms of saying that living as a worldless Jew during the National Socialist period brought out a certain humanity in people that was lost when the war was over and Jews gained Israeli citizenship that guaranteed them rights and a national identity ("world," in her terms).

Arendt herself is very aware of the conflicts and contradictions she is raising when she talks about world and worldlessness or fraternity and friendship.

> In the first place, belonging to a group is a natural condition. You belong to some sort of group when you are born, always. But to belong to a group in the way you mean, in the second sense, that is, to join or form an organized group, is something completely different. This kind of organization has to do with a relation to the world. People who become organized have in common what are ordinarily called interests. The directly personal relationship, where one can speak of love, exists of course foremost in real love, and it also exists in a certain sense in friendship. There a person is addressed directly, independent of his relation to the world. Thus, people of the most divergent organizations can still be personal friends. But if you confuse these things, if you bring love to the negotiating table, to put it bluntly, I find that fatal. […] I find it apolitical. I find it worldless. And I really find it to be a great disaster. I admit that the Jewish people are a classic example of a worldless people maintaining themselves throughout thousands of years.[17]

Arendt continues by pointing out that the worldlessness "which the Jewish people suffered in being dispersed … generated a special warmth among those who belonged [which] changed when the state of Israel was founded."[18] However, friendship, warmth, and love are insufficiently political to establish a space in which one can be politically effective as someone with rights and agency—voice and the power to enact change.

Hardly lost on Derrida is the fact that *Arendt is saying there cannot be a politics of friendship*, because friendship and politics are mutually exclusive. Contrary to her remarks on the *polis* in the Lessing Prize speech, in the televised interview, the political is related to the kind of belonging that is fraternal in the context of being a member of a group. Aporetic is the relation of fraternity/friendship in that each excludes something in the other: One can have friendship (love) but only with the exclusion of politics; one can have politics (fraternity) but only with the exclusion of friendship (love). In the lecture course *The Politics of Friendship*, Derrida will question the concept of the friend as itself aporetic ("O my friends, there is no friend"). But in *Fantom* Derrida wonders if Arendt's statements in the televised interview and the Lessing Prize address are sufficiently thought through, not that he should be surprised, because in the case of texts drawn from newspapers, radio, and television, he was looking for statements that had to be said expediently, telegraphically, and in many cases marginally as commentary on writings that had been worked out elsewhere in far more detail.

Arendt's plea for worldlessness may be oddly formulated, but this isn't so much a slip or mistake as it is a conviction about the inadequacy of the nation-state relative to what she calls humanitarianism. In *The Origins of Totalitarianism*, Arendt gives a full-throated account of why statelessness is an appalling fate for any social group, given that statelessness (worldlessness) is the abrogation of "the right to have rights," whereas citizenship affords one the legal protection (due process) of a nation-state, not that she is uncritical of such a state. In the television interview with Gaus, Arendt suggests that the nation-state's legal apparatuses ensure that people can live isolated, atomized existences and therefore don't have to express their humanitarianism, since that has been replaced by social services, the police, courts, and the penal system. As Derrida realized, this speaks to an aporia in which both world (a space of political redress) and worldlessness (a space where political redress is foreclosed) are injurious. Whatever Arendt says relative to this sort of double jeopardy is bound to be full of unresolved problematic or contradictory consequences, which Derrida says are far too numerous to be unpacked in the current seminar.

Of course, a major reason that Derrida examines Arendt's television interview concerns her affirmation that most fundamental in terms of identification is one's relation to one's mother tongue. In this conviction Arendt and Adorno overlap and say almost the same things. Arendt:

> But the general, and the greatest experience when one returns to Germany—apart from the experience of recognition, which is always the crux of the action in Greek tragedy—is one of violent emotion. And then there was the experience of hearing German spoken in the streets. For me that was an indescribable joy.[19]

Again,

> **Arendt:** The German language is the essential thing that has remained and that I have always consciously preserved.
> **Gaus:** Even in the most bitter time?
> **Arendt:** Always. I thought to myself. What is one to do? It wasn't the German language that went crazy. And, second, there is no substitution for the mother tongue.[20]

As to there being no substitute for the mother tongue, Adorno would have agreed entirely. With respect to English, Arendt says she speaks it unidiomatically and with a heavy accent, which again parallels Adorno more or less exactly, and, as Derrida notices, since this is his central theme, Arendt too recognizes the crucial importance of idiom as the bedrock of a thinker's identity and work, which is again a view underscored in Adorno. That Arendt and Adorno express views that are not only very similar but that agree with views on language that one can find in Heidegger's works, not to mention work by Schlegel and Fichte, emphasizes once more how strongly the theme of the Jew and the German is making itself known. If over the years to follow, Derrida will develop this theme, he always does so in terms of pulling together various texts brought together by means of a certain kind of free association as if one were doing a psychoanalysis of the Jew and the German relation, rather than an exhaustive, systematic historical investigation. No doubt, this had disadvantages, among them, omissions. The foray into Arendt's work left out her masterpiece *The Origins of Totalitarianism* on the subject of what could be called philosophical nationalism. Had Derrida revised *Fantom*, he no doubt would have had to engage with Arendt's seminal social history of the rise of the nation-state and its totalitarian development.

Wittgenstein: *Wir stehen im Kampf mit der Sprache*

> The Jew is a desert region, but underneath its thin layer of rock lies the molten lava of spirit and intellect. [*Der Jude ist eine wüste Gegend, unter*

deren dünner Gesteinschicht aber die feurig-flüssigen Massen des Geistigen liegen.]—L. Wittgenstein, *Culture and Value* [*Vermischte Bemerkungen*] (1931)

In turning to Wittgenstein, Derrida considers a Jewish thinker who unlike Arendt and Adorno has a hostile relationship with language. Derrida notes that for Wittgenstein language, in place of giving us paths and places to cross over or stay, sets up traps. Instead of being a refuge from all nationalism, from all renounced *patrie*, language is the place where obstacles are lain, the place where one is tripped up. Derrida specifies that if one ends by falling *upon* or *in* language, a falling or fall that connotes at once a chance and a mishap, this does not have the same meaning for Adorno or Arendt that it does for Wittgenstein for whom it is scandalous and upsetting. Rather than a friend, language is viewed by Wittgenstein as an enemy that is plotting against him and that intentionally misleads and derails. Hence Derrida quotes Wittgenstein as follows:

> Language sets everyone the same traps; it is an immense network of easily accessible wrong turnings. And so we watch one man after another walking down the same paths and we know in advance where he will branch off, where he will walk straight on without noticing the side turning, etc. etc. What I have to do then is erect signposts at all the junctions where there are wrong turnings so as to help people past the danger points.[21]

"*La langue c'est le cas, casus, la chute, le piège*, (Language is the case, the misfortune [accident, occasion] the fall, the trap)," Derrida says. For Wittgenstein the concept of language is a matter of *Kampf* in which we are engaged, as opposed to being what Arendt called the *Muttersprache*, the maternal language in which we find refuge and solace. This is a struggle or fight both for and against language. One opposes oneself to language's detours, misdirections, figures, if not its many misleading and untranslatable idioms, all of which lay traps for the philosopher who is engaged in "a philosophy of philosophy," wherein is encountered a certain intersection between a national giftedness or genius (*génie*) and the "non-génie du judaisme" (e.g., the absence of Jewish genius) where one will find, in this particular type of exilic person, the same kind of self-denegation, conflictedness, and proud self-accusation that one sees also in the case of Hannah Arendt. As Wittgenstein puts it,

> Amongst Jews 'genius' is found only in the holy man [*ist nur ein Heiliger*]. Even the greatest of Jewish thinkers is no more than talented. (Myself for instance.) [*Der größte jüdische Denker ist nur ein Talent.* (Ich z.B.).] I think there is some truth in my idea that I really only think reproductively. I don't believe I have ever *invented* a line of thinking. I have always taken one over from someone else.[22]

This view overlaps with Adolf Hitler's central claim in *Mein Kampf* that Jews are derivative and parasitical, that they are only able to think reproductively and lack real national genius and for that reason are motivated out of jealousy to disparage and sabotage true German genius. This supposed inferiority of the Jew is reflected in Wittgenstein's self-deprecating "Often my writing is nothing but 'stuttering.'"[23]

Derrida wonders how the philosophy-of-doing-philosophy crosses paths with Judaism. The link, in Derrida's view, is probably language. Derrida credits Wittgenstein with the thought that philosophical differences are not founded on clashing theses concerning truth, or on issues that are to be debated, but on idiomatic differences. According to Derrida, this is what Wittgenstein means when he writes that "philosophy is a matter of temperament (*Temperamentssache*)."[24] I would call this "idiom," Derrida says, because it refers to personal preferences for metaphors, likenesses, and comparisons—in short choices regarding how something is to be figured. Idioms, of course, are figures of speech that reflect an approximation with something that is mediated by temperament which in the case of each person is being privileged to choose this or that figure of speech or idiom. "A preference for certain similes could be called a matter of temperament and it underlines far more disagreements than you might think," Wittgenstein writes.[25] For Derrida this implies that philosophical disagreements may well concern idiomatic differences that relate to what Heidegger called *Stimmung* or mood. Another indication that Wittgenstein is gesturing in the direction of idiom occurs in the statement, "Perhaps what is inexpressible (what I find mysterious and am not able to express) is the background against which whatever I could express has its meaning."[26] The temperamental idioms of language therefore could be imagined to make up this background of the inexpressible that can only be approximated by idioms, which are often statements containing comparisons.

Having lightly touched on idiom, Derrida moves on to Wittgenstein's conviction that Jews are not original thinkers because they merely appropriate other people's ideas, much in the way in which one cleverly appropriates idioms. For Derrida, this is where the philosophy-of-philosophy (Wittgenstein's meta-philosophical fragments) and Jewish identity intersect. That is, this is where "We are struggling with language. We are engaged in a struggle with language" ("*Wir kämpfen mit der Sprache. Wir stehen im Kampf mit der Sprache*)."[27] crosses over into *we are struggling with our Jewish identity; we are engaged in a struggle with Jewishness, Judaism, Jews.* Derrida avoids the obvious, which would be to invoke the idiom of *mein Kampf* as a struggle with the Jewish Question. For readers today, Wittgenstein's *Vermischte Bemerkungen* may remind one of Heidegger's *Schwarze Hefte*, since they are written in a similar fragmentary style and weave in and out of alternatively brilliant and lamentable speculations, both containing shocking anti-Semitism.

Of note is that in 1930 Wittgenstein states that the spirit of the main current of Western civilization inherent in "fascism and socialism ... is alien and uncongenial to the author (*ist dem Verfasser fremd und unsympathisch*)."[28] Although he claims to be at odds with socialist and fascist political tendencies, he draws from the same well of anti-Semitism as they do, with its stock of idioms concerning the derivative, parasitical, and imitative tendency of the Jew who supposedly counterfeits existence in a rather spectral manner. Again, as seen from our contemporary twenty-first-century perspective, this isn't so different from Heidegger who also displayed such conflicts in his controversial notebooks wherein he repudiates National Socialism while repeating aspects of it at the same time.

Wittgenstein maintains that the Jew is fake, not real. As he puts it, the Jew sees to it that "all things are as nothing to him." This statement recalls Arendt's remarks on what Derrida translates as *acosmie* (worldlessness). The Jew is an entity who is essentially in a state of dispossession, who has, as Wittgenstein says, money in place of physical property. "He [the Jew] has nothing that is peculiarly his."[29] Because the Jew is a nothing that appears as a something, it could be said to make its appearance as *fantom of the other*. As such, the Jew haunts and even takes possession of what is not proper to him or her.

Associated with the notion of the fantom as trespasser who maliciously haunts places that should be rid of ghosts is Wittgenstein's statement that "It is typical for a Jewish mind [*es ist dem jüdischen Geiste typisch*] to understand someone else's work better than he understands it himself."[30] Because "*es ist dem jüdischen Geiste typisch*" can refer to mind as well as to spirit in a way that alludes to the ghost or fantom, Wittgenstein's statement continues the suggestion that the Jew is a sort of specter intent on usurpation. The Jew breaks into and steals the minds of others by displaying an "understanding" superior to the one that was originally entered into.

It is not unlikely that Derrida, who is quite critical of Wittgenstein's attitude, was probably annoyed by such remarks concerning understanding as usurpation. In *Of Grammatology* we read that

> The reading must always aim at a certain relationship, unperceived by the writer, between what he commands and what he does not command of the patterns of the language that he uses. The relationship is not a certain quantitative distribution of shadow and light, of weakness or of force, but a signifying structure that critical reading should *produce*.[31]

One could easily substitute the word "understanding" for "critical reading," which in this case understands the text better than its original author and on account of this better understanding *produces* (cogitates or constitutes) a signifying structure. Such a critical reading (by Derrida, in this case) is able to see what the author presumably could not: the relationship between what the author did and didn't have under control ("what he commands and what he doesn't command").[32] From Wittgenstein's perspective, and not just his alone, such a critical reading is characteristic of the Jew in the role of cultural mediator who usurps the author's understanding by taking over its place in order to take the place of that understanding. Absent would be recognition of the fact that German thinkers unrelated to Judaism, such as Friedrich Schleiermacher and Wilhelm Dilthey, accepted as foundational the principle that the interpreter should know the mind of the author better than did the author himself or herself.

However, there is another reason why Derrida might have been annoyed enough by Wittgenstein's point of view to include him in *Fantom*. Recall Michel Foucault's "My Body, This Paper, This Fire," in *History of Madness*, which was a blistering attack on Derrida's "meticulous" reading of a passage on Descartes.

> It might well be asked how an author as meticulous as Derrida, and one so attentive to texts, managed not only to allow so many omissions, but also to operate so many displacements, interventions, and substitutions. But perhaps we should do that while remembering that Derrida is recalling an old tradition in his reading.

But what is that "old tradition"? This is code for the Rabbinical tradition of Talmudic interpretation in which displacements, interventions, and substitutions are legion. This charge appears to be buttressed by the fact that Foucault will refer to a Pauline distinction between the letter (which is blind, Jewish) and the spirit (which is that of revelation, Christian) that in his vocabulary contrasts text with discourse. "It is part of a system, a system of which Derrida is today the most decisive representative, in its waning light: a reduction of discursive practices to textual traces; the elision of events that are produced there, leaving only marks for a reading."[33] In other words, Derrida is a Jewish master of the dead letter, which is textual, and not the spirit, which is living and discursive. Foucault argues that Derrida is advancing "a historically well-determined little pedagogy ... which teaches the student that there is nothing outside the text, but that in it, in its interstices, in its blanks and silences, the reserve of the origin reigns." This is "a pedagogy that inversely gives to the voice of the masters that unlimited sovereignty that allows it *indefinitely to re-say the text*."[34] The re-saying is, of course, easily identified with Jewish scriptural interpretation if not with the identity of the Jew as a mere repeater who claims something for himself in the mastery of repetition and mere secondary elaboration.

Derrida doesn't make such connections explicitly in *Fantom*, but he could not have been unaware of how Wittgenstein's anti-Semitic view of Jewish thinking had been used in a very different context and by a very different thinker whose wounded pride led him to demean Derrida in a highly public dispute. Derrida as Jewish intellectual had a significant stake in these matters from the perspective of his academic career, given an incipient prejudice within French society and certain areas of academic life that were from time to time directed at him, in this case, for being too meticulous, hyper-intellectual, overly textual, pitilessly rigorous, and so on, criticisms that could be (and were) viewed as coded language for insulting Jewish thinkers, something Jean-Paul Sartre noticed in *Anti-Semite and Jew* when he referenced how anti-Semites speak of "the destructive intelligence" of the Jew.[35] Wittgenstein at least had been more overt than Foucault. His "anti-Semitic clichés," as Derrida calls them, often reinforce the idea that if Jews have genius it is only in the context of their religion, which is to say, of the holy man: a person of testimony, suffering, martyrdom, exemplarity, sacrifice, and the sacred. In contrast, the secular Jew is merely a talent, which Wittgenstein owns as pertinent to himself.

As mere talent, Wittgenstein adds, the Jewish thinker cannot find a new way or path. Derrida explicitly raises the question of Wittgenstein's sense of *Denkbewegung* or *chemin de pensée*, a way or route taken by Wittgenstein but, as he says, not invented by him.

> Incidentally, when I was in Norway during the year 1913–14, I had some thoughts of my own ... I have the impression that at that time I brought to life new movements in thinking [*neue Denkbewegungen geboren*] (but perhaps I am mistaken). Whereas now I seem just to apply old ones.[36]

Derrida observes that Heidegger is confident about "*un signe vers le Weg*," some indicator that directs one to the road which the philosopher can assume as his own. Wittgenstein to the contrary displays considerable insecurity; there is no road or path that is his own. Perhaps there never is a clear-cut way or path, or something about taking a path is problematic. "Philosophers use a language that is already deformed as though by shoes that are too tight."[37] This suggests that thinking is like walking, that walking requires language as shoes, and that it is language that binds and hurts because it never fits. There are passages more directly related to the path. "It is as though I had lost my way and asked someone the way home (*den Weg nach Hause*). He says he will show me and walks with me along a nice smooth path. This suddenly stops. And now my friend tells me: 'All you have to do now is find your way home from here.'"³⁸ In fragments such as this, one senses Arendt's antinomy of world and worldlessness, of being on the way and losing the way. That should remind readers familiar with Wittgenstein's *Philosophical Investigations* that he is often wondering in what *way* is one to take a direction or expression. That too relates to idiom. Can one be secure in how one takes idiom or innuendo, for that matter. In what way should one take Foucault's statement about re-saying?

Can one ever be secure about the way? Meta-textually this relates to the way in which are we to take Wittgenstein's self-hatred. What is or should be this way? In *Fantom*, Derrida is taking only preliminary steps in order to figure this out.

Among the advances in these preliminary steps is Derrida's sense that the movement or path of thinking relate to the conviction that every thought is a picture that in a certain manner is a re-production; in short, there is no other way of thinking than in terms of the picture. For example, in the *Notebooks* (1914–16), we read "the proposition is the picture of the fact (*der Satz ist das Bild der Tatsache*)."³⁹ As a corollary, "the possibility of all similes, of the whole pictoral character of our language, is founded in the logic of portrayal (*Logik der Abbildung*).⁴⁰ Again, in the *Tractatus Logico-Philosophicus* we are told that "A proposition can be true or false only in virtue of being a picture of reality."⁴¹ In *Culture and Value* the Jew and not the proposition is associated with picture making: the fashioning of comparisons, metaphors, allegories, pictures—in short, reproductions. In *Culture and Value*, portrayal is the Jew's way, literalized as drawing: "[The Jew's] way is rather to make a drawing of the flower or blade of grass that has grown in the soil of another's mind and to put it into a comprehensive picture."⁴² If there is a danger in such statements, Derrida says, it concerns the compulsion to make comparisons, in this case between that of the Jew and the German. Racism, he suggests, has a basis in putting kinds into relation, of making pictures whereby one is confined to an original/copy distinction. Even Heidegger attests to this abuse. "Having found its pure essence [a] people could never have any time left over for comparing itself with others, be this in an overestimating or in an underestimating manner."⁴³ No doubt, Derrida realized that Wittgenstein's German/Jew distinction is analogous to the voice/writing distinction in *Of Grammatology*, which could be taken as a template for a certain kind of racism in which the actual and the fake are presupposed as an essential condition for imagining social relations, for example, relations of class (upper class/bourgeois), of religions (Christianity/Judaism), of languages (German/Dutch, French/Quebecois), of old and new (native/immigrant, old money/new money), and of race (German/Jew, White/Black). Foundational is the Platonic abhorrence of imitations, simulacra, and copies. In this context, Derrida sees in Wittgenstein a retrograde thinking operating on the cutting edge of philosophy. This speaks to a major aim in *Fantom* which is to expose how even the most innovative thinkers, who have produced work of compelling demystification, in fields such as philosophy and social science, harbor what one might call regressive thinking, by which is meant, in part, the backsliding into metaphysical crudity. How the progressive is mediated by the retrograde and vice versa is one of Derrida's major interests throughout the 1980s.

Although the discussions of Adonis, Adorno, Arendt, and Wittgenstein are largely preliminary investigations (thumb-nail sketches), retroactively one can see the emergence of some dominant themes: that of the exile, of relationships to language, of world versus worldlessness, and of overtures of self-effacement if not, in exceptional cases, self-loathing. Of considerable interest in this part of the course should be that what appears nascent but emerging in terms of discussing Adonis, Adorno, Arendt, and Wittgenstein is the sense of worldlessness (*acosmie*) that they all have in common. Adonis embraces it; Adorno accepts it melancholically and, in the case of Auschwitz, as unprecedented and unrepresentable. Additionally, whereas Arendt is ambivalent about worldlessness, Wittgenstein is not.

> Put a man in the wrong atmosphere and nothing will function as it should. He will seem unhealthy in every part. Put him back into his proper element and everything will blossom and look healthy. But if he is not in his right element, what then? Well, then he just has to make the best of appearing before the world as a cripple.[44]

Notes

1. Hannah Arendt, *The Origins of Totalitarianism* (New York: Harcourt, 1968), 275.
2. Hannah Arendt, "On Humanity in Dark Times: Thoughts about Lessing," in *Men in Dark Times* (New York: Harcourt Brace, 1968), 14.
3. Ibid.
4. Ibid., 24.
5. Ibid., 25.
6. Ibid.
7. "'What Remains? The Language Remains': A Conversation with Günter Gaus," in *Essays in Understanding: 1930–54* (New York: Schoken, 1994), 16. The headnote

states that "on October 28, 1964, the following conversation between Hannah Arendt and Günter Gaus … a high official in Willy Brandt's government, was broadcast on West German television. The interview was awarded the Adolf Grimme Prize and was published the following year under the title, 'Was bleibt? Es bleibt die Muttersprache' in Günter Gaus, *Zur Person* (Munich, 1965)." Notice that in German "mother-tongue" is used, not the word "language."

8   Martin Heidegger, *Letters to His Wife: 1915–70*, trans. R.D.V. Glasgow (Cambridge: Polity, 2008), 24.
9   Ibid., 127.
10 Hannah Arendt and Martin Heidegger, *Letters 1925–1975: Hannah Arendt and Martin Heidegger*, trans. Andrew Shields (New York: Harcourt, 2004), 53.
11 Ibid., 93.
12 "A Conversation," 6.
13 Ibid., 7.
14 Ibid., 8.
15 Ibid.
16 Ibid., 17–18.
17 Ibid., 17. The opening statement about belonging to a group resonates in *Fantom* with the idea of a group being a *Geschlecht*. Here as elsewhere in his remarks on Arendt, much is being left in suspension that could have been taken up at great length. Arendt's aversion to "belonging" and "identitarianism" was something Derrida himself shared. This is brought out by Benoît Peeters in *Derrida* (Cambridge: Polity, 2013), 502. "Derrida's attitude to every form of communitarianism had always been ambivalent and somewhat distant."
18 Ibid.
19 Ibid., 15.
20 Ibid., 13.
21 Ludwig Wittgenstein, *Culture and Value*, trans. Peter Winch (Chicago: Chicago University Press, 1984), 18c. Translation corrected. Page numbers are accompanied by small case letters in this edition. The quotation was written in 1931.
22 Ibid., 18e–19e.
23 Ibid., 18e.
24 Ibid., 20e.
25 Ibid., 20e.
26 Ibid., 16e.
27 Ibid., 11e.
28 Ibid., 6e.
29 Ibid., 19e.
30 Ibid. Italics mine.
31 Jacques Derrida, *Of Grammatology*, trans. G.C. Spivak (Baltimore: Johns Hopkins, 1976), 158.

32 Ibid.
33 Michel Foucault, "My Body, This Paper, This Fire," in *History of Madness* (London: Routledge, 2009), 573. Where italics appear, they are mine. The entire sentence reads, "It is part of a system, a system of which Derrida is today the most decisive representative, in its waning light: a reduction of discursive practices to textual traces; the elision of events that are produced there, leaving only marks for a reading; the invention of voices behind the text, so as not to have to examine the modes of implication of the subject in discourses; the assignation of the originary as said and not-said in the text in order to avoid situating discursive practices in the field of transformation where they are carried out." The argument throughout is that Derrida is eliding voice as a rhetorical determinant in order to stress effects of textuality.
34 Ibid. Italics mine.
35 Jean-Paul Sartre, *Anti-Semite and Jew*, trans. J.G. Becker (New York: Schocken Books, 1976), 113.
36 Wittgenstein, *Culture and Value*, 20e.
37 Ibid., 41e.
38 Ibid., 46–7.
39 Ludwig Wittgenstein, *Notebooks 1914–1916*, trans. V.E.M. Anscombe, 2nd ed. (Chicago: University of Chicago Press, 1979), 46.
40 Ibid., 48.
41 Ludwig Wittgenstein, *Tractatus Logico-Philosophicus*, trans. D.F. Pears and B.F. McGuinness (London: Routledge and Kenan Paul, 1974), 23. (Sec. 4.06.)
42 Wittgenstein, *Culture and Value*, 19e.
43 Martin Heidegger, "Evening Conversation," in *Country Path Conversations*, trans. B.W. Davis (Bloomington: Indiana University Press, 2005), 152.
44 Wittgenstein, *Culture and Value*, 42.

Part Two

Geschlecht as Social Relation: Nation, Sex, Race, Kith, and Kind

5

Das Geschlecht

Lectures six to thirteen of *Fantom* were at one point intended by Derrida to be published as "Geschlecht II" and "Geschlecht III," two chapters meant for a four-chapter monograph on Heidegger's appropriation of the idiom *Geschlecht*. "Geschlecht I: Sexual Difference, Ontological Difference" had already appeared by 1983 in *Heidegger*, edited by Michel Haar (in the series *Cahier de l'Herne*). "Geschlecht II: Heidegger's Hand" appeared in Derrida's *Psyche* in 1987. Only much later did "Geschlecht IV: Philopolemonology" appear as an addendum on Heidegger in the French publication *Politiques de l'amitié* (1994). "Geschlecht III" on Heidegger's "Die Sprache im Gedicht: Eine Erörterung von Georg Trakls Gedicht (1953)" wasn't composed, though the materials for such a piece exist, comprising lectures eight to thirteen of *Fantom*. Essentially, these lectures are a commentary on Heidegger's essay in which one is given an exegesis and amplification of key passages of significance to Derrida from the point of view of problematization, critique, and deconstructive radicalization. They inform the latter pages of "Geschlecht II" as well as the last chapters of *Of Spirit*.

Lectures six and seven of *Fantom* correspond to what was published as "Geschlecht II." We have already seen that in the first five lectures of *Fantom*, Derrida had been engaging with *Geschlecht* in ways that were both direct and indirect, with an often tacit awareness that in certain contexts—in particular, that of National Socialism—this idiom has been used in ways that are not just "menacing and extreme," as Derrida puts it early in the course, but, as in the case of so-called Nazi science, lethal. Lectures six and seven focus on the "monstrosity" of *Geschlecht* as philosophical and linguistic idiom. The larger context for this perception of monstrosity in Heidegger's writing goes beyond language, of course, which Derrida explores when he discusses the meaning of Heidegger's raised hand during the Nazi period whereby a social-political relation was being affirmed.

Derrida never says it outright, but he expects one to see that his inquiry into *Geschlecht* is essentially an interrogation of a word within which there is a complex matrix of social relations that etymologically are proto-deconstructed. *Geschlecht* both affirms and negates the social relation, something that has a corollary in the *Politics of Friendship* when Derrida says of the social relation of the friend: "O my friends, there is no friend," or when in *Monolinguism of the Other*, he says, "I only have one language; it is not mine."[1]

Given that *Geschlecht* is an idiomatic term for the social relation as used by Heidegger, it is important to recognize some of the features of Heidegger's understanding and treatment of the social, particularly in relation to philosophical nationalism. An oddity about Heidegger that Derrida doesn't mention, but that has to stand out for those who have read him at length, is the fact that Heidegger tends to exclude the social as a category even in texts where one might expect to see it. In Heidegger's philosophical-politico-ontico seminars of 1933–34, there is actually no mention of society *stricto sensu*, but rather talk of Being, *das Volk*, nation, and the State. "We established formally that the people is the being that *is* in the manner of a state, that being that is or can be a state."[2] By state Heidegger means primarily "the mode of Being of a people."[3] By contrast, notice the sociological work of Max Weber, Heidegger's famous contemporary at the University of Heidelberg. For him a society (*Gesellschaft*) is the hierarchical organization of various peoples on a superstructural level that rationalizes human activity in such a way as to make lives coherent, meaningful, manageable, and humanly fulfilling. In Weber's *Economy and Society* (1925) relations of significance are said to be established far less on the basis of blood relations (*Geschlecht*) than through "social actions" that connect individuals to all members of society in some respect or other. A true social action, Weber says, is not merely imitative or performed under duress, but is initiated for the sake of rational ends, values, and affects (*Zweckrational, Wertrational, Affektuel*), and, too, for reasons of tradition (custom), as together these aims give meaning and hence motivate individuals to behave in ways that are socially constructive in that they contribute to forging social bonds (relations) and hence cooperative relationships without which a society collapses.[4]

In Heidegger one never hears of social actions in such terms, nor does one hear anything about state apparatuses, class formations, economic systems and the disparities they produce: civic virtues (social constructions of morality), juridical principles of right, let alone what Michel Foucault has called the heterogeneous layers within society where discipline (philosophy, for example) and sovereignty (power) meet, not to mention the social-historical constructions of race, ethnicity, and national identity. Whereas Heidegger easily identifies race with *das Volk*, as if this were a self-evident ontological relation, social theorists such as Foucault have demonstrated a far more vexed and complicated nexus of social, cultural, and historical relations concerning race that exceed ontology.[5]

Furthermore, if one reads texts by Heidegger such as "Origin of the Work of Art" or "Building, Dwelling, Thinking," one will notice a conspicuous absence of any mention of the social. The peasant woman in "Origin" is supposed to depend upon "equipmentality," not the society of her kin or neighbors, which isn't recognized. In "Building, Dwelling, Thinking," we hear a great deal about dwelling but nothing about any social relations among the dwellers.[6] Heidegger's famous Fourfold of earth, gods, mortals, and sky certainly can't be considered a social order of any kind that would have been recognizable to a sociologist. Moreover, in Heidegger's reading of Trakl, one suspects that what attracted Heidegger to the poet was emphasis upon lyrics in which a wanderer leaves society behind and a soul connects with the earth, not society.

Notable for Derrida is that when Heidegger in 1953 came around to seizing on a term for the *social* relation, he seized upon what is essentially a monstrous word, *Geschlecht*, that grotesquely overdetermines the meaning of the social relation to such an extent that its measure cannot be established and stabilized. The more one analyzes it, the more whatever social relation it is supposed to depict withdraws into obscurity. In that sense, *Geschlecht* is a term that functions rather like the word "being" in "Concerning 'the Line'" ("Über 'die Linie'") when crossed out and put under erasure.[7] This, of course, is already the case in Trakl's lyrics where the word *Geschlecht* is invoked, not that in his poetry an argument couldn't be made that much else is also *en retrait* (decline, *Untergang*). For example, Trakl's use of the word *Abendland* (Evening Land: Occident, Europe) is taken up by Heidegger with some enthusiasm precisely because it indicates effacement, withdrawal, retreat.

In "The Retrait of Metaphor," Derrida once spoke of erasure as a "Withdrawing by displaying itself or determining itself *as*."[8] What withdraws in *Geschlecht*, assuming it is under erasure, is the social relation in its very being affirmed *as*. But as *what*? Here Derrida's text about Being *en retrait* is apposite.

> Being does not let itself be named except through a metaphorico-metonymical divergence. One is tempted to say, then: the metaphysical, which corresponds in its discourse to the withdrawal of Being, tends to assemble, in resemblance, all its metonymic divergences in a great metaphor of Being or of the thought of Being. This assembly is *the* language of *the* metaphysical.[9]

What is said of Being is also true for *Geschlecht*: that it can't be named except through metaphorical substitution (*Schlag* for *Geschlecht*) and metonymical displacements (kith, kin, family, generation, race, sex, kind, species, and type). Because *Geschlecht* too withdraws or retreats, its metaphorico-metonymical divergences proceed etymologically by means of a gathering or assembly that is the language of philosophical nationalism: in this case, one with considerable metaphysical baggage. However, under erasure, *Geschlecht* comprises a withdrawal of the social relation if not its deconstruction and with it the overcoming of the metaphysical per se.

Given that Derrida's work is so concerned with the social relation, he is, of course, strongly drawn to consideration of *Geschlecht*, particularly since it confirms his suspicion, displayed in his other writings, that the social relation is aporetic, paradoxical, under erasure, spectral, or a matter of the *faux bond*, as he put it in the mid-1970s. Moreover, it must have been compelling to look into the fact that Heidegger, who had so little interest in talking about the social in his philosophical writings, would latch on to a word such as *Geschlecht*, given its monstrous overdeterminations as a term denoting the social relation. Anticipating the writing of a "Geschlecht III" in 1983, the year before delivering *Fantom*, Derrida wrote in a footnote to "Geschlecht I" that the text "toward which this reading is heading, and by which, in truth, I know it is already being drawn as toward a magnet" is Heidegger's 1953 essay on Trakl.[10]

In particular, what must have drawn Derrida to Heidegger's retrieval of *Geschlecht* out of the poetry of Georg Trakl is that in "Die Sprache im Gedicht" Heidegger unpicked its etymological locks with the consequence, for Derrida, of confirming his hypothesis that the social relation is founded by an inceptual violence. *Fantom of the Other* is one of the most sustained inquiries into the inceptual violence of the social relation, though one sees it too in later courses, among them, *The Theological-Political* in which the inceptual violence of the social relation is viewed from the perspective of Jewish religious thought in Spinoza and Gershom Scholem. In the short monograph of 1989, *Force of Law* (*Force de loi*), Derrida returns to this theme in the context of Walter Benjamin's thoughts on violence.[11] What stands out in *Fantom*, however, is the fact that by way of Heidegger, Derrida could make a direct etymological connection within the word *Geschlecht* with inceptual violence, simply because *Geschlecht* is pregnant with the word *Schlag* which as a noun means cast, kind, or race and as a gerund means a blow, hit, or thwack. In short, *Schlag* speaks or says the inceptual violence of *Geschlecht*, something that was not lost on Trakl and certainly not Heidegger, Trakl's close reader.

All of that said, for reference here is a relatively full-scale etymological account of *Geschlecht*.

Das Geschlecht is a neuter noun that stems from the Middle High German *geslehte*, Old High German *gislathti*. The prefix "gi" or "ge" refers to what is gathered around, assembled, or collected together. Such words are related to the verb *schlagen* (*gislathti/ geschlagen*): to hit, beat, strike, stamp, coin, but also to pluck a musical instrument.

Duden's *Das Herkunftswörterbuch: Etymologie der deutschen Sprache* offers the idiom, "*das, was in dieselbe Richtung schlägt, (übereinstimmende) Art*": that which strikes us the same way (agreement). *Aus der Art schlagen* (struck from the same kind), *nach dem Vater schlagen* (a knock-off of the father). These idioms suggest something being struck, stamped, minted or cast into existence as a certain type that is of the same sort as its progenitor.

Idiomatically, *schlagen* was used many centuries ago as a synonym for *ficken* (sexual hitting, banging: fucking), which suggests that *nach dem Vater schlagen* has a sexual connotation wherein we are brought into being by violent sexual congress. *Flügelschlag*, which Trakl employs and Heidegger cites, means both wingbeat and song.

As nouns, *Schlag* and *Geschlecht* are synonyms, which Heidegger exploits. Like *Geschlecht*, *Schlag* also refers to genus, race, and kind; moreover, *Schlag* determines kinds by means of violence (hitting, banging). Phrases such as *geschlagene Geschlechter* (minted, struck types or kinds) are relevant in this context. Related is the word *Verschlagen*, "cast" in the senses of throwing (casting aside) and forming (casting an entity).

Geschlecht, according to Duden, means "*Menschen gleicher Abstammung*" (people of the same stock), which relates to the Latin *genus*—people with a similar ancestry. As genus, *Geschlecht* also directly refers to gender and/or sexual difference, male and female as distinct types. Furthermore, as *genus*, *Geschlecht* can refer to animal species. Related is *Menschengeschlecht*, which refers to the human species or race.

Geschlecht may refer to *generation*, the time frame in which a group of people exist together. However, *Geschlecht* can also denote kith and kin, tribe and stock. A *Geschlecht* can also refer to a noble family dynasty.

In the 18th century, *Geschlechtsteil* is the German translation for the Latin *membrum genital*, and *Geschlechtsverkehr* denotes sexual intercourse. *Geschlechter*, moreover, is used grammatically in German to differentiate nouns that are masculine, feminine, and neuter (*Geschlechtslos*).[12]

Monstration: the Hand, the Monster

As noted, "Geschlecht II" conforms to the lectures given in *Fantom of the Other*, beginning with the sixth lecture that ends on remarks by Heidegger on the difference of man and ape. Derrida begins with a number of precautions, among them, that "Geschlecht I" will not be recapitulated and that the contextual background of "Philosophical Nationality and Nationalism" will remain largely invisible, despite the intention "to make the presentation of these few reflections, still preliminary, as intelligible and independent of all these invisible contexts as possible."[13] Of course, auditors of *Fantom* would know that the materials on *Geschlecht* were largely motivated and justified as an interrogation of a national, if not nationalist, German idiom, something that is not highlighted in the published text of these lectures. When Derrida introduces the word *Geschlecht* in the essay, it is not so much in terms of its idiomaticity but in terms of its untranslatability that the word is problematized. "Doubtless I shall translate it at no moment."[14] Derrida returns to the beginning of the lecture course in noting that *Geschlecht* was encountered earlier in *Fantom of the Other* in Fichte's *Addresses to the German People* and that in one particular passage the French translation does not translate the word *Geschlecht* because of conditions during or just after the Second World War that "made the word 'race' particularly dangerous and moreover not pertinent for translating Fichte."[15] The untranslatability and even omission of the word *Geschlecht* speaks to its being under a sort of erasure, of its being withdrawn in being posited, in this case, in terms of its French translation and censorship. Is *Geschlecht* present only by way of its absence?

At the outset of "Geschlecht II," Derrida mentioned that he would be stitching together various fragments preliminary to what one could expect to be a fully developed study in the future. Among them is consideration of Fichte's idea of *Bund* and *Kreis*, of an alliance and a circle that "constitutes precisely belonging to 'our *Geschlecht*.'"[16] The idea of the circle and the circular is broached in *Fantom* in the materials on Fichte, but it is not developed much until the lectures on Trakl, in particular, the final lecture in which homecoming and return are stressed. This suggests that *Heimat* (return to the homeland) and *Geschlecht* (our kin, kith, or race) are related in the context of Heidegger's thinking.

In drawing from and compressing materials from the beginning of *Fantom*, Derrida recalls that *Geschlecht* relates to "the eternal and progressive formation of this spirituality through freedom," something that relates oddly to nationalism insofar as spirituality through freedom indicates cosmopolitanism, republicanism, and humanism.[17] Here Derrida is exploring an issue that will come up more pointedly later, whether *Geschlecht* is a term that is restricted or unrestricted. In short, does the word have limits? Is *Geschlecht* any one thing? If it is a marker of identitarianism, why does it seem to be lacking an identity? Why isn't *Geschlecht* proper to itself? Derrida asks if Fichte uses the word *Geschlecht* because its indeterminacy enables him to bridge the nationalistic with the cosmopolitan. In reprising not only Fichte, but some of what was covered earlier in relation to Marx and Engels, Derrida remarks, "One of the themes of the seminar I am currently working on concerns just the paradoxical but regular association of nationalism with a cosmopolitanism and with a humanism," which are all part of our *Geschlecht* as *Menschengeschlecht* (humanness, humanity). "So this *Geschlecht* is not determined by birth, native soil, or race, has nothing to do with the natural or even the linguistic." Derrida then raises the contradiction, explored earlier in the course, that Fichte's claim is made through a *German* idiom and by means of an appeal to *German* spirit foundational to determining a "we" or "us."

> Certain citizens, German by birth, remain strangers to this idiom of the idiom; certain non-Germans can attain it since, engaging themselves in this circle or this alliance of spiritual freedom and its infinite progress, they would belong to "our *Geschlecht*." The sole analytic and unimpeachable determination of "*Geschlecht*" in this context is the "we," the belonging to the "we" who are speaking at this moment, at the moment when Fichte addresses himself to this supposed but still to be constituted community, a community that *stricto sensu* is neither political, nor racial, nor linguistic, but that can receive his allocution, his address, or his apostrophe (*Rede an* …), and can think with him, and say 'we' in some language and from whatever birthplace.[18]

Derrida concludes that *Geschlecht* is "an ensemble" or "gathering together" in a sense that is not incompatible with Heidegger's conceptions of *Versammlung* in his writings on the pre-Socratics. The question, once more, is that of limitation. Fichte addresses the Germans by addressing an "infinite progress of the spirit through freedom. So it is an infinite 'we,' a 'we' that announces itself to itself from the infinity of a *telos* of freedom and spirituality."[19] If the "we" is without limit and bound to "an infinite will," as Fichte says, does this not ontologically override the social by means of subsuming the particular into the universality of spiritual beings? Is this not but another instance where the social is being withdrawn? Again, Derrida asks: "how is *Geschlecht* to be translated?" Is it the trait of an alliance that remains unassimilable within it?

As Derrida said on more than one occasion, there is always a fantom in the seminar, by which is usually meant the silent presence of an intertext, whether recognized or not. For example, in lecture eight of *The Theological-Political*, Derrida says that Nietzsche hangs around as the great fantom of this seminar (*"Nietzsche reste le grand fantôme de ce séminaire"*). However, a text such as "From Restricted to General Economy" may well be one of these unseen fantoms too in the sense of being an intertext that stalks "Geschlecht II." Especially pertinent in this context is the following statement:

> An absolutely *unique relation*: of a language to a sovereign silence which toler*ates no relations,* tolerates no symmetry with that which tilts itself and slides in order to be related to it. A relation, however, which must rigorously, *scientifically*, place into a common syntax both the subordinated significations and the operation which is nonrelation, which has no signification and freely keeps itself outside syntax. Relations must scientifically be related to nonrelations, knowledge to unknowledge.[20]

Sovereignty in this passage refers to Georges Bataille's conception wherein sovereignty is distinguished from lordship in terms of a certain negativity whereby control is relinquished and a nonrelation of relations is introduced. Self-maintenance, integrality, coherence, sense, self-identity, and so on are all sacrificed by sovereignty—given up. "Sovereignty has no identity, is not *self, for itself, toward itself, near itself.* In order not to govern, that is to say, in order not to be subjugated, it must subordinate nothing." Sovereignty "must expend itself without reserve, lose itself, lose consciousness, lose all memory of itself and all interiority of itself."[21] Put simply, sovereignty is lordship under erasure. Lordship is weaker than sovereignty, according to Bataille, because its metaphysics of identity (selfhood, control, rationality, will) has to be protected from threat, whereas sovereignty expends identitarian relations without reserve with the result that it has nothing that can be taken away from it. For Derrida, the relationship between lordship and sovereignty is, in fact, one of "imperceptible difference," one that "is not even the symmetry of an upper and lower side" (i.e., of lordship's hierarchical relation with sovereignty).[22]

Derrida's account of sovereignty is very much in line with his reading of *Geschlecht* that in terms of its untranslatability has sacrificed meaning and expended its identitarian relations as a manifestation of its power as sovereign. At the same time, *Geschlecht* functions in the role of lordship to the extent that it "reconstitutes presence"[23] in terms of itself as a marker of an identity that governs itself in terms of those characteristics that are proper to it alone. At stake in lordship is self-awareness as self-preservation and an ability "to be near oneself," that is, to live among others who are of the same genus and of the same place. This, in Derrida's parlance, is restricted economy (metaphysical discourse). General economy refers to the effects of sovereignty as a discourse that produces "destruction, without reserve, of meaning."[24] Is sovereignty a thing in itself? Derrida answers that "sovereignty is the impossible, therefore it *is not.*"[25] Here, once again, one can sense the logic of *retrait* (withdrawal) at work: that sovereignty is the *retrait* of lordship at once the same and different, powerless and powerful, weak and aggressive. Would that be the case for *Geschlecht* as well? That its untranslatability speaks to its sovereignty within lordship, above lordship, or below it? As the general economy that does violence to philosophical nationalism as a restricted economy, *Geschlecht* would perform the "relation to [a] loss of meaning." Of course, in the context of nationalism questions of sovereignty, lordship, relation, and meaning are always at issue. Also, one has to wonder if Heidegger's inceptual philosophizing—his interrogation of *Seyn/Sein*—is imagined by Derrida as an instance of methodological sovereignty, a destruction without reserve that also conserves, a thinking that "must expend itself without reserve, lose itself, lose consciousness, lose all memory of itself and all interiority of itself."[26]

When Derrida asks, "How is '*Geschlecht*' to be translated under these conditions (of infinite will)?" he is speaking of a general economy that is immediately mediated by a restricted national one, that of speaking in German. "Despite what he says: anyone, in whatever language he or she speaks, '*ist unsers Geschlechts*,' he says this in German, and this *Geschlecht* is an essential *Deutschheit*." The word's "connotations belong irreducibly to German, to a German more essential than all the phenomena of empiric Germanness, but to some German. All these connoted senses are co-present in the use of the word *Geschlecht*, they virtually appear in that use, but no sense is fully satisfying. How is one to translate?"[27] One can omit the word, Derrida says, as the French translator did or judge the word so open-ended and undetermined that omission wouldn't matter much. Unmentioned but critically at issue is the relation/non-relation of the social relation inherent in *Geschlecht*, its impossibility, as it were, that emerges even as the relations withdraw into indeterminability and infinitization.

The "we" that announces itself to itself from the infinity of a telos of freedom and spirituality "finally comes down to the humanity of man, to the teleological essence of a humanity that is announced *par excellence* in *Deutschheit*. '*Menschengeschlecht*' is often said for '*genre humain*,' 'humankind,' 'human species,' 'human race.'" This speaks to a universal alliance, convergence, or relatedness under the sign of the human, despite its being announced in *Deutschheit*. Of course, this would be characteristic of philosophy as a discourse that is by its very nature cosmopolitan and transnational even to the point of imagining an infinite we. Philosophers speak of "the problem of man, of man's humanity, and of humanism,"[28] which is how Derrida will transition from Fichte to Heidegger, since both of them abandoned the cosmopolitan Latinate *Humanität* for *Menschlichkeit*, which obviously privileges their national mother tongue. Derrida will explicate Fichte's remarks in the *Addresses* on the concrete nature of German versus the abstract nature of Latin. For Fichte language, image, and symbol are constituted in terms of a "national imagination," for example, with respect to *Menschheit*, which is a "sensible concept," versus *Humanität*, which is not. This consideration, Derrida says, underlines "the difficulty of translating" this "sensible, critical, and sensitive (*névralgique*) word *Geschlecht*."[29] In other words, despite the word's general economy of loss, there is an aspect in which such a word is very concrete and sensible to the German speaker for the whom the idiom makes a strong impression.

At this point, discussion turns to Heidegger, who in a letter of 1945 to the Academic Rectorate of Albert-Ludwig University "explains his own attitude during the Nazi period. He had thought, he said, that he would be able to distinguish between the national and nationalism, that is, between the national and a biologicist and racist ideology."[30] Heidegger says that he said no to nationalism and "the intellectual and metaphysical grounds on which the biologism of the Party doctrine rested." Rather Heidegger identifies with the social (he only refers to it in the most abstract, denuded sense) and the national, because they "were not essentially tied to a biologicist and racist ideology." Derrida cites texts in which Heidegger performs this division and says "I shall not reopen today the dossier of Heidegger's 'politics,'" as that has been done elsewhere.[31]

Instead, Derrida says he will speak of a monstrosity (not unrelated to the dossier on Heidegger's politics) that will require "another detour through the question of man (*Mensch* or *homo*) and of the 'we' that gives its enigmatic content to a *Geschlecht*."[32] This monstrosity concerns revenance, the return of monstrosities that exist out of relation to their proper places and times and that are therefore perceived as uncanny. We usually think of monsters as entities that are out of proportion: deformed, grotesque in size, violating laws of kind or type, and possessing powers that do not obey the usual rules of nature, to say nothing of social behavior. *Geschlecht*, Derrida says, is "*un monstre*."

> You know the polysemic gamut of this word, the uses one can make of it, for example concerning norms and forms, species and genus/gender: thus concerning *Geschlecht*. I shall begin by privileging here another course [*direction*]. It goes in the direction, the *sens*, of a less known sense, since in French *la monstre* (a changing of gender, sex, or *Geschlecht*) has the poetico-musical sense of a diagram that shows [*montre*] in a piece of music the number of verses and the number of syllables assigned to the poet. *Monstrer* is *montrer* (to show or demonstrate), and *une monstre* is *une montre* (a watch). I am already

settled in the untranslatable idiom of my language, for I certainly intend to speak to you about translation. *La monstre*, then, prescribes the divisions of a line of verse for a melody. *Le monstre* or *la monstre* is what shows in order to warn or put on guard. In the past *la montre*, in French, was written *la monstre*.[33]

That the French word for watch (*la montre*) was once written as *la monstre* orthographically bears out Derrida's thesis that monstrosity as hideous, measureless showing is inherently connected to an uncanny temporality in which the measure (chronology) of time is violated. In this case, *Geschlecht* is the monster or monstrosity that is embedded in a national imagination that has returned from its various states of historical obsolescence as a sign whose exhibition would be privileged by the National Socialists for monstrous ends—e.g., in the context of arresting, deporting, and experimenting on homosexuals. That the word suddenly returns within Heidegger's writings of the 1950s in connection with the poetry of Georg Trakl is another instantiation of a monstrosity, one that is quite detached from the technological utilitarianism of the Nazis in their pursuit of remaking humankind in their Aryan image, though, as we will see, Heidegger in 1953 was entertaining the narrative of a rebirth of the Germans insofar as that can be unearthed in Trakl's lyrics about the decline, death, and rebirth of a wandering stranger who turns his back on modern society *c.* 1914.

If Trakl's lyrics of the very early twentieth century were appropriated in the 1950s in order to condemn and retrieve something from National Socialism of the 1930s and '40s, one could argue that perhaps a case could be made for time being "out of joint," to borrow a phrase from Derrida's *Specters of Marx* in which historical revenance and monstrosity are theorized.[34] As it happens, Derrida himself doesn't speculate on this curious handling of Trakl, nor does he comment on the fact that, as Derrida well knows, deconstruction itself is implicated in the return of the word *Geschlecht* in Heidegger insofar as both Heideggerian and Derridean modes of philosophical *Abbauen/Déconstruction* invite monstrous formulations, vocabularies, and logical connections in terms of their encounter with this word.

Relative to the theme of monstrosity in "Geschlecht II," Derrida introduces a displacement by way of a citation from Friedrich Hölderlin's "Mnemosyne" that occurs in Heidegger's *What Is Called Thinking?*

Ein Zeichen sind wir, deutungslos,
Schmerzlos sind wir, und haben fast
Die Sprache in der Fremde verloren.

Nous sommes un monstre privé de sens
Nous sommes hors douleur
Et nous avons perdu
Presque la langue à l'étranger.

We are a 'monster' void of sense
We are outside sorrow
And have nearly lost
Our tongue in foreign lands.[35]

The German word *Zeichen* would usually be translated into French as *signe*, not *monstre*. Derrida says that at first he found this translation of Heidegger into French to be "mannered and gallicizing," but he finds it hermeneutically enlightening, nevertheless. "We are a monster, and singular, a sign that shows and warns." This sign (or monstration) shows, designates, and signifies, though it is "void of sense (*deutungslos*)."[36] Here the logic of withdrawal or *retrait* and the notion of sovereignty, from "From Restricted to General Economy," are in evidence. The sign

> says itself void of sense, simply and doubly monster, this 'we': we are sign–showing, informing, warning, pointing as sign toward, but in truth toward nothing, a sing out of the way (*à l'écart*), in a gapped relation to the sign (*en écart par rapport au signe*), display (*montre*) that deviates from the display or monstration, a monster that shows (*montre*) nothing. [37]

This speaks to a "monstrosity of monstrasity (*monstrosité*)," a loss of the German in the French tongue, which concerns one of the impasses of the cosmopolitan, which Derrida has been thematizing throughout the course in terms of the untranslatable.

Can one untranslatable idiom translate another? That seems to be a monstrous idea, though Derrida takes up the challenge. (1) "The translation of *Zeichen* by *monstre* has a triple virtue." *Zeichen*, *zeigen*, and *Aufzeigen* suggest a relation between sign and monstration. In *Being and Time*, "*Zeigen eines Zeichens*" concerns the "showing of the sign." In *On the Way to Language*, *Zeichen* and *Zeigen* are hooked up with *Sagen* or the Old High German idiom *Sagan*. "'Sagan' heisst: zeigen, erscheinen-, sehen- und hören-lassen." Again, *die Sage* (the said) is named by means of an old word, *die Zeige* (*la monstre*). (2) "The second virtue of *monstre* occurs within the Latin idiom, since the translation stresses this gap concerning the normality of the sign, of a sign that for once is not what it should be, shows or signifies nothing, shows the *pas de sens*, no-sense, and announces the loss of the tongue." Later, Derrida will wonder if *Geschlecht* refuses sense and displays its absence. (3) "The third virtue of this translation poses the question of man," who is monstrously determined by *Geschlecht* as well as by the *Zeichen*. This leads to Derrida's main exhibit concerning man and monstrosity, the human and the inhuman: namely, Heidegger's hand.[38]

In the course entitled *Eating the Other: The Rhetoric of Cannibalism* (1989–90), Derrida wrote a lengthy passage on the polymorphous perversity of the mouth, which speaks, murmurs, spits, sucks, chews, swallows, vomits, smiles, kisses, and viciously bites. The mouth, he was saying, cannot be considered any one thing and has to be thought of as a monstrosity, one that continually distorts, and in so doing shows a breakdown of differences that exceeds any one sort of identity. Yet, the mouth can be drawn or photographed as if it were but a singular feature of someone in particular, which clearly it is. That too replicates the sovereignty/lordship difference given that as sovereign the mouth is polymorphous perverse, whereas in terms of lordship it is a singular apparatus. Derrida, not surprisingly, works on breaking down this difference, especially since in the cannibalism course the mouth ambiguates the difference between man and animal.

Heidegger's hand is a somewhat similar case of the polymorphous perverse, given that like the mouth, it too is objectifiable as some thing in particular that is specific to a unique individual, though what it is in terms of its performativity wouldn't be so easy to restrict. The hand touches, strikes, caresses, grasps, holds, releases, points, pushes, pulls, and much else besides. In fact, "the hand cannot be spoken about without speaking of technics,"[39] that is, without objects, implements, or what Heidegger prefers to call equipment. Unlike the mouth, which all animals pretty much have in common, only the human hand is supposedly proper to man in a way that differentiates him absolutely from all other forms of life. The hand, as we know from the fine arts, is often the sign of man's humanity. Complex hand gestures in Asian forms of dance often stress this signifying aspect of the hand as sign that not only separates man from beast, but as that which signifies the social relation as a refined and complex interplay of significations. In that sense, the hand is related to social monstration. But the hand is also the necessary condition for fabrication, which Heidegger will discuss in terms of handiwork (*Handwerk*).

"The hand," Derrida says, "will be the (monstrous) sign (*le monstre*), the proper of man as (monstrous) sign, in the sense of *Zeichen*."[40] This presupposes the question of whether the hand is a perverse monstrosity or the semiotic showing of what is essentially most human. In *What Is Called Thinking?* we read about the hand reaching, extending, receiving, and welcoming. The hand reaches not just for the object but "receives its own welcome in the hand of the other." The hand, keeps, holds, carries. "The hand designs and signs, presumably because man is a (monstrous) sign (*Die Hand zeichnet, vermutlich weil der Mensch ein Zeichen ist*)."[41]

Derrida indicates that we are not to associate the hand with man, simply, because Heidegger in *What Is Called Thinking?* has left that sort of metaphysical formulation behind; rather, we are to think of the hand as the gift, of the "es gibt" of *Sein*. That connection is not developed, though one could consult Derrida's *Given Time: I. Counterfeit Money* for thoughts along this line that circle back to the early work on unrestricted/restricted economy. "The gift, like the event, as event, must *remain* unforeseeable, but remain so without keeping itself. It must let itself be structured by the aleatory." Again, "the condition of the gift and the event is a certain unconditionality ... The gift and the event obey nothing, except perhaps principles of disorder, that is, principles without principles." Not explainable "by a system of efficient causes, [the gift] is the effect of nothing." This, then, speaks to general economy. Derrida, however, will immediately turn to restricted economy, "and yet—effects of pure chance will never form a gift that has the meaning of a gift," which has to do with "the intention to give" and "wanting to say," which endow the gift with a meaning.[42] Of course, this concerns a thing (the gift, the hand) which makes possible a social relation that involves exchange and debt, one that requires the gift to be understood as part of an order of circulation whereby a social bond is articulated. Here too one can see the withdrawal ("the effect of nothing") and a coming forth into being (the gift *as* gift). But is the hand a gift? Can one really give a hand? What about the intention to give? Isn't the handshake inseparable from such intention? Is there something unforeseeable, something due to chance in the extension of the hand? We will return to this in a bit.

Heidegger's hand, Derrida implies, is both the gift to philosophy and the gift of philosophy. As such, the hand is inceptual: the "*es gibt*." Yet, the hand that writes great philosophy is believed to be literally human, as well, which is why Heidegger had his own hands photographed in terms of what Derrida calls the "theatre of hands" and "demonstration of hands"—"the deliberately craftsman-like staging of the hand play" that was made into an album Derrida bought in Germany in 1979 when he had had his séance with Heidegger's ghost as recollected in *The Post Card*. Exhibited is the handling of the pen, in particular, which depicts a certain meditation, stillness, and piety of thought. Yet as Derrida sees it, "the hand is monstrasity (*monstrosité*), the proper of man as the being of monstration. This distinguishes him from every other *Geschlecht* (species), and above all from the ape."[43] In that sense of man versus animal, the hand symbolizes difference, not identity. The hand absolutely distinguishes human from beast.

After Derrida gave "Geschlecht II" as a lecture at Loyola University of Chicago in 1985, I had a chance to ask him about an allusion to the hand that had immediately come to mind as he read. Isn't there a sense in which one will be thinking of Heidegger's raised hand that must have given the Nazi salute during the Hitler years? Derrida's response was "of course." He didn't elaborate, but I take it the point is that in the context of the salute, the distinction between the human and the beast isn't really so clear cut. In addition, we shouldn't lose sight of the fact that with respect to the word *Schlag* in its relation to *Geschlecht*, which Derrida discusses later, it is likely the hand that is doing violence by striking, hitting, punching, beating, and so on. This also points to *Geschlecht* as sexual difference in terms of what has been called a battle of the sexes in which the hand strikes. That too can be assumed to be part of the monstrosity of the hand, which in certain cases can do things that are unforeseeable, given the chances. Already at this point we can see that many sorts of differences are in play: the human being versus the monster, man versus animal, the giving of being versus the literal hand of the thinker, the pious versus the violent hand, the individual hand of the thinker versus the collective hand of a political demonstration of allegiance to a leader.

Instead of examining all these differences at once, Derrida follows Heidegger's discourse on handwork, a move that transitions from monstration to fabrication, showing to making. Derrida is interested in the photographs of the hand that Heidegger had taken that were meant to thematize the thinking hand as working hand. "The noble *métier*, as *Handwerk*, will also be that of the thinker or the teacher who teaches thinking."[44] *Handwerk* requires being in direct contact with the essence of the thing that one is manipulating or fabricating with. Nothing is said of workers in relation to one another (the social), but of the relation of hand to thing in which there is "an accord." The hand should be in touch with the essent. This relates as well to the poet. "At any rate," Heidegger says, "it (thinking, *das Denken*) is a handiwork."[45] This reprises the idea of the hand as the "*es gibt*," the hand in relation with inceptual being.

The hand in Heidegger is significant, Derrida tells us, because (1) it "binds thinking" to "a situation of the body ... of man and of human being (*Menschheit*)"; (2) in Heidegger "the hand thinks before being thought; it is thought, a thought, thinking (*la pensée*)"; this suggests that the difference between hand and thought has been dismantled. "The hand cannot be thought as a thing."[46] (3) "The meditation on the authentic *Hand-Werk* also has the sense of an artisanalist protest against the hand's effacement or debasement in the industrial automation of modern mechanization."[47] In all three of these points,

Derrida sees in Heidegger the aim of deconstituting the commonplace subject–object relation of hand and thing.

The idea that the hand is an instrument for grasping or manipulating insists on such a subject–object relation. However, for Heidegger,

> the hand's being (*das Wesen der Hand*) does not let itself be determined as a bodily organ of gripping (*als ein leibliches Greiforgan*). It is not an organic part of the body intended (*destinée*) for grasping, taking hold (*prendre*), indeed for scratching, let us add even for catching on (*prendre*), comprehending, conceiving, if one passes from *Greif* to *begreifen* and to *Begriff*.[48]

If the hand thinks, it is not for the sake of conceptual grasping. "Rather, this thought of the hand belongs to the essence of the *gift*, of a giving that would give, if this is possible, without taking hold of anything."[49] Here Heidegger is turning to an inceptual conception of the hand in terms of giving as an originary determination of being. Derrida naturally sees this as a repudiation of a biologistic understanding of the hand that undermines the man/animal distinction Heidegger imagines elsewhere.

At the end of the sixth lecture, Derrida says that he objects to Heidegger's introduction of a difference when he says "Apes, *for example* [my emphasis, J.D.], have organs that can grasp, but they have no hand." Derrida subsequently remarks: "In its very content, this proposition marks the text's essential sense, marks it with a humanism that wanted certainly to be nonmetaphysical."[50] Can one make an argument for human *Geschlecht* (kind, genus) independent of a "biologistic determination" that imposes an "absolute oppositional limit"? Such a limit, Derrida says, "effaces the differences" of what we could call a general economy "and leads back, following the most resistant metaphysico-dialectic tradition, to the homogeneous." Not only that, but Derrida accuses Heidegger of imposing a crude, *unthinking* distinction between man and animal, one that "knows nothing about this [zoological knowledge] and wants to know nothing."[51] Ironically, the philosopher's hand, in this case, is an unthinking hand that contradicts the discourse on the hand in relation to thought. Heidegger's discourses on the hand are therefore massively conflicted.

That Heidegger "has no doubt studied neither the zoologists (even were it to criticize them), nor the apes of the Black Forest" is said by Derrida to be "serious."

> Because what he says traces a system of limits within which everything he says of man's hand takes on sense and value. Since such a delimitation is problematic, the name of man, his *Geschlecht*, becomes problematic itself. For it names what has the hand, and so thinking, speech or language, and openness to the gift.[52]

Derrida is pointing out that by imposing a dogmatic difference, Heidegger has reintroduced a restricted economy within what was being de-restricted and that this will have implications for the philosophemes of thinking, speech, language, and gift. We shouldn't lose sight of the fact that fundamentally at issue in terms of the hand is showing (monstration), making (fabrication), and offering (stretching out, giving the hand). Derrida sets aside fabrication when he speaks of "the hand's double *vocation*," which is "to show (*montrer*) or point out (*zeigen, Zeichen*) and to give or give itself, in a word the *monstrasity* (*monstrosité*) *of the gift or of what gives itself.*"[53] Why fabrication is left out is unclear, given Derrida's lengthy discussion of it, but apparently he wanted to point out that a sign and an offering or gift are related: that the sign proffers something. Again, the fantom of the Nazi salute comes to mind insofar as the hand as sign is outstretched, given, as it were, to others as a reciprocal gift that makes a social bond or relation. Not just the hand, but "man is himself a sign, a monstrous sign."

From *What Is Called Thinking?* Derrida finally cites the complete tutor text that he has had on his mind from nearly the beginning of "Geschlecht II" that begins, "The hand designs and signs (*zeichnet*), presumably because man is a [monstrous] sign (*ein Zeichen ist*)." It ends, "all the work of the hand is rooted in thinking. Therefore, thinking (*das Denken*) itself is man's simplest, and for that reason hardest, *Hand-Werk*, if it would be properly accomplished (*eigens*)."[54] Of interest is that, according to Derrida,

> the nerve of the argument seems to me reducible to the assured opposition of *giving* and *taking*: man's hand *gives and gives itself, gives and is given,* like thought or like what gives itself to be thought and what we do not yet think, whereas the organ of the ape or of man as a simple animal, indeed as an *animal rationale*, can only *take hold of, grasp, lay hands on the thing.*[55]

Since Derrida is concerned with delimitations, he will turn to the well-known distinction of *Vorhandenheit* (present-to-hand) and *Zuhandenheit* (ready-to-hand) in *Being and Time* in order to point out another example of how hand and difference come into play. Also another differend of interest to Derrida is that of pragma and praxis in Heidegger's seminar *Parmenides*. Pragma, praxis, *Vorhandenheit*, and *Zuhandenheit* are all "in the domain of the hand." And to this will be added yet another differend familiar to readers of Derrida, namely the speech/writing distinction.

Heidegger speculates that the hand as pointer is determinative of speech—in other words, that speech is an innate determinant of the hand, rather than the hand being a gesture that mimics speech. On account of the hand's innate relation to speech (*logos*), typographic mechanization of speech in the form of typewriting is to be considered debased. "The typewriter tends to destroy the word: the typewriter 'tears (*entreisst*) writing from the essential domain of the hand, that is, of the word,' of speech."[56] Also, Heidegger claims that writing is but a copy or transcription of speech based on a technical intermediary that is itself incapable of thinking. For Derrida, who analyzed the voice/writing at length in Husserl and Plato, this claim is as crudely metaphysical as the claim concerning the human hand versus the ape's paw and speaks to the repeated attempt to establish markers of difference whose history in terms of Heidegger's decades of writing consists of both subtle and gross distinctions. Speech versus writing, man versus ape are, of course, typical of what Derrida above calls "the most resistant metaphysico-dialectic tradition" that has the performativity of a certain revenance in Heidegger, a stunning and monstrous return in plain sight that occurs from within what can be apprehended as a subtle disarticulation of differences threatening to metaphysics.

The purpose of Derrida's investigation of the hand in Heidegger is precisely to exacerbate the multiplicity of differentials that Heidegger formulates relative to the hand, a master signifier of *Geschlecht* (e.g., *Menschengeschlecht* [human kind or race]). The hand, whose philosophical differentials decompose it as a thing in itself, nevertheless synecdochically refers us to what *kind* (*Geschlecht*) of being man is. Kind, in turn, refers to *Wesen*, essence as a *particular* sort. The question is, of course, whether the hand can convincingly determine human kind, given its interplay of differences, and whether failure to convince means it is at best just a superficial, conventional sign that fulfills a prejudice? Anyway, why should the hand be privileged? What about the brain? Or the tongue?

One should bear in mind that in general Derrida has been critical of *Dasein* as an abstraction and has, in various texts, mischievously given *Dasein* a body or, at least, body parts. The hand, the ear, the foot, the arm, if not the physical sex of *Dasein* serve in Derrida's writings to give *Dasein* a physical body that it otherwise doesn't appear to have. What we witness in his work, in fact, is the thematization of the body part, or what Derrida, thinking along the lines of French psychoanalysis, would have identified as the "part object." Are the various meanings of *Geschlecht* part objects too? Should they be considered as an interplay of differentiality or effraction? Is *Geschlecht*, like *Dasein*, an abstraction that has to be embodied: given a body by way of a helping hand? This, in fact, occurs in "Geschlecht I" on sexual difference.

Derrida's theme of monstrosity is a part of a long-term interest in Freud's concept of body parts as polymorphous perverse. As noted, polymorphous perverse organs such as the mouth are as violent as they are gentle and mild. Of the hand, Heidegger says, "only the being that, like man, 'has' speech (*Wort, mythos, logos*) can and must have the hand thanks to which prayer can occur, but also murder, *the salute* or wave of the hand, and thanks, the oath and the sign (*Wink*), *Handwerk* in general."[57] Prayer, murder, the salute, the oath, and the sign are in correspondence polymorphously and, one might argue, perversely as well. Again, note that they speak to social relations. In this context, Heidegger also mentions the *Handschlag* or hand shake in which the inceptual violence of the *Schlag* (punch, strike) is latent. One shakes instead of hits, though the threat of the hit is not completely absent. This is said to ground an accord, alliance, or bond. *Geschlecht* in terms of stock, community, or race requires that people handle each other physically. As we know, that can turn violent.

Such violence speaks to a register in Derrida's thinking that emerges too in *Of Spirit* in which again there is an intuition that the social relation is founded upon an originary violence, one that can be detected, for example, in all those differentials or splittings that obsess Heidegger's analyses, splittings whereby various elements are both separated and constellated (gathered). Derrida even embodies this differential between splitting and gathering when he talks about the one hand versus two hands and Heidegger's tendency to speak of the hand as if man had only one. In prayer, however, there is mention of two hands that gather or join into one. "Gathering together (*Versammlung*) is always what Heidegger privileges."[58]

Nothing, however, is "said of the caress or of desire"; no mention is made of loving with the hand, which would concern an alliance between the sexes foundational to *Geschlecht*: generation, kin, family, etc. This suggests that Heidegger has not quite worked out the conflictual relation within *Geschlecht* between the hand's *Schlag* (or strike) and the hand's caress, which is to say, the fundamental *social* division between difference/identity, separation/unification, and hate/love. In fact, what Derrida wrote out in *Fantom* is a bit different from "Geschlecht II" in that Derrida writes not just of the caress, but of "all the other symbolic or physical gestures" of the man who goes so far as "to give a military salute, show political party adherence, or who tortures."

Given all that has been said about *Geschlecht*, Derrida almost interrupts himself by coming to a very key insight upon which future lectures will be more or less based.

> I just said "the word '*Geschlecht*'": that is because I am not so sure it has a determinable and unifiable referent. I am not so sure one can speak of *Geschlecht*

beyond the word "*Geschlecht*"—which then is found necessarily cited, between quotation marks, mentioned rather than used. Next, I leave the word in German. As I have already said, no word, no word for word will suffice to translate this word that gathers in its idiomatic value stock, race, family, species, genus/gender, generation, sex.

Derrida takes this further by concluding provisionally,

> Perhaps it is no longer a word. Perhaps one must begin by gaining access to it from its disarticulation or its decomposition, in other words, its formation, its information, its deformations or transformations, its translations, the genealogy of its body unified starting from or according to the dividing and the sharing of the words' morsels. We are going then to concern ourselves with the *Geschlecht* of *Geschlecht*, with its genealogy or its generation.[59]

To put this in the context of a general economy, as sovereign, *Geschlecht* is a word that is not a word. Parenthetically, Derrida adds: "After saying the word '*Geschlecht*,' I amended or corrected myself: the 'mark *Geschlecht*,' I clarified." Derrida will add that his genealogical understanding of *Geschlecht* will be "inseparable … from the decomposition of human *Geschlecht*, from the decomposition of man."[60] This remark alludes to a passage on *Geschlecht* in Heidegger's "Die Sprache im Gedicht" in which *Geschlecht* in the context of generation is thought to be de-essenced and de-composed because it "has been removed from its kind of essential being."[61] For Derrida, this decomposition refers to the word *Geschlecht* per se, if not to Trakl's "Die Sprache im Gedicht" generally. In short, for Derrida decomposition is going to be considered a major Heideggerian philosopheme.

Situating Trakl

In the seventh lecture of *Fantom*, incorporated in "Geschlecht II," Derrida references Heidegger's "Die Sprache im Gedicht: Eine Erörterung seines Gedichtes" published in the journal *Merkur* in 1953 and republished in *Unterwegs zur Sprache* in 1959. Both the title and subtitle, Derrida writes, "are already practically untranslatable," hence Derrida's interest in how Jean Beaufret and Wolfgang Brokmeier rendered their French translation of Heidegger's text.[62] Moving on, Derrida initiates his first major inquiry by saying,

> Before any other preliminary, I jump suddenly to the middle of the text in order to throw light as from a first flash on the site that interests me. On two occasions,

in the first and the third parts [of "Die Sprache im Gedicht"], Heidegger declares that the word "*Geschlecht*" has in German, "in our tongue" (it is always a question of "we"), a multitude of significations ....While recalling here that *Geschlecht* is open to a kind of polysemy, he heads, before and after all, toward a certain unity that gathers this multiplicity. This unity is not an identity, but guards the simplicity of the same, even in the form of the fold. Heidegger wants this primordial simplicity to give rise to thought beyond all etymological derivation, at least according to the strictly philosophical sense of etymology.[63]

A statement of crucial significance for Derrida occurs in Heidegger's commentary on Trakl's "Autumn Soul" ("*Herbstseele*") when we read that "the travelers who follow the stranger find themselves immediately separated from 'Loved Ones' (*von Lieben*) who are for them 'Others.' The 'Others,' let us understand the ruined stock of man." In German this reads: "*Die Wanderer, die dem Fremdling folgen, sehen sich alsbald geschieden 'von Lieben' 'die fur sie' 'Andre' sind. Die Anderen– das ist der Schlag der verwesten Gestalt des Menschen.*" Peter Hertz, the English translator of *Unterwegs*, renders Heidegger's commentary a bit differently than John P. Leavey did within his translation of Derrida's essay. "The wanderers who follow the stranger soon find themselves parted 'from loved ones' who to them are 'others.' The others—that is the case of the decomposed form of man."[64]

Without attempting to introduce, explicate, and interpret "Autumn Soul," Derrida jumps into the thick of things by seizing upon "*der Schlag der verwesten Gestalt des Menschen*" in which *Schlag* functions as a synonym for *Geschlecht*.

> "*Schlag*" means several things in German. In the literal sense ... it is *blow* [*coup*] with all the associable significations; but in the figurative sense, says the dictionary, it is also race or species, the stock [*la souche*] (the word chosen by the French translators). Heidegger's meditation will let itself be guided by this relation between *Schlag* (at once blow and as stock) and *Geschlecht*.[65]

Also to be taken into consideration is the word *Verwesen* ("*Der Schlag der verwesten Gestalt des Menschen*"), which "literally understood according to the usual code of bodily decay" speaks to what is decomposed, but also, in Heidegger's lexicon, to what is dis-essenced. Derrida avoids the suggestion that *Verwesen* might also point to a certain degeneracy whereby Trakl could be saying of "the others": "the race (*Schlag*) of a degenerate (*verwesten*) form (*Gestalt*) of man." That, of course, would be taking poetic license with "*verwesten*," though poetic license is almost everywhere being taken by Heidegger. Given all the talk about monstrosity and the fantoms of Nazism that course through "Geschlecht II," it is hard not to make a mental note of a possible race-degeneracy connection.

Derrida himself focuses on the crucial point that "Heidegger's meditation will let itself be guided by this relation between *Schlag* (at once as blow and as stock) and *Geschlecht*."[66] *Verwesen*, Derrida says, denotes bodily decay and the corruption of being. Does that mean the "loved ones" Trakl denotes in "Autumn Soul" are dead? We're not told. Apparent, however, is that Derrida is keen on *identifying Schlag as a primordial violence required in order for Menschengeschlecht to come into being*. This is fundamentally at issue in the following quotation and explication of Heidegger, which I quote initially in Derrida's original for semantic reference.

> Notre langue appelle [*nennt*: nomme] l'humanité [*Menschenwesen*] ayant reçu l'empreinte d'une frappe [*das aus einem Schlag geprägte*] et dans cette frappe frappée de spécification [*und in diesen Schlag verschlagene*: et en effet *verschlagen* veut dire couramment spécifier, séparer, cloisonner, distinguer, différencier], notre langue appelle l'humanité ... 'Geschlecht'.[67]

In Leavey's translation:

> Our language calls [*nennt*: names] humanity [*Menschengeschlecht*] having received the imprint of a striking [*das aus einem Schlag geprägte*] and in this striking struck with/as species determination [*und in diesen Schlag verschlagene*: and in effect *verschlagen* means commonly to specify, separate, cast adrift, partition, board-up, distinguish, differentiate], our language calls humanity ... 'Geschlecht'.[68]

Later Derrida will concern himself at length with the word *verschlagen*. For now, he brings out the extent to which people or races are struck in a way analogous to minting coins. However, at stake is something far less abstract than being stamped out, given that it is also the sexes that are being struck in a way that is itself sexual if one understands *Schlag* in terms of the sexual hitting or banging that centuries ago have been associated with the word *Ficken*. In other words, the production of *Menschengeschlechter* requires the violence of *Schlagen* (slamming against) associated with the sexual act, and not only that, but with the social violence whereby types are kept distinct through segregation, as in the case of aristocratic dynasty, or by means of subjecting members of an ordinary family to the blows of the one who enforces rule, which speaks to regulatory, domestic violence. *Schlag*, not surprisingly, is also to be associated inferentially with the battle of the sexes and hence human reproduction, which in turn relates to identity as social control over kin, stock, and tribe. Such social violence was, of course, explicit under National Socialism, particularly with respect to literally beating supposedly "degenerate" peoples to death, among other modes of violent persecution. Of course, none of this is spoken of in Heidegger, though the line that is of such interest to Derrida about *Schlag* and *Verwesen* seems to be some kind of revenant that is temporally (historically) out of joint.

Derrida has a light touch regarding racism, but he does emphasize sexual violence. Derrida comments that Heidegger speaks of two blows, the first initiating the duality (*das Zwiefache*) of *Geschlecht* as differentiated sexually, and the second, *die Zweitracht der Geschlechter*, "the duality of the sexes as dissension, war, disagreement, opposition, the duel of violence, and of declared hostilities"—in a word, a battle of the sexes.[69] The remarks on *Schlag* compress what otherwise would have been a much lengthier discussion of effraction that includes not just the *coup* or *blow* whereby generations are produced and/or maintained as separate entities but in terms also of *the difference of difference* that Heidegger speaks of in terms of duality/discord. Odd, of course, is that the *Schlag* is actually quite unspecified. Heidegger speaks of it above in terms of a "having received the imprint of a striking (*das aus einem Schlag geprägte*)." But as to who or what does the striking, with what in specific one is struck with, and so forth are left in abeyance, something Derrida doesn't question or explain. He is, however, keenly aware that difference and differentiation in terms of *Schlagen* both establishes and divides the identity and unity of the type or genus that Heidegger particularizes as *Menschenwesen* and *Menschengeschlecht*. This is why Derrida's second major exhibit in "Die Sprache im Gedicht" is Heidegger's mention of "*das* Ein."

In a very prolix and opaque passage, simplified here somewhat, Derrida announces,

> The second passage [by Heidegger] will be taken from the third part [of "*Die Sprache im Gedicht*"] in the course of a passage that will have indeed displaced things: "'*One*' [in quotation marks and italics in the German text: '*das* "Ein"'] in the words '*One* race' (*im Wort* 'Ein *Geschlecht*': citation of a verse by Trakl; this time the French translators chose, without apparent or satisfactory justification, to translate *Geschlecht* by 'race') does not mean 'one' in place of 'two' [*meint nicht 'eins' statt 'zwei'*]. *One* does not signify either indifference of an insipid uniformity. [...] The words 'One race' [*das Wort* 'Ein *Geschlecht*'] name here no biologically determinable state of things ... neither 'unisexuality' ... nor the 'undifferentiation of the sexes ...' In the *One* underlined [by Trakl] ... does the unity take shelter, the unity that, starting from the matching azure of the spiritual night, reunites [*einigt*].[70]

Derrida, apparently, prefers that *Geschlecht* be translated in terms of sex rather than race. In arguing that the *One* is not one, he contrasts unisexuality with undifferentiation of the sexes: an effraction of identity into non-identical identicality. In part, Derrida objects to the French translation of *Geschlecht* as race, because "*ein Geschlecht*" *retreats* from the determinability of types or categories insofar as it precedes distinguishability and the division of identity/ difference. In that sense, *Geschlecht* is a mark or trait of what Derrida famously called "*la différance*," except that here "*la différance*" is situated within Heidegger's inceptual thinking that was undertaken on a vast scale in Heidegger's private notebooks of the late 1930s in which ap-propriation, a gathering that elides distinctions of the one and the many, is at issue. Gathering, in this sense, is not considered formalizable or structurally bounded, which speaks to Derrida's understanding that for Heidegger the interpretation of Trakl lacks a certain formalizable method, given that for Heidegger, even if Trakl is thought to be the expression of just one thought—one genus (*Geschlecht*)—his poetry is a gathering of verses whose identity holds difference open and, at certain points, disseminatively so.

For Derrida, *Geschlecht*, as invoked by both Trakl and Heidegger, is conceivable as a marker for *la différance* as a phenomenological interplay (*Ereignis, ap-propriation*) of multiple constructions that establish and dis-establish the notion of a unitary genus or kind. This may be seen to correlate to what Heidegger in the late 1930s called the enactment of the truth of being wherein we are to understand truth as an unconcealedness within concealment that concerns restraint, a chief characteristic of Trakl's poetry.

In *Contributions to Philosophy (of the Event)*, Heidegger states that "restraint disposes (*Verhaltenheit stimmt*) each grounding moment of a sheltering (*Bergung*) of truth in the coming *Dasein* of the human being." This entails "the concealed history of the great stillness (*die verborgene Geschichte der großen Stille*)." Moreover, "only in such history can a people still *be*. This restraint alone can gather humans and human assemblies to themselves, i.e. into the destiny of their assignment: the enduring of the last god (*Diese Verhaltenheit vermag allein Menschenwesen und Menschenversammlung auf es selbst, d.h. in die Bestimmung seines Auftrags: die Beständnis des letzten Gottes, zu sammeln*)."[71] For Heidegger, Trakl's poetry is the enactment of such restraint, reservedness, or withdrawal: the concealed history of a great stillness that concerns an inceptual thinking of being that precedes the kind of objectification that distinguishes clearly between identity and difference.

Heidegger's point that restraint and reservedness alone can gather a people to themselves underlies mention of "*ein Geschlecht*" in "Die Sprache im Gedicht" given that "*ein Geschlecht*" is this gathering that is inceptual and as such historically determinative. For Derrida the inceptual gathering is essentially etymologically determined, which means that for him (as for Fichte) what gathers a people to themselves is language or, in this case, an idiom whose "multiple fullness of signification" concerns an interplay (or *Zuspiel*, as Heidegger puts it in *Contributions*) between metaphysics and its overcoming (deconstruction).

At issue for Heidegger in *Contributions* is the transition, as he calls it, to "an other beginning" by which he means an inceptual thinking more radical than that of metaphysics. Deconstruction performs the kind of interplay that recognizes a more radical understanding of an inceptual beginning that is brought into confrontational relation (or *Auseinandersetzung*) with metaphysics—in the case of *Fantom*, with philosophical nationalist metaphysics. As if to put in his lot with Derrida's project, Heidegger himself writes *c.* 1936:

> All biologisms and naturalisms (which proffer "nature" and the nonrational as the matrix from which everything arises, or as the universal life in which everything simmers, or as the dark versus the light, etc.) remain entirely rooted in the soil of metaphysics and need metaphysics, even if only to rub up against in order to produce a spark igniting the knowable, sayable, and—for these "thinkers"—writeable.[72]

Not only is this a direct condemnation of the metaphysics of philosophical nationalism but disparagingly mentioned are Richard Wagner and Houston Stewart Chamberlain, figures accused of resurrecting ("this 'resurrection' of") metaphysics by "making use of the Christian churches."[73] Clearly, their sort of philosophical nationalism covers over an *interplay* (a Heideggerian term that in certain respects is very roughly synonymous with deconstruction) whereby an "other" inception of Western thought might be disclosed and the traditional inception surpassed as an "overcoming of metaphysics." Of course, it is in this context that *Geschlecht* ought to be interpreted as a term that performs the interplay between a metaphysical inception and its overcoming by means of enacting restraint, withdrawal (erasure), reservation, and even silence: the unspoken.

Derrida, it seems, is on the same page with Heidegger when he writes,

> *Ein* then will give the fundamental tone, the fundamental note [*Grundton*]. But it is the *Grundton* of *Gedicht* and not of *Dichtung*, for Heidegger regularly distinguishes *Gedicht*, which always remains unspoken [*ungesprochene*], silent, from poems [*Dichtungen*], which themselves say and speak in proceeding from *Gedicht*. *Gedicht* is the silent source of written and spoken poems [*Dichtungen*] from which one must start in order to situate [*erörtern*] the site [*Ort*], the source, to wit, *Gedicht*. That is why Heidegger says of this 'Ein *Geschlecht*' that it shelters

the *Grundton* from which the *Gedicht* of this poet silences [*schweigt*] the secret [*Geheimnis*].⁷⁴

Gedicht is more inceptual than *Dichtung* and between them is an interplay of speaking and not speaking, of revealing and concealing, which has the consequence of deconstituting and overcoming metaphysics. That *Gedicht* (restraint, withdrawal, silence, not-speaking) should have a ground tone is paradoxical if what we expect is to hear that tone when in fact that tone is being sheltered. This obviously raises questions about what we can or cannot hear, whether the tone is hearable or not, whether it is a tone as something present-to-itself, and so forth. *Gedicht* is the "other inception or beginning" relative to *Dichtung* that is the manifest text ready to hand from which we must begin in order to get our bearings—to situate the site.

> *Gedicht* (an untranslatable word once more) is, in its place, what gathers together all the *Dichtungen* (the poems) of the poet. This gathering together is not that of a complete corpus, of the *œuvres complètes*, but a unique source that is not presented in any part of any poem. This gathering is the site of origin, the place from which and toward which the poems come and go according to a 'rhythm.' [...] What Heidegger wants to indicate, to announce rather than show, is the unique Site (*Ort*) of this *Gedicht*.⁷⁵

In his writings on Heraclitus, Heidegger characterizes *Logos* in terms of gathering, collecting, and gleaning (*Lesen*), a parallel Derrida expects us to know. In line with his earlier account of Schlegel in *Fantom*, Derrida reminds his auditors of a certain *Wechselbezug* (relation of reciprocal exchange) not only between *Gedicht* and *Dichtung* but between two associated terms that Heidegger specifies at the outset of "Die Sprache im Gedicht": the *Erörterung* (of *Gedicht*)—i.e., the situation and site of the unspoken—and the *Erläuterung* (of *Dichtung*), the elucidation and clarification of what is written. This speaks to Heidegger's manner or idiom of reading, one that Derrida says "always resorts in its decisive moments to a resource that is idiomatic, in other words, untranslatable."⁷⁶ *Gedicht*, in that sense, is inherent in the idiom insofar as the idiom holds something in reserve that can't be translated, though it can be known intuitively by the native speaker to whom the idiom is a part. This resource that is restrained or withheld within idiom is what Derrida earlier called "the idiom of idiom," something that is overdetermined in Trakl and Heidegger and that is "not only the resource of German, but most often of an idiom of the Old High German idiom," what Heidegger often refers to, according to Derrida, as "in our tongue (*in unsere Sprache*)" that "signifies originally (*bedeutet ursprünglich*)."⁷⁷

Having noted inceptual signification, Derrida makes a move that is familiar within the lecture courses, namely the presentation of a seemingly hurried list of topics that could be investigated if one had the time and space to do so. In this case, that list presents a number of words "of morsels of words, or of sentences." The final itinerary begins, redundantly, with the etymology of *Schlag* and its derivatives (*einschlagen, verschlagen, zerschlagen, auseinanderschlagen*). Added, as if belatedly, is quotation of the lengthy and very informative explication of *Schlag* and *Geschlecht* by David Farrell Krell in his chapter "Strokes of Love and Death" from *Intimations of Mortality*.[78] Other complex idiomatic words of concern to Derrida include *Ort* (place, site), *Geist* (spirit), *Fremd* (strange), and *Wahnsinn* (senseless), which Derrida begins to unpack somewhat.

Also, as sometimes occurs in Derrida's lectures, he gives a summative itinerary for further consideration that will be taken up—in this case, mainly in lectures eight to thirteen. These include:

1. Explication of the meanings and function of the word *Schlag* in "Die Sprache im Gedicht."
2. Explication of the word *Ort*: as site, tip, point of gathering, the indivisibility of *Gedicht*, *Erörterung* as situating, and so on.
3. The "untranslatable opposition" of *geistig/geistlich*. "This opposition authorizes withdrawing the *Gedicht* or the 'site' of Trakl both from what is gathered together ... [as] the 'western metaphysics' and of its Platonic [and Christian] tradition[s]." (Derrida takes this up at some length in *Of Spirit*.)
4. Explication of Heidegger's use of the word *fremd* not in the Latin sense of what is outside but in the High German context of *fram*: "forward toward elsewhere, in the act of making one's own path ..."
5. Explication of Heidegger's invocation of *Wahnsinn* from the High German *wana*, without, and its relation to *Sinnan*: "to travel, to strive toward, to carve open with a blow a direction ... [*eine Richtung einschlagen*]." (This speaks to Trakl's figure of the wanderer/madman/stranger.)[79]

To the previous itinerary, Derrida adds several supplementary questions: "If the 'situation (*Erörterung*)' of *Gedicht* is thus found to depend on its decisive moments on recourse to the idiom of *Geschlecht* or to the *Geschlecht* of idiom, how is one to think the relation between the unspoken of *Gedicht* and its belonging, the appropriation of its very silence, to one tongue and to one *Geschlecht*?" How does this situation relate to "Occidental man, since this whole 'situation' ... is preoccupied ... with concern for the place, the site, the path, and the destination of the Occident."[80] How are we to consider *Geschlecht* in terms of its *Verwesung* or decomposition? This corruption is to be considered a "*second blow* that comes to strike the sexual difference and to transform it into dissension, war, savage opposition. The primordial sexual difference is tender, gentle, peaceful; when that difference is struck down by a 'curse' ... the duality or the duplicity of the two becomes unleashed, an indeed bestial, opposition."[81] Inherent in these remarks is continued interest in the difference between man and animal, which is of concern to Derrida in Trakl.

Also, Derrida sees the double articulation of discord/duality as a "schema" that in Heidegger "is neither Platonic nor Christian," despite "all the appearances and signs of which he is well aware." Such a schema "would come under neither metaphysical theology nor ecclesial theology. But the primordiality (pre-Platonic, pre-metaphysical, or pre-Christian) to which Heidegger calls us and in which he situates the proper site of Trakl *has no other content and even no other language* than that of Platonism and Christianity." Derrida goes even further in saying that

> this primordiality is simply that starting from which things like metaphysics and Christianity are possible and thinkable. But what constitutes their arch-morning origin and their ultra-Occidental horizon is nothing other than this hollow of a repetition ... And the form or the "logic" of this repetition is not only readable in this text on Trakl but in everything that, since *Sein und Zeit*, analyzes the structures of *Dasein*, the *Verfall*, the *Ruf*, care [*Sorge*], and regulates this relation of the 'most primordial' according to what is less so, notably Christianity.[82]

Heidegger's argument that Trakl is not a Christian poet is at once too laborious and too simplistic, according to Derrida. Moreover, just as Heidegger presupposes there can be only one "gathering site" for Trakl's *Gedicht*, he presupposes a single site "unique and univocal, for the metaphysics and the Christianity. But does this gathering take place? Has it a place, a unity of place? That is the question I leave suspended."[83]

Notes

1   Jacques Derrida, *The Politics of Friendship*, trans. George Collins (London: Verso, 1997), xiii. *Monolinguism of the Other*, trans. Patrick Mensah (Stanford: Stanford University Press, 1998), 1.

2   Martin Heidegger, *Nature, History, State*, trans. Gregory Fried, Richard Polt (London: Bloomsbury, 2013), 38.

3   Ibid., 41.

4   Max Weber, *Wirtschaft und Gesellschaft* (Tubingen: Mohr, 1956).
5   Michel Foucault, *Society Must Be Defended*, trans. David Macey (New York: Picador, 2003). See 258 ff.
6   Martin Heidegger, "Origin of the Work of Art," in *Poetry, Language, Thought*, trans. A. Hofstadter (New York: Harper and Row, 1975). "Building, Dwelling, Thinking" in *Poetry, Language, Thought*.
7   Martin Heidegger, "Concerning 'The Line,'" in *The Question of Being*, trans. William Kluback and Jean T. Wilde (New Haven: College and University Press, 1958).
8   Jacques Derrida, "The Retrait of Metaphor," in *Psyche*, vol. 1 (Stanford: Stanford University Press, 2007), 64.
9   Ibid. 65.
10 Jacques Derrida, "*Geschlecht* I," in *Psyche*, vol. 2 (Stanford: Stanford University Press, 2007), 7.
11 Jacques Derrida, *Force de loi* (Paris: Galilée, 1994).
12 My account is informed by David Farrell Krell's expansive etymological depiction in *Phantoms of the Other* (Albany: SUNY, 2015). Another chief source for me is *Duden: Das Herkunftwörterbuch, Etymologie der deutschen Sprache*, vol. 7, 5th ed. (Mannheim: Dudenverlag, 2014).
13 Jacques Derrida, "Geschlecht II," in *Deconstruction and Philosophy*, ed. John Sallis, trans. John P. Leavey, Jr. (Chicago: University of Chicago Press, 1987), 161.
14 Ibid., 162.
15 Ibid. As pointed out in my introduction, this translation issue reoccurs in Gregory Moore's translation of the *Addresses*. Fichte, *Addresses to the German Nation*, trans. Gregory Moore (Cambridge: Cambridge University Press, 2008). In the translator's notes Moore explains that he translates *Geschlecht* as either race or generation.
16 Ibid.
17 Ibid.
18 Ibid., 162–3.
19 Ibid. Telos is spelled out in Greek script in the text and has been transliterated for better accessibility.
20 Jacques Derrida, "From General to Restricted Economy: A Hegelianism without Reserve," in *Writing and Difference*, trans. Alan Bass (Chicago: University of Chicago Press, 1978), 264.
21 Ibid., 265.
22 Ibid.
23 Ibid.
24 Ibid., 270.
25 Ibid.
26 Ibid., 265.
27 Derrida, "Geschlecht II," 163.
28 Ibid.

29 Ibid., 165.
30 Ibid.
31 Ibid.
32 Ibid., 166.
33 Ibid.
34 Jacques Derrida, *Specters of Marx*, trans. Peggy Kamuf (London: Routledge, 1994).
35 Derrida, "Geschlecht II," 166–7.
36 Ibid., 167.
37 Ibid.
38 Ibid., 167–8.
39 Ibid., 169.
40 Ibid., 168.
41 Ibid.
42 Jacques Derrida, *Given Time: I. Counterfeit Money*, trans. Peggy Kamuf (Chicago: Chicago University Press, 1992), 122–3.
43 Derrida, "Geschlecht II," 169. Italicized single letter "a" is my interpolation to ensure one not think this spelling is a mistake.
44 Ibid., 170.
45 Ibid., 171.
46 Ibid.
47 Ibid., 172. Derrida recognizes a National Socialist dimension to Heidegger's rejection of modern technicity. The reader is supposed to know that Heidegger associated such techne with Americanization and Bolshevism.
48 Ibid., 172.
49 Ibid., 173.
50 Ibid.
51 Ibid., 174.
52 Ibid.
53 Ibid.
54 Ibid., 175. The passage from Heidegger is too long to quote here. The interpolations in brackets are Derrida's.
55 Ibid.
56 Ibid., 179. What neither Heidegger nor Derrida reveals is that Heidegger's brother, Fritz Heidegger, was an assiduous typist who faithfully typed out Heidegger's writings.
57 Ibid., 178.
58 Ibid., 182.
59 Ibid., 183.
60 Ibid.
61 Martin Heidegger, "Language in the Poem," in *On the Way to Language*, trans. Peter Hertz (New York: Harper and Row, 1971), 170.

62 Derrida, "Geschlecht II," 183.
63 Ibid., 184.
64 Emphasis mine. *On the Way to Language*, 170. *Unterwegs zur Sprache*, 8th ed. (Pfulligen: Günther Neske, 1986), 49. *Unterwegs zur Sprache* is republished in Heidegger's *Gesamtausgabe*, vol. 12 (Frankfurt am Main: Vittorio Klostermann, 1985). Pagination of the Neske edition is reproduced in the margins of *GA 12*. Derrida used the Neske edition; his copy is archived in the Derrida Library that is currently housed at Princeton University. Throughout, Derrida marks the keywords.
65 Derrida, "Geschlecht II," 185.
66 Ibid.
67 *Psyché* (Paris: Galilée, 1987), 442.
68 Derrida, "Geschlecht II," 185. The sentence by Heidegger in the original reads: "*Unsere Sprache nennt das aus einem Schlag geprägte und in diesen Schlag verschlagene Menschenwesen das 'Geschlecht.'*"
69 Ibid., 186.
70 Ibid.
71 Martin Heidegger, *Contributions to Philosophy (of the Event)*, trans. Richard Rojcewicz and Daniela Vallega-Neu (Bloomington: Indiana University Press, 2012), 29. *Gesamtausgabe 60, Beitrage zur Philosophie (vom Ereignis)* (Frankfurt am Main: Vittorio Klostermann, 1989), 34–5.
72 Ibid., 136. In German, 172.
73 Ibid., 137. In German, 172–3.
74 Derrida, "Geschlecht II," 187.
75 Ibid., 190.
76 Ibid.
77 Ibid., 191.
78 David Ferrell Krell, *Intimations of Mortality* (University Park: Pennsylvania University Press, 1986).
79 Derrida, "Geschlecht II," 192–3.
80 Ibid.
81 Ibid. Translation slightly modified.
82 Ibid., 193.
83 Ibid., 194.

6

Retreat into the Inceptual

Lectures eight through thirteen have recently been published by Éditions du Seuil under the title *Geschlecht III: Sexe, race, nation, humanité*. The editors have employed a double reference wherein *"Geschlecht III"* refers both to lectures eight to thirteen in general and to a typescript bridging lectures seven and eight of *Fantom*, dubbed "The Loyola typescript." Derrida distributed this typescript to some of his confidants at Loyola University of Chicago where he had delivered the whole of "Geschlecht II" in March of 1985. Mention of the typescript was made at the end of delivering "Geschlecht II" when Derrida began making remarks on what was then announced as the forthcoming "Geschlecht III" on Martin Heidegger and Georg Trakl, a work then said to be in progress.[1]

Because the Loyola typescript revises *Fantom*'s original lecture scripts, the editors of *Geschlecht III* have substituted it in place of what they call the "seminar version" with the stipulation that they have provided footnotes wherein text from the original lecture script is provided in order to show how the two texts differ. In fact, upon checking the published typescript against the original, one will see that various discrepancies are ignored. In addition, the substitution of one typescript for another introduces a bit of confusion, for the Loyola typescript does not respect how lectures seven and eight are divided, but cuts across them, starting with the latter part of seven and finishing before the end of eight. Given that the editors of *Geschlecht III* have edited what are in the main the lectures from *Fantom*, it seems odd to have substituted a script that does not conform to *Fantom*'s divisions. More logical would have been to include the Loyola typescript in an appendix and retain *Fantom*'s original lectures. As to discrepancies, just one example follows so as not to get bogged down in comparisons (others will be mentioned in endnotes). Consider, for instance, how Derrida's "il y a du rassemblement (*Versammlung*)" in *Fantom*'s script has been changed by the editors to "il y a ou il doit y avoir du rassemblement (*Versammlung*)."[2] This is not just a minor change, since "il y a" is a Heideggerian locution for "es gibt."

Indeed, E*s gibt Versammlung* (*il y a rassemblement*) translates into English as "'there is' gathering," or, more precisely, "it gives gathering" in which the "it" is undetermined as something inceptual that can give, send, or destine, as Heidegger explains in the essay "Time and Being."[3] Because Derrida is clearly adopting a Heideggerian idiom relative to the word gathering in *Fantom*, it is problematic to have some other locution thrown into the mix within the Loyola typescript without any explanation from the editors as to whether they or Derrida made this change.

The question of the specifics of editorial practice aside, readers more generally will have to decide for themselves whether the Loyola typescript comprises the long lost "Geschlecht III" that Derrida never published, as the editors suggest, or whether it is work in progress and just part of a much larger whole, an option the editors confusingly hold open. Technically, whereas Derrida referred in print to the Loyola typescript as "Geschlecht III," anyone who reads this text in the context of *Fantom* will see it is but a restricted installment of a much bigger project, one that was never formally executed as a publication intended to be called "Geschlecht III." Moreover, when I discussed the question with Derrida in the fall of 1997 of whether a "Geschlecht III" would ever appear, he responded that this essay would never be written. He didn't say "Geschlecht III" existed as a typescript that he didn't intend to publish. In my view, what we have to work with are materials, some more preparatory than others, that form the basis for an essay that was never achieved. These materials include the latter part of lecture seven plus the last six lectures of *Fantom*, the Loyola typescript, a fragment called the "Intermediate Version" (on the subject of reading) that was included in the notes of *Geschlecht III*, and the pages derived or borrowed from *Fantom* that were included in the last two chapters of *Of Spirit*.

Of course, it is hardly surprising that intense interest has been paid on the part of scholars to the whereabouts of a "Geschlecht III" or its drafts, given that the essay was supposed to be the crown jewel of the *Geschlecht* series of essays in which the themes of monstrosity, animality, sex, violence, madness, and race would converge within the reading of a major thinker with a tainted political past under National Socialism. Of course, as we have seen, these themes were already opened up in "Geschlecht II" where they were exposed in close readings of passages in *What Is Called Thinking?* and related texts by Heidegger. The last six lectures of *Fantom* by contrast consist of a much slower and detailed exegesis of Heidegger's "Die Sprache im Gedicht" that is itself a highly compressed and secretive literary sort of text, given Heidegger's poetic approaches to the German language, to say nothing of the essay's baffling transitions and surprising leaps of association that Derrida will query. Nevertheless, despite what Derrida cautions with respect to how one should go about reading Heidegger's essay, we need to bear in mind that fundamentally Derrida's reading of "Die Sprache im Gedicht" is, in spite of everything else, written in the tradition of an exegesis that works its way linearly from the beginning to the end of a tutor text. That said, Derrida does not provide a wholistic reading of Heidegger's essay, pulling all of its parts together; rather, he selectively touches on those parts of Heidegger's essay that he finds to be problematic or in need of the kind of exposition that reveals the more radical aspects or potentials of Heidegger's discourse.

In lecture eight Derrida tells his audience that the lectures on Trakl will proceed slowly and that they will be rhythmically irregular. Derrida adds that the lectures will not follow a strictly linear trajectory and that his method at times will be unable to advance on account of a certain circularity in which steps have to be retraced. However, there will be sudden leaps, if not a certain zigzagging, the consequence of various ruptures that may well be incalculable.[4] This description should not surprise us, because in the essay "Passions: An Oblique Offering," Derrida insists that a deconstructive discourse should be oblique. "We should not above all approach in a direct, frontal *projective*, that is, thetic or thematic way," given that according to Derrida this is to be considered violent. A responsible approach to a text should be oblique, mobilizing the "discretion of the ellipse."[5] In fact, this is also how Heidegger approaches Trakl, obviating a direct approach to discussion of topics such as *Geschlecht* by avoiding, say, (1) discussion of Trakl's extremely difficult poem "Passion" in its three versions, where *Geschlecht* is so prominent a word, signaling incest ("*dunkle Liebe eines wilden Geschlechts*") and (2) the discreet avoidance of Trakl's "Dream and Derangement" ("*Traum und Umnachtung*") that speaks to a cursed race, "*O des verfluchten Geschlechts*."

Ort, Ortschaft

Given its exegetical approach, lecture eight's analysis begins at the beginning of Heidegger's essay by making remarks on Heidegger's use of the word *Ort* (place, site). Derrida is, in fact, making his audience aware that he is touching on a philosopheme as complex as *Geschlecht*.[6] Heidegger begins by saying that the word *Erörterung* (discussion) has to be considered in terms of the original meaning of *Ort* as the situating of a site whereby thought orients itself and is oriented. Of immediate concern is investigation of the nature of the site of the poetic work.

> We use the word "discuss" here to mean, first, to point out the proper place or site of something, to situate it, and second, to heed that place or site. The placing and the heeding are both preliminaries of discussion (*Erörtern meint hier zunächst: in den Ort weisen. Es heißt dann: den Ort beachten. Beides, das Weisen in den Ort und das Beachten des Ortes, sind die vorbereitenden Schritte einer Erörterung*).[7]

For English readers, it is problematic that the word "discussion" completely obscures the fact that the word *Ort* is embedded in *Erörterung*.[8] As Heidegger stresses, the site is not just some place or location, but a place in which *everything is concentrated and comes together*. "Originally the word 'site' means the tip of a spear where everything comes together. The site gathers unto itself, supremely and in the extreme (*Ursprünglich bedeutet der Name 'Ort' die Spitze des Speers. In ihr läuft alles zusammen. Der Ort versammelt zu sich ins Höchste und Äußerste*)."[9] Derrida maintains that access to "*cette langue primitive*" occurs by means of a jump or leap, because the origin is itself a leap ("*car l'origine est un saut [Sprung]*)." Heidegger himself will say that one cannot approach the poetic site in the absence of a leap that is also a blow ("*un coup*," in Derrida's text) that is "brought by means of a sudden leap to the site of the statement (*durch einen Blicksprung an den Ort des Gedichtes zu bringen*)."[10]

In citing this passage, Derrida is tacitly alluding to the *Schlag* mentioned in the previous lecture, which will become clear later on. Initially Derrida explains that it is by means of leaping that literary criticism proceeds in Heidegger in terms of what one may consider arbitrary jumps in the middle of a poem or verse of a poem. In fact, the blow, leap, or jump comprises the rhythm of a reading, no matter how slow or sinuous. Such rhythm will be recontextualized shortly in terms of Heidegger's subsequent remarks on waving or oscillation. At this point, however, this will also concern the themes, motifs, and significations that Heidegger will treat by means of "a blow (*Schlag*, jump, and leap [*Sprung*])," or in Derrida's original: "*un coup* (Schlag, *du bond, et du saut* [Sprung])". Whereas in "Geschlecht II" Derrida was thinking of the *Schlag* in terms of a violence associated with sexual intercourse and the consequent production of stock or race, here *Schlag* pertains to a practice of Heideggerian reading which *pounces* on the text in order to assemble it, as if some form of originary violence were required in order to make sense by bringing elements into relation through convergence: jumping from one verse (or poem) to another. Later, Derrida will discuss this in terms of Heidegger's metonymical understanding of Trakl's poetry.

Of special interest to Derrida, given the earlier discussion in *Fantom* of Heidegger's hand, is Heidegger's connection of *Ort* (site) with the tip of a spear or sword, a weapon carried in the hand, that is made in order to carry out violence by means of stabbing, dismemberment, beating, and so forth. *Schlag* and *Schlagen* are the consequence of the sword and the spear that one generally associates with combat and war. For Fichte, who was discussed earlier in the course, there would be no question that the site certain people of the same stock inhabit is secured with the spear and the sword. However, for Heidegger the value of the sword and the spear, and of the *Ort* or area that is their point, is not that of division but of *Versammlung* (*de rassemblement*): gathering, concentrating, drawing together. This gathering together converges on what Derrida calls an indivisible point, not that, as he puts it, this could be thought of in geometrical terms. Hence "Il y a *du rassemblement (Versammlung)*," a gathering which gives place to place as indivisible unicity and singularity. Derrida, of course, has borrowed the "*il y a*" in his translation of Heidegger from the "Letter on Humanism" where Heidegger speaks (in French) of the "*il y a l'Être*," the "there is/it gives Being (*Es gibt Sein*).[11] In the "Letter" Heidegger says that "the self-giving into the open, along with the open region itself, is Being itself."[12] Rather than saying "Being is," Heidegger wants to stress the performativity of Being as a giving or coming to be (in terms of *An-wesen*, presencing). Key is Parmenides's phrase, *esti gar einai*, "for *there is* Being." Derrida links this discussion in the "Letter", by means of allusion to Heidegger's writings on Heraclitus in which Being is considered in terms of gathering or, to be more precise in terms of Heidegger's vocabulary, ap-propriation of which *Er-eignis* (en-owning, converging) is yet another synonym. This speaks to the tip of the spear as an appropriative site where "everything meets up."

As Heidegger puts it, the site gathers and appropriates unto itself what is most elevated and *extreme (Äusserste)*, which, as Derrida explains, is the most exterior, the limit of what is most outside, the end of the sword. This pointed, elevated place is, in fact, what Derrida calls the limit between the exterior and the interior; it is the tip or summit of the thing (the sword), which penetrates and swipes, though in this case not as a weapon that vanquishes enemies, though certainly it can't lose that sense, but to the contrary as a point that determines a gathering, an assembling (say, of community) that preserves and assures the protection of all that isn't without relation. Analogously one might think, for example, of knighting someone by resting the end of the sword on the shoulder, hence affirming a social bond or connection, the social as propriation.

In the context of Trakl's poetry, "the truth of the sword" is said to be the place that assures meaning its origin and orientation as "*la pointe extrême*." The poem, then, is to be considered an extreme point of extension that metaphorically corresponds to the point of a spear or sword protecting what gathers, collects, or comes together. The idea that a place has the attributes of a weapon is arguably a strange catachresis that traverses the difference between splitting and gathering, or, if one prefers, dividing and unifying. But this is hardly odd for Derrida who is implicitly arguing that the *place* of the poem in Heidegger is, in fact, characterized by *la différance*, an effraction characterized by deferral, differing, differentiating, etc.

Typical of the lecture courses are moments when Derrida will take a detour by way of making a free association. In what opens up a sidebar, Derrida says, with respect to the tip of the spear, "I think naturally of Lacan."[13] Does the extreme point of the spear or sword symbolize a phallic signifier insofar as the sign (*Zeichen*) shows what must be in place in order to support a signifying chain, namely a topology within which signifiers are gathered (Lacan's "treasury of signifiers")? Rather than contrast Lacan and Heidegger, Derrida says he will dwell on the point of an indivisibility, of the indivisible gathering of place as a point, as indivisible simplicity of the place or indivisibility of the letter, of which the definition in Lacan is that of "the place of the signifier," as pointed out in Lacan's "Seminar on the Purloined Letter" in *Écrits*. As Derrida puts it, "the letter is for Lacan the place of the signifier."[14] This letter, Derrida says, does not support partition and division.

In Derrida's "Le Facteur de la vérité" on Lacan's reading of Poe—the text to which Derrida is alluding here—we're told that "the signifier, in its letter, as a sealed text and as a locality, remains and falls in the end."[15] Moreover, "the notions of indivisibility (protection from partition) and of locality are themselves indissociable; they condition each other."[16] According to Lacan, "the real carries its place glued to its heel, ignorant of what might exile it from it."[17] Place is therefore glued to the heel of the signifier as a material sign whose reality, whatever upheaval we subject it to, is always situated in terms of a fundamental site. "Lacan leads us back to a truth, to a truth which itself cannot be lost. He brings back the letter, shows that the letter brings itself back toward its *proper* place via a *proper* itinerary, and, as he overtly notes, it is this destination that interests him, destiny as destination."[18] Derrida is suspicious of the determinability of this destination, a suspicion he shares with Heidegger, whose notion of *Ort* as inceptually self-differentiated and withdrawn does not share Lacan's sense of security about place as determinable destination. Relative to *Geschlecht*, Derrida will also question Lacan's notion of the phallus in terms of its secure place in Lacan's theory wherein "transcendental reappropriation" insures its status.

In returning to "Die Sprache im Gedicht," Derrida considers Heidegger's distinction between *Gedicht* and *Dichtung*, a topic that Derrida will come back to more than once in later lectures. Heidegger says that "our task is to discuss the site that gathers Georg Trakl's poetic Saying into his poetic work—to situate the site of Trakl's work." Derrida notes that for Heidegger "every great poet creates his poetry out of one single poetic statement only," which suggests from one single place.[19] Derrida comments that (1) the unique (*einzige*) marks a conception of place as an indivisible singularity, "*l'idiome absolu*"; (2) the notion of a great poet in Heidegger is one who devotes himself to what is special or unique with respect to *Gedicht*: the unity of the place of *Gedicht* which is secured by "*son dire poétique [dichtendes Sagen]*"[20]—his poetic utterance; and (3) the notion that *Gedicht* cannot be translated because of its unicity and uniqueness as something absolutely idiomatic to the person that cannot be adequately pronounced in words and therefore cannot be reduced or rendered in terms of what the poet has written. "*Le Gedicht est non-dit, imparlé, improoncé [ungesprochen]*."[21] That is, the poetic is unspoken, not said, not pronounced. Hence Heidegger's remark: "the poet's statement remains unspoken. None of his individual poems, nor their totality, says it all. Nonetheless, every poem speaks from the whole of the one single statement (*Gedicht*), and in each instance says that statement (*Gedicht*)."[22] One therefore has to listen to the "*non-dit de Gedicht*" (the not spoken, unsaid, of the poetry) which speaks ("*qui parle*") throughout all the poems. Here Derrida is closely following Heidegger's text sentence by sentence, lightly emphasizing points that are of concern, particularly with respect to *Fantom*'s major theme, the place of idiom in philosophical nationalism.

What does it mean, Derrida wonders, that immediately after speaking of the single *Gedicht* Heidegger avers that "from the site of the statement there rises the wave (*Dem Ort des Gedichtes entquillt die Woge*) that in each instance moves [the poet's] Saying as poetic saying. But that wave, far from leaving the site behind, in its rise causes all the movement of Saying to flow back to its ever more hidden source (*verhüllteren Ursprung*)."[23] The wave ("*l'onde ou de la vague*"), according to Derrida, isn't a metaphor, but the character of a relation between *Gedicht* and *Dichtung*, the not-said and poetic utterance, whose place is to be considered originary, an *Ursprung* that can be associated with a spring or source (*Quelle*). "This is more and something other than a metaphor," Derrida says, because it speaks to poetic rhythms, regular undulating movements within the source of the poem, unique to this place, which are themselves unspoken and unpronounced.[24] As Heidegger puts it, "The site of the poetic statement, source of the movement-giving wave, holds within it the hidden nature of what, from a metaphysical-aesthetic point of view, may at first appear to be rhythm (*Rhythmus*)."[25] In other words, rhythm is but an outer manifestation of a movement within the origin or source of *Gedicht* that is withdrawn and concealed. Derrida comments that otherwise put, if one wants to think rhythm beyond the study of prosody, one would have to consider the singular relation between a place of the un-said—of *Gedicht* as unpronounced— and the poem which emerges from and returns to it. This coming and going of the wave is the rhythm, a circular coming and going or hermeneutic circle, as Derrida puts it, out of which one might think about escaping.

As it happens, Heidegger will circulate or course among Trakl's poems, given that each is considered an elucidation of the other in the sense of commentary, explication, clarification. As Heidegger puts it, "Clarification (*Erläuterung*) is what brings to its first appearance that purity which shimmers in everything said poetically."[26] Derrida stresses the extent to which this speaks to manifestation: "first appearance [*paraître premier*," but also "*phénomène premier*," and "*première brilliance*]."[27] This is what is shown in the utterance of the poem, though this clarification or elucidation presupposes *Erörterung* (situating, situation). One must have access to an indivisible and unique place, to a pure idiom, in order to begin elucidating, and explicating texts, since it is from the source of the place and the place of the source that the wave proceeds. Inversely, however, and here Derrida asks us to be mindful of the circle/circularity, the situation or *Erörterung* of the site that is unspoken has need of a preliminary access made possible by moving through an explication or elucidation of the poems, whereas inversely elucidation of the poems requires access to the site or source of the *Gedicht*.

Heidegger stipulates, "The individual poems derive their light and sound only from the poetic site. Conversely, the discussion of the poetic statement must first pass through the precursory clarification of individual poems."[28] Derrida notes that Heidegger doesn't call this a circle but rather a *Wechselbezug*, a relation of reciprocal exchange between *Erörterung* (discussion) and *Erläuterung* (clarification). This exchange or "conversion" is that of a conversation or dialogue (*Zwiesprache*) within which thinking comes to pass. For Derrida, dialogue or *Zwiesprache* concerns the difference of saying and not saying, what is uttered (*Dichtung*) and what remains silent (*Gedicht*), though it also concerns *Denken und Dichten*, thinking and poetizing: the thinker (Heidegger) and the poet (Trakl). This emphasis upon difference per se is only implicit in Heidegger, whereas for Derrida it is part of a circle of reciprocity between the different and the same, the two and the one, which make up an interplay that broaches the deconstructive logic of neither one nor two, both one and two. Here the determinacy of a circularity that simultaneously affirms and negates distinctions and categories is at issue. If it is true that all thinking dialogue with a poet's poetic statement (*Gedicht*) stays within this reciprocity between discussion and clarification, what is it that determines or fuels this reciprocity? Of course, this relates to the dialogue between thinking and poetry as well, a dialogue or conversation that is circular and brought about by something in the origin or source of the *Gedicht* that determines and requires reciprocity, something that in Heidegger refers to rhythm and an oscillation (as in the case of waves). In *Beiträge zur Philosophie (Vom Ereignis)*, Heidegger speaks of a *Wesung des Seins*, which Parvis Emad and Kenneth Maly have translated as the swaying of Being, something that Heidegger may well have had on his mind when he spoke of there being a wave or oscillation whose rhythm relates to not only *Gedicht* but *Dichtung*. Is dialogue itself akin to the swaying of Being? Is it what essences being? This is a question we are in a better position to ask, given the appearance of Heidegger's posthumous writings unavailable to Derrida in 1984–85.

Toward De-cease

Having explored the introductory pages of "Die Sprache im Gedicht," Derrida moves on to discuss Heidegger's reference to *Abgeschiedenheit*, a word with a considerable number of meanings: departure, isolation, solitude, separation, death, decease. *Abgeschiedenheit* defines the situation of the stranger who is wandering— "*L'étranger en migration*." Jean Beaufret and Wolfgang Brockmeier introduce neologisms whereby to translate Heidegger: *dis-cès* for *Abgeschiedenheit* and *dis-cédé* for *Abgeschiedene*, to which Derrida adds *vers le décès* (toward death). Dominique Janicaud in *Heidegger in France* comments that whereas Heidegger hyphenated an ordinary German word that is readily understandable (*Ab-geschiedenheit*) in order to emphasize withdrawal or retreat, in the French translation familiarity or intelligibility is lacking, although this seems intentional insofar as the French wording speaks to a more inceptual or originary separation than death.[29]

David Krell too has weighed in on the French terminology.

> Derrida hears in the word *Abgeschiedenheit* its double tonality. A recluse or solitary knows the meaning and the importance of living apart. And the defunct, the deceased, the dead, if they know anything at all, know what it means to be departed. The French translation says *Dis-cès* playing upon *décédé*, deceased,

but retaining the *dis-* of separation and the critical capacity as in dis-cernment, the perspicacity of the recluse. The coinage—itself the result of a *Schlag* of *Geschlecht*—attempts to retain the being under way of departure and to indicate a dying that is fateful but not fatal. [To Derrida] in a second note I suggested that this might be related to the theme of the unborn, *des Ungeborenen*, a theme that haunts Trakl throughout his poetry.[30]

Whereas Janicaud stresses the question of withdrawal more or less in the context of Heidegger's posthumous writings of the late 1930s, Krell stresses personhood: for example, the recluse. Krell, drawing from Trakl, casts *Abgeschiedenheit* in the role of the unborn (social subjects to be) as opposed to, say, the not-born.[31]

Derrida, for his part, stresses originary separation in terms of the notion of the strange or *fremd*, which Heidegger translates *idiomatically* (as Derrida notes) by way of the Old High German *Fram* as "forward to somewhere else, underway toward … onward to the encounter with what is kept in store." Heidegger himself personifies the strange as stranger. "The strange goes forth, ahead. But it does not roam aimlessly, without any kind of determination. The strange element goes in its search toward the site where it may stay in its wandering. Almost unknown to itself, the 'strange' is already following the call that calls it on the way into its own."[32] For Heidegger, this strange element relates to Trakl's verse, "Something strange is the soul on the earth." As Heidegger says further,

> The soul is called to go under [*Die Seele ist in den Untergang gerufen.*] Then it is so after all: the soul is to end its earthly journey and leave the earth behind! Nothing of the sort is said in the verses [above]. And yet they speak to "going under." Certainly. But the going under of which these verses speak is neither a catastrophe nor is it a mere withering away in decay [*Wegschwinden in den Verfall*]. Whatever goes under, going down the blue river "Goes down in peace and silence" ["Transfigured Autumn," l. 30]. Into what peace does it go? The peace of the dead [*des Toten*]? But of which dead? And into what silence?[33]

To read Heidegger as if he were commenting on what is denoted in Trakl's lines would be to misunderstand a meditation that seeks to comprehend the arche-traces of the text's language that makes up its *Gedicht* in terms of proto-significations. Above, Heidegger is talking about a decline or return to an inceptual condition of Being that is neither dead nor alive, a movement *vers le décès*.

That Heidegger would define the strange or *Fremd* in terms of the Old High German *Fram* imitates the *Schritt zurück*, or step back, which is already a movement toward what inceptually precedes the saying of the verse. For Derrida idiom in terms of a word such as *Fram* is itself made up of proto-significations, a manifestation of *Gedicht* relative to what is concretely spoken, which is what

Derrida means much earlier in *Fantom* when he speaks of "the idiom of idiom." Indeed, an argument could be made that the whole of Heidegger's encounter with Trakl's writings is pulled back into the idiomatic insofar as this is constitutive of the archaic site out of which *Dichtung* emerges.

The Animal, the Strange, and Man

Unexplored in both Heidegger and Derrida are specific verses in Trakl concerning the relation between animal and man. Are they too *"ein Geschlecht"* or strangers? Heidegger has only general thoughts on Trakl regarding an indeterminacy between the animal, the strange, and man. Citing Nietzsche, Heidegger explains that man is not yet an entirely fixed type of being. As Derrida notices, this contradicts *What Is Called Thinking?* when Heidegger speaks of the human hand versus that of the ape's. In his essay on Trakl, however, Heidegger writes,

> Who is this blue wild game to whom the poet calls out that it recall the stranger? Is it an animal? No doubt. Is it just an animal? No. For it is called on to recall, to think. Its face is to look out for ..., and to look on the stranger. The blue game is an animal whose animality presumably does not consist in its animal nature, but in that thoughtfully recalling look for which the poet calls. The animality [*Tierheit*] is still far away, and barely to be seen. The animality of the animal here intended thus vacillates in the indefinite [*Unbestimmten*]. It has not yet been gathered up into its essential being. This animal—the thinking animal, *animal rationale*, man—is, as Nietzsche said, not yet determined [*noch nicht fest gestellt*].[34]

As Heidegger puts it, Nietzsche is saying that "this animal's animality has not yet been gathered up onto firm ground, that is to say, has not been gathered 'home,' into its own, the home of its veiled being ... This animal not yet determined in its nature is modern man."[35] Derrida comments that the vocabulary of home (*Heimat, Heim*) aren't images or just metaphors, but a *"catastrophe de la métaphore"* insofar as, in Heidegger's words, "Western European metaphysics has been struggling to achieve [such gathering into home] ever since Plato. It may be struggling in vain. It may be that its way into the 'underway' is still blocked (*der Weg in das 'Unterwegs' noch verlegt*)."[36] Poetically, Trakl speaks of this in terms of the blue wild game who are metaphorically the mortals who sojourn in the foreign and who wish to return to the *"chez soi"* which is close to our essence as humans. In the eleventh lecture Derrida will return questions of home and their relevance to political nationalism, which in the 1950s Heidegger is expanding to embrace Europe and the West.

In terms of the figure of the stranger-wanderer who departs, one can see overtones of earlier discussions in *Fantom* concerning exile and return—in the cases of Arendt and Adorno—though perhaps more uppermost at issue at this point of the course is the question of human *Geschlecht* in terms of genus, which in the context of the book *Khōra* (drawn in part from the lecture course of 1985–86) will be the separation into distinct kinds or essents that are not indeterminate.[37] Throughout the eighth lecture of *Fantom*, we are continually confronted with the conviction that differences cannot be maintained and are to be swallowed up into the kind of unfixity that leaves entities vacillating and indeterminate, so much so, that even the animal/man distinction breaks down. Hence the poet, Derrida says, encompasses the non-bestiality of the animal's experience in terms of a certain strangeness, one that will be associated with "*déperdition* (loss, wastage) *et de décomposition*," which stresses identity over difference.[38]

In a key statement, Heidegger explains that

> the name "blue game" [*blaues Wild*] names mortals who would think of the stranger and wander with him to the native home of human being [*das Einheimische des Menschenwesens erwandern möchten*]. Who are they that begin such a journey? Presumably they are few, and unknown, since what is of the essence comes to pass in quiet, and suddenly, and rarely …. The blue game [*das Blaue Wild*], where and when it is in being, has left the previous form of man's nature behind. Previous man decays in that he loses his being [*sein Wesen verliert*], which is to say, decays [*verwest*].[39]

In Trakl's "Seven-Song of Death" ("*Siebengesang des Todes*"), Heidegger cites the verse "*O des Menschen verweste Gestalt* (O man's decomposed form)." Of importance, Derrida says, is how the words *Wesen* (existing) and *Verwesen* (decomposing) oscillate in the essay. *Verwesen* denotes the decomposition of a corpse, but Derrida adds that in Heidegger's ontological idiom it means dis-essencing. "This is why the 'something strange' that is being called is also referred to as 'something dead' (*Darum heißt das so gerufene Fremde auch 'ein Totes'*)."[40] Death in this case means that only a certain form of man has decayed. Is this just a matter of *Gestalt*? In Heidegger's text, we are to read everything inceptually, which amounts to an idiomaticity that overtakes and revises customary denotations by means of a certain proto-signification. Also we shouldn't lose sight of the fact that Peter Hertz's English translation obscures Heidegger's emphasis upon the "*ein*" or *one* that circumscribes the strange and death (ein *Fremdes;* ein *Todes*), just as later it will circumscribe *Geschlecht* (*Ein Geschlecht*). This stress upon the *Ein* in all three of these cases is not picked up by Derrida.

Taking up once more the theme of exile, Derrida notes that the decomposition of man's form is itself exilic. Not just the form but man as kind is expelled, unsituated, unhoused. This leads Derrida to consider Heidegger as follows. Heidegger, in explicating the decayed form of man (*der verwesten Gestalt des* Menschen), writes that the "decomposed form" (*der verwesten Gestalt*) is what the poet calls a decomposing kind. "It is the generation (*Geschlecht*) that has been removed from its kind of essential being (*aus der Art seines Wesens herausgesetzt*), and this is why it is the 'unsettled' kind (*darum das 'entsetzte' Geschlecht*)."[41] Speaking of *Geschlecht*, Heidegger says,

> In our language a human cast, cast in one mold and cast away into this cast, is called a kin, of a kind, a generation. The word refers to mankind as a whole as well as to kinship in the sense of race, tribe, family—all of these in turn cast in the duality of the sexes. The cast of man's "decomposed form" is what the poet calls the "decomposing" kind. It is the generation that has been removed from its kind of essential being, and this is why it is the "unsettled" kind.[42]

Here, of course, the original German is crucial, given how much of it is obscured in translation.

> Unserer Sprache nennt das aus einem Schlag geprägte und in diesen Schlag verschlagene Menschenwesen das "Geschlecht." Das Wort bedeutet sowohl das Menschengeschlecht im Sinne der Menschheit, als auch die Geschlechter im Sinne der Stämme, Sippen und Familien, dies alles wiederum geprägt in das Zwiefache der Geschlechter. Das Geschlecht der "verwesten Gestalt" des Menschen nennt der Dichter das "verwesende" Geschlecht. Es ist aus der Art seines Wesens herausgesetzt und darum das "entsetzte" Geschlecht.[43]

When Heidegger intones "our language," he is, of course, stressing what the German language delivers or gives, thanks to its ancestral German speakers, in terms of a people's idiomatic specificity and untranslatability, to say nothing of idiomaticity as affect. The paronomasia of "*diesen Schlag verschlagene*"—the casting away of the cast, as the English translator would render it—linguistically displays a violence, obscured in the translation, in which *Schlag* means hitting or striking of what is into sorts or kinds, a violence that is thrown away once the kind or genus is struck into a proper form.

By way of comparison, Derrida's later lectures on *Khōra* in 1985–86 are very relevant in that they too are about the production of forms out of what is formless.

> Socrates is not *khōra*, but he would look a lot like it/her if it/she were someone or something. In any case, he puts himself in its/her place, which is not just a place

among others, but perhaps *place* itself, the irreplaceable place. Irreplaceable and unplaceable place from which he receives the word(s) of those before whom he effaces himself but who receive them from him, for it is he who makes them talk like this.[44]

Here Derrida is speaking in allegorical terms. As if he were the *khōra*, Socrates converts inchoate thoughts and words, which he receives from others, into the formally distinct entities that he enables these others to articulate. That Socrates as *khōra* has no proper place, however irreplaceable, introduces the exilic sense of a place as a no-place essential for the production of forms by means of casting words a certain way, of striking out at statements in order to shape them up into logical propositions. Taken most generally, it should be apparent that the particulars aside, Derrida is inherently fascinated by not just genus but genesis as a philosophical problematic, one that does not presuppose a god-like agency dividing chaos up into distinct things that are arranged within a preconceived world. Of course, both Heidegger's account of *Geschlecht* and Plato's account of *khōra* represent alternative accounts of Genesis. Incidentally, that Derrida has long been fascinated with the topic of genesis goes back to his master's thesis, *The Problem of Genesis in Husserl's Philosophy*, in which he noticed a certain oscillation: "the genesis of sense is always a priori converted into a sense of genesis" and vice versa.[45]

"Curse (*Fluch*) Means *plege* in Ancient Greek, Our Word *Schlag*"

In his reading of Trakl, Heidegger states that the "decomposing kind" (*verwesende Geschlechtes*) is the consequence of a curse that has struck humankind. Whereas in "Geschlecht II" none of this is worked out, in the eighth lecture Derrida will take a detailed interest in this curse because it relates so strongly to an inceptual violence of the social relation that "strikes humankind." Indeed, the implication is that to be human means to have been struck by this violence that creates discord. Heidegger:

> What curse has struck this humankind? Here curse [*Fluch*] means *plege* in ancient Greek, our word *Schlag*. The curse of the decomposing kind [*verwesenden Geschlechtes*] is that the old human kinship [*dieses alte Geschlecht*] has been struck apart [*auseinandergeschlagen*] by discord [*Zwietracht*] among sexes, tribes, and races [*der Geschlechter*]. Each strives to escape from that discord [*Zwietracht*] into the unleashed turmoil [*losgelassenen Aufruhr*] of the always

isolated [*vereinzelten*] and sheer wildness of the wild game [*bloßen Wildheit des Wildes*]. Not duality [*Zweifache*] as such, the discord is the curse [*die Zwietracht ist der Fluch*]. Out of the turmoil of blind wildness it carries each kind [*Geschlecht*] into an irreconcilable split [*Entzweiung*], and so casts it [*verschlägt es*] into unbridled isolation [*losgelassene Vereinzelung*]. The "fragmented kind" [*verfallene Geschlecht*] so cleft in two [*entzweit und zerschlagen*], can on its own no longer find its proper cast [*rechten Schlag*]. Its proper cast [*Schlag*] is only with that kind [*Geschlecht*] whose duality [*Zwiefaches*] leaves discord behind [*Zwietracht weg*] and leads the way, as "something strange" [*ein Fremdes*] into the gentleness [*Sanftmut*] of simple twofoldness [*einfältigen Zwiefalt*] following in the stranger's footsteps.[46]

Given how crucial the German diction is throughout (the English almost totally obscures the wordplay), I have provided translations within the English passage; though for the sake of preserving the syntax, the German text also needs to be cited in full.

Womit ist dieses Geschlecht geschlagen, d.h. verflucht? Fluch heißt griechisch *plege*, unser Wort "Schlag." Der Fluch des verwesenden Geschlechtes besteht darin, daß dieses alte Geschlecht in die Zwietracht der Geschlechter auseinandergeschlagen ist. Aus ihr trachtet jedes der Geschlechter in den losgelassenen Aufruhr der je vereinzelten und bloßen Wildheit des Wildes. Nicht das Zwiefache als solches, sondern die Zwietracht ist der Fluch. Sie trägt aus dem Aufruhr der blinden Wildheit das Geschlecht in die Entzweiung und verschlägt es so in die losgelassene Vereinzelung. Also entzweit und zerschlagen vermag das "verfallene Geschlecht" von sich aus nicht mehr in den rechten Schlag zu finden. Den rechten Schlag aber hat es nur mit jenem Geschlecht, dessen Zwiefaches aus der Zwietracht weg in die Sanftmut einer einfältigen Zwiefalt vorauswandert, d.h. ein "Fremdes" ist und dabei dem Fremdling folgt.[47]

Metaphorically speaking, the passage is linguistically radioactive in terms of how the words are interacting, as in the case of *Zwiefaches*, *Zwietracht*, and *Zwiefalt* (duality, discord, twofold); *Schlag* and *Geschlecht* change places and reiterate one another, as in *Geschlecht geschlagene*, amplified by the words *ausgeschlagen* (beaten out of, violently separated from) and *zerschlagen*. Essentially, the passage performs deconstruction in the context of what in Heideggerian terminology is called dis-appropriation: a fusion within fragmentation and fragmentation within fusion, identity within difference and difference within identity, the coalescence into kinds as splitting and splitting as the coalescence into kinds. The German language does not simply describe such a philosophical dynamic, but enacts it, which, of course, Derrida seizes upon, given that denotation gives way to manifestation: that is, to phenomenolization, which threatens concrete, ostensive reference, hence Derrida's remark in "Geschlecht II" about whether *Geschlecht* can even be considered a word anymore.

To recapitulate, in the passage above Heidegger is referring to Trakl's reference to kinds being struck by *two blows*, the first "*un bon Schlag*," as Derrida says, and the second "*un mauvais coup*" (the first a good stroke and the second a bad blow).

> There are then two blows, two strikes, two imprints. The first blow comes knocking in order to leave its imprint (its mark) or rather by way of the imprint to constitute a "first" *Geschlecht*. However, the second blow appears to be bad. It is an evil, the evil.[48]

This speaks to an ethical differentiation of difference into two kinds of difference, the one good, the other evil. Are these two kinds of difference different? Are they kinds? The first blow or *Schlag* is right, "*un coup juste*," whereby sexual difference is established, whereas the second creates dissension between the sexes, "*de mauvaise différence sexuelle, de guerre sexuelle*," that is, of a bad sexual difference, a battle of the sexes.[49] Here the difference between *Zwiefache* (duality) and *Zwietracht* (discord) comes into play with the implication that being separated into kinds cannot be kept apart from the kinds being at war with one another, a view that, as Derrida must have known quite well, would apply to not just sex but race. "Out of the turmoil of blind wildness it (the *Schlag*) carries each kind (*Geschlecht*) into an irreconcilable split (*Entzweiung*), and so casts it (*verschlägt es*) into unbridled isolation (*losgelassene Vereinzelung*)."[50] Derrida translates *Vereinzelung* as individuation, singularization. *Losgelassene* is translated as *déchainer* (to unleash, rage, set off, trigger). This unleashing is to be imagined as a frenzied cutting off of all connections, of all contracts or of all associations. "*C'est la dissémination*," Derrida writes in between the lines, as he does a bit later when "singularization in separation" is again identified with dissemination, which in the essay "Dissemination" was associated with triggering, releasing, unhooking, unchaining, and so on.[51]

Apparently, for Derrida the curse of the second blow is to be associated with the breaking of the social relation in favor of a singularization that is synonymous with dissemination or, as Derrida also puts it, "*démariage*," which is a French agricultural term for what English gardeners would call "thinning out," the removal of certain plants in order that others may grow.[52] "*C'est un opération démographique*" which consists of limiting dissemination, of limiting births. *Le démariage* is also the marriage, that is to say, the normalization of births for avoiding an anarchic proliferation and for obtaining the best possible population. This is a calculation that one can also translate into a national context of eugenics.

Not surprisingly, mention is made of the turmoil (*Aufruhr*) and "blind wildness" that can be viewed as an originary violence that makes beings into the kinds that they are but that also isolates them. "Out of the turmoil of blind wildness it carries each kind (*Geschlecht*) into an irreconcilable split (*Entzweiung*), and so casts it (*verschlägt es*) into unbridled isolation (*losgelassene Vereinzelung*)."[53] What is fragmented thus cannot retrieve what was once its proper cast or strike. "The 'fragmented kind' (*verfallene Geschlecht*) so cleft in two (*entzweit und zerschlagen*), can on its own no longer find its proper cast (*rechten Schlag*)."[54] As Derrida puts it, the fragmented or split up kind (*verfallene Geschlecht*) is no longer the same, cannot any longer recover itself in terms of the initial good, proper, and just blow (*in den rechten Schlag*), given that duality, dissension, and twofoldedness are de-differentiated in their differentiatedness. And yet by means of an emigration, Trakl can imagine how duality leaves discord behind "and leads the way, as 'something strange' (*ein Fremdes*) into the gentleness (*Sanftmut*) of simple twofoldness (*einfältigen Zwiefalt*) following in the stranger's footsteps."[55] Derrida calls this twofoldedness the simplicity of a duplicity, the one fold of the double fold ("*un pli' du 'double pli'*") or the not fold of the fold ("*le sans pli du pli*").[56] Reference to the fold speaks to the undecidability of what is (ironically?) being called a simple duality wherein difference follows the Heideggerian logic of dis-appropriation (*Er/Ent-eignis*). Indeed, Derrida's mention of a fold without fold indirectly references Heidegger's problematic of ontological difference that in *Nietzsche II* is said to separate and connect and not simply on the basis of an act of differentiation. In fact, the differentiation of Being and beings is to be considered an ungrounded ground (outside of any strict sort of formalism or structure) that negates simple duality by calling into question the act of differentiation as decisive blow or *Schlag*.

In the late 1930s, of course, Heidegger began theorizing ontological differentiatedness in terms of *Ereignis*, which is to be understood as a primordial or inceptual process of appropriation cognate with *Wesung* (essencing). In a late but key text that Derrida knew, *Zur Sache des Denkens*, Heidegger states that "appropriation (*Ereignis*) withdraws what is most fully its own from boundless unconcealment. Thought in terms of Appropriating, this means: in that sense it expropriates itself of itself. Expropriation (*Enteignis*) belongs to Appropriation (*Ereignis*) as such. By this expropriation, Appropriation does not abandon itself—rather, it preserves what is its own (*bewahrt sein Eigentum*)."[57] In terms of duality and dissension, which relates to the two blows in Trakl, the two are appropriated into one even as something is being expropriated such that the one is expropriated of itself. That *Enteignis* belongs to *Ereignis* means that they are not different even if they are not the same, either. To put this a bit more concretely, when Heidegger and Derrida reference the stranger or wanderer in Trakl as the naming of the strange (and the stranger), what they are referencing is *Enteignis*, the dis-appropriation within appropriation that is essential to appropriation. This is what Derrida associates with the departed and the deceased.

States of Being-Apart

Fantom's ninth lecture takes up part two of Heidegger's "Die Sprache im Gedicht" and cautions from the outset that "fatally" Derrida will be more selective, and even more brutal, perhaps, in putting Heidegger's text "in perspective" so that he can begin to ask some questions germane to *Fantom*. Central to Heidegger's thinking in part two is that the place or *Ort* of the poem is the wanderer's withdrawal, departure, or decease. Heidegger asks: "Is it possible to bring apartness [*Abgeschiedenheit* (leave taking, departure, decease)] itself before our mind's eye, to contemplate it as the poem's site (*Ort des Gedichtes*)?" Recall from the eighth lecture that the *Ort des Gedichtes* relates to the tip of a sword, which in the ninth lecture now relates to apartness in terms of cutting, dividing, ripping things apart. As noted earlier, the connection of the tip of the sword with *Ort* suggests that both are linked in terms of a violence that could be considered inceptual and "gathered." For Derrida, metonymy is the linguistic expression of such a gathering that is assembled within words such as *Schlag* and *Geschlecht*: beating, pounding, cutting, hacking, casting (molding, throwing), banging (sexually), and so on.

In the gathering together of metonymies we see an overall effect that concerns splitting: the violent setting apart of things. Heidegger's reference to *Abgeschiedenheit* is the overarching philosopheme for apartness whose violence in Trakl is usually not that of the tip of a sword but that of a calm withdrawal, leave taking, decomposition, decease, and setting apart. In *Beiträge* (*Contributions*) Heidegger had explored such apartness in terms of what he called reservedness. "[*Die Verhaltenheit*] ... *ist der Stil des anfänglichen Denkens* ([Reservedness, holding or standing back, keeping apart] ... is the style of inceptual thinking)." Moreover, "reservedness (*Verhaltenheit*) attunes (*stimmt*) each grounding moment (*grundenden Augenblick*) of a sheltering (*Bergung*) of truth in the future Dasein of man (*des Menschen*)."[58]

Indeed, Heidegger's Trakl reading can be seen to substitute *Abgeschiedenheit* for *Verhaltenheit*. This is quite apparent when in *Beiträge* one reads statements such as "reservedness [considered] as origin of stillness and as law of the gathering" or "reservedness [considered] as openness for the reticent nearness of the essential swaying of be-ing (*Wesung des Seyns*), tuning to the remotest enquivering (*Erzittern*) of hints (*Winke*) that enown from the distance of what is undecidable (*Ferne des Unentschiedbaren*)."[59] The English translation here is that by Emad and Maly and is usefully accompanied by the more recently translated version by Rojcewicz and Vallega-Neu: "Restraint [considered] as openness for the reticent nearness of the essential occurrence of being, disposing toward the most remote trembling of appropriative intimations out of the remoteness of the undecidable."[60] "Restraint" in Rojcewicz and Vallega-Neu's rendering accentuates a sense of an actant's will to hold back, whereas Emad and Maly's selection of "reservedness" suggests a certain amount of passivity. In fact, *Abgeschiedenheit* in the essay on Trakl reflects both the active and the passive modalities of *Verhaltenheit*. But notice too Heidegger's mention of undecidability, which refers to the withdrawal of difference/identity within the remoteness of the inceptual.

Although Derrida didn't have access to *Beiträge* at the time he gave *Fantom*, he certainly was very aware of Heidegger's well-known rhetoric of *Verhaltenheit*, which speaks to idiomaticity insofar as Heidegger's invocation of German idioms often puts a significant restraint on presupposing that the modern usual denotation of a word is what Heidegger has in mind. In that sense, many of the words Heidegger invokes take their leave of modern or commonplace German. We will see the extent to which Derrida is very aware of this linguistic departure when he begins to acknowledge how Heidegger's use of the word *Wahnsinn* steps back from modern, commonplace, everyday German usage.

In the ninth lecture, Derrida is attentive to Heidegger's remark at the beginning of part two of "Die Sprache im Gedicht": "If we now follow the stranger's path (*Pfad*) with clearer eyes (*helleren Auges*), [we] ask: Who is the departed one (*der Abgeschiedene*)? What is the landscape of his paths?"[61] Heidegger himself stresses that "departed also means deceased," the point Derrida and the French translators cannot underscore enough, because they read this in terms of a fold without fold. To be departed is to be dead and not dead. To be dead is to be dead and departed (not dead). "The dead one *lives* in his grave," Heidegger remarks.[62] Apparently the grave is a site where the difference between life and death no longer holds.

Heidegger cites Trakl's line, "In his grave the white magician plays with his snakes,"[63] and comments that because these snakes (in the poem "Psalm") have not been strangled, their malice has been transformed. Derrida wonders if this figure of the magician belongs to a metonymical chain of such references not only within the poem but within Trakl's corpus. In "Psalm," for example, Derrida wonders if the magician is metonymically related to the madman and the stranger who are also said to have died. Are they appropriated or gathered into the Same as metonymies? Are they one kind or genus? Or are they different figures? In *Nietzsche II*, Heidegger writes that in terms of difference, entities are set apart, separated, and yet connected to one another "indeed of themselves" and not just on the basis of an act or blow of differentiation. Heidegger claims that "differentiation as 'difference'" means that a settlement (*Austrag*) exists between what is differed, which in the context of the figures Derrida is addressing speaks to metonymy as *Austrag*, the condition upon which things are settled, posed, or situated in terms of their interrelations.[64] In other words, metonymy (a sort of "gathering") functions as a ground that serves as the condition for identifying the madman, the magician, the stranger, and so forth, who are neither the same nor different, both the same and different. If "*ce mort étranger blanc vivant magician est le Dément*," which is to say, if this living-dead white stranger magician is the madman, stress for Derrida falls on the German idiom, *Wahnsinnige* ("l'idiome intraduisible [untranslatable idiom])."

Heidegger himself writes "The dead one is the madman." But "does the word mean someone who is mentally ill?"[65] Heidegger argues that *Wahnsinn* (madness) "does not mean a mind filled with senseless delusions. The madman's mind senses—senses in fact as no one else does. Even so, he does not have the sense of others. He is of another mind. The departed one is a man apart, a madman, because he has taken his way in another direction."[66] To understand *Wahnsinn* correctly, Heidegger says one has to retreat and return to Old High German in which *wana* signifies *ohne* (without). Derrida in turn asks: "What does Heidegger mean to do with this 'without?'" The play on *sans/sens* (without/sense) in French is self-evident. Here the play of *sans/sens* intrigues Derrida because again there appears a fold without fold, given that *sans/sens* mirrors pairs such as *différence/différance* or *Seyn/Sein*. "'*Der Wahnsinnige sinnt* [*le dément songe* ...]', *il songe mais si der Wahnsinnige sinnt, c'est qu'il a le sens, le fou est dans le sens. Il n'est pas dépourvu de Sinn* ('The madman dreams': he dreams ... but if so, that is because he has sense, is within the sense. Not devoid of *Sinn* [sense] the madman '*sinnt*' [senses, dreams]."[67] Heidegger explains,

> The madman's mind senses—senses in fact as no one else does. Even so, he does not have the sense of the others. He is of another mind. "*Sinnan*" originally

means: to travel, to draw towards (to pursue) ... to set out on a direction [Derrida translates this as *voyager, tendre vers, prendre une direction*]: the Indo-Germanic root *sent* and *set* means way [*Weg*]. The departed one is a man apart, a madman, because he has taken his way in another direction. From that other direction, his madness may be called 'gentle' for his mind pursues a greater stillness.[68]

[Der Wahnsinnige sinnt, und er sinnt sogar wie keiner sonst. Aber er bleibt dabei ohne den Sinn der Anderen. Er ist anderen Sinnes. "*Sinnan*" bedeutet ursprünglich: reisen, streben nach ..., eine Richtung einschlagen; die indogermanische Wurzel *sent* und *set* bedeutet Weg. Der Abgeschiedene ist der Wahnsinnige, weil er anderswohin unterwegs ist. Von dorther darf sein Wahnsinn ein "sanfter' heißen; den er sinnt Stillerem nach.][69]

Heidegger's understanding of *Wahnsinnige* mirrors his thinking on *Verhaltenheit* insofar as one steps back from the notion of "madman" to something more fundamental and originary that concerns apartness, separation, and withdrawal into a state that is to be considered "otherwise" ("strange" [*fremd*]). Speaking of this withdrawn condition, Derrida says of *Sinne*, "*il est d'un autre sens*," a sense that separates itself ("*se sépare*") from others. The sense associated with the so-called madman is not that of others—i.e., of the common man—though this hardly means that such sense is senseless ("*privé de sens*").

It is at this point that Derrida notes again that Heidegger is drawing us back into German idioms that have long passed out of currency in German society, idioms that are untranslatable out of German but perhaps not entirely translatable into modern German, either. By means of withdrawing into idiomaticity and hence untranslatability, one retreats into a place apart in order to restrain a certain *sens* for the sake of releasing "other" meanings. In Husserlian terms, this is somewhat reminiscent of bracketing. One steps back from ordinary apprehensions by bracketing them (restraining or temporarily excluding them) for the sake of occupying a different place or place apart whereby a more primordial understanding of apperception may come about. Derrida thinks of the step back into idiom (the bracketing of standardized, commonplace language) as a mode of restitution, which is to say, as a means of restituting meaning.

Derrida says that we have to ask ourselves how the philological affinity of the German word *Sinn* (sense) with *Fram* (strange) concerns a restitution of meaning that orients the entire situation that Heidegger calls *Erörterung*. What are the consequences, Derrida wonders, taken from the fact that "*un mot signifiant*," alien or strange to us, doesn't actually signify in an entirely alien or strange way and has a meaning or sense that has to be figured out by means of the "*frontières d'une langue*."⁷⁰ Derrida notes that for Heidegger the situation entails a retreat to the place of origin where translation is always at work, say, "in the interior of German, by way of Germans of different ages, of different generations"⁷¹—hence the attention paid to Old High German, Middle High German, modern German, and so on. Here Derrida also notices a rhythm or oscillation between modern and older forms of German that is the fundamental condition of translation as philosophical need and activity.

Having made that point, Derrida turns to the meaning of *Sinnan* in Middle High German and cites Heidegger's reference to *Sinnan* as *reisen* (*voyager*, journeying), *streben nach* (*tendre vers*, stretching out to, drawing toward, hence *tendre la main*: to stretch out the hand, but also in terms of archery to draw back [*tendre vers*] the string of a bow). Heidegger also translates *Sinnan* as taking a direction (*eine Richtung einschlagen*). Derrida notes the phrase *Den falschen Weg einschlagen*, which means taking the wrong route by means of making a bad decision. Derrida accents the word *Schlag* within *einschlagen*, signifying the decisive *coup* for taking off in one direction over another.

Heidegger, as quoted above, specifies that the Indo-German roots *sent* and *set* signify way (*Weg*). Duden's *Herkunfts-wörterbuch* has an ample entry on *Sinn* and notes that although the Indo-Germanic *sent* does indeed mean way, *set* means "gehen, reisen, fahren" (going, travelling, driving), contrary to what Heidegger states. *Sentire* is the Latin forbearer, which means to feel, to apprehend. Related is the Latinate *sensus* (feeling, meaning, sense) and the Lithuanian *sintéti*, which means "thinking." In Old High German, *unsinnig* means mad, crazy, or raving. Thinking, deciding, traveling, going, drawing toward, feeling, sensing, apprehending, and sense/meaning form a constellation of meanings or senses that are gathered in the place of a Middle High German word, *Sinnan*, out of which they can spring forth and disseminate.

Summarizing, Derrida cites Heidegger's statement that the "departed one (*le dés-cédé*) is a madman (*le dément* [*Wahnsinnige*]), a man apart, because he has taken his way in another direction (*parce qu'il est en chemin vers ailleurs*)."⁷² Derrida adds that the madman is without the sense of others, which is why he has taken a different path. Certainly the madman could be viewed as a figure for a complex set of verbal relations held back in the philology of the German Middle Ages. As figure, this marker or *point de capiton*, as Lacan would have called it, is on the way toward an elsewhere, an *Ort* that is to be associated with *Einschlag*, the decision to deviate, to separate. The decision in this context is to be related to the sword as *Ort*. In fact, this mad person does not "vagabond" and is not errant, because this person decides upon a way and a destination. Such a person is what Heidegger called *Fram*.

Heidegger's Own *Wahnsinn*

Derrida makes a biographical turn when in considering the figure of the madman he opens "a long parenthesis," as he puts it, in which he wonders if Heidegger himself is not this person who has made a decision to depart from familiar ways, as if he were someone who appears mad to others, as someone who is to be considered strange. Derrida asks "What is Heidegger doing? What movement, what way, what craziness, what sense or other sense is he describing, of what and to whom is he speaking relative to the purported situation of Trakl's *Gedicht*?"[73] Heidegger reads Trakl in a way that literary critics, philologists, and philosophers would consider mad. He appears to be in error, jumping from one poem to another, one verse to the next without any reasonable cause or method. He says that Heidegger wanders alone as a stranger over the trace of the other. He is at once "*le mort et l'étranger*," the dead and the stranger, and it is he who plays in his own grave. Hence Heidegger is speaking of himself when he speaks of the other who is mad. "He [Heidegger] speaks of his own place in speaking of the place of the other, or rather he is in search of his place in following the steps of the other."[74]

If Heidegger's text can be considered an analysis, it is one decided by a *coup* or *Schlag* in terms of the direction and way it undertakes, something reflected in the title *Unterwegs zur Sprache*, the collection in which "Die Sprache im Gedicht" is to be found. No doubt, Heidegger has a destination in mind, which is not of the order of knowledge in any academic sense, but rather an orientation or way, a *Sinn* which pre-orients his excursion. No doubt, this excursion predetermines how Trakl is to be read, a method that the scholars repudiate, but this hardly matters, given that Heidegger sets himself apart, departs from the commonality of literary criticism and philosophy, given that he has chosen his own place, his own step, his own route, his own signature whereby conversation with Trakl is to take place. Derrida says that in his view there is nothing objectionable here in that this is the condition of any situation, presumably of reading. If Heidegger has chosen a route, it is that of idiomaticity which plays a determining role that is destinal.

Derrida assumes his auditors should know that "Die Sprache im Gedicht" is deceptive in that by the time we enter part two of this essay we are no longer encountering a discourse that is denotatively familiar but one that departs from our mimetic correlation of words with things in the world around us. *Wahnsinn* means something entirely different from madness even as it refers to madness denotatively in some ordinary sense. The retreat into the *Verhaltenheit* of a far more originary German language where distinctions are in the process of coming about reflects Heidegger's general aim, which is to enter reservedness linguistically as a mode of access to inceptual thinking (*anfänglichen Denkens*). To step back into reservedness means to enter a place or situation in which words and the things they refer to are not objectified to the point that one can sort them out in terms of presence/absence, identity/difference, gathering/dispersal. It is crucial to realize that this place of reservedness or retreat that Heidegger discusses in *Beiträge* is being poetically performed in "Die Sprache im Gedicht," dis-closed in the poetry of Trakl generally.

Heidegger enters a regional ontology (one of *Ortschaft*) of sorts whose contours, such as they are, reflect the conditions of what is most ontologically inceptual or, if one prefers, transcendental in the phenomenological sense of most archaic. Heidegger's audacious statement in *Beiträge* that beings can still "be" (exist) within an "abandonment of Being" (*Seinsverlassenheit*)[75] speaks to a withdrawing to an inceptual point where beings (entities) as we encounter them in daily life exist otherwise in a state or situation characterized by an abandonment or withdrawal of Being that in Trakl corresponds to *Abgeschiedenheit* and decease. There beings have a different nature (*Wesen*). Hence in that place the dead needn't be dead. In terms of what Husserl called the natural attitude, such a contradiction isn't tenable, but in the place of withdrawal and apartness it is as if a very different set of ontological laws are in operation. Indeed, the analysis of language in Trakl is intended to reveal these laws or relations situated in an inceptual or originary region.

The idea that inceptual ap-propriation leads to a *Kehre im Ereignis* (turning in the event, ap-propriative turn) is performed by Trakl's poetry in terms of an inceptual ontological history "grounded in Da-sein" that is "the hidden history of deep stillness." Heidegger comments: "In this stillness alone there can still *be* a people."[76] "Die Sprache im Gedicht" is, in fact, about a turning whereby out of the hidden history of a deep stillness, Europe is reborn. It is the story of how there can still be an Occidental people and how that cosmopolitan vision is, as in Fichte, brought about by the leadership (*Führung*) of someone embodying a German spirit, in this case, Georg Trakl. This, of course, links the Trakl lectures to the earlier part of *Fantom*.

The Re-turn

Rebirth for Heidegger requires return, a step back into the inceptual where difference and identity are not clearly distinguishable even as they are not merely collapsed either. In that context, we ought to recall what Derrida said about the word *Geschlecht* in "Geschlecht II" concerning it not being a word. What he did not say explicitly is that for Heidegger in terms of inceptual thinking, words aren't words quite. Indeed, the basis for that conviction can be found in *Beiträge*. "The word fails, not as occasional event ... but originarily. The word does not even come to word, even though it is precisely when the word escapes one that the word begins to take its first leap."[77] The leap is that into ap-propiation, the *Schlag* into kinds. The word casts. That is, the word in distinguishing kinds by means of categorization (separation, division) contributes to the disclosure of the essent—beings as the beings that we objectify and in that sense produce for ourselves. This utilitarian employment of words in order to produce things as particular kinds is akin to that second blow Heidegger associates with *Geschlecht* whereby kinds are thrown into dissension on account of their differentiatedness, which raises issues of value: what kind is better or worse, what kind is to be privileged, eradicated, and so on.

It is this blow or *coup* of the word that Heidegger is retreating from when he speaks of a withdrawing into the inceptual where the word escapes utilitarian categorization and manipulation. "The word's escaping (*die Verschlagung*) is the inceptual condition for the self-unfolding possibility of an originary-poetic-naming of *Seyn* (Being's originary moments)."[78] If we think of *Geschlecht* in its inceptual context as a failure to categorize and establish differences by means of not quite "coming to word," which is what *Verschlagung* suggests, we enter a place of undecidability that Heidegger associates with reservedness (*Verhaltenheit*) as openness, reticence, and stillness that appropriates undecidability unto itself as an event of standing back and apart. This is the disavowal on Heidegger's part of the second *Schlag* that produces dissension.

With respect to the inceptual, Derrida references discussion by Heidegger on the figure of Elis who personifies the one who retreats into "earliness" where the difference between presence/absence, life/death, is de-differentiated. "Elis is the dead whose being moves away into earliness. This stranger unfolds human nature forward into the beginning of what is yet to be borne."[79] The "situation" or "place" of Elis is entirely contradictory and paradoxical in terms of Husserl's natural attitude—that is to say, the world as we commonly perceive it. However, in the inceptual region, one goes back in order to go forward, one dies in order to live, one is born as unborn, and so forth. Terms such as the dead, the unborn, the departed, and the stranger are, as Derrida puts it, metonymically substitutive, though in a way that compromises our ability to identify them or separate them, given the undecidability that permeates the signifying chain. "Elis would name a place older and more peaceful than the old (or prior idea of) *Geschlecht* (an older or previous kind or sex) that has received the bad blow, the second blow of malediction that has created the twoness of dissension, sexual difference as dissension."[80] Here, without having had access to *Beiträge*, it is evident once more that Derrida is cognizant of the rhetoric of *Verhaltenheit* in Heidegger and the extent to which the essay on Trakl by Heidegger is an allegorization of this *Verhaltenheit*, a translation of it into lyric poetry.

Of special interest to Derrida is that in Elis's retreat into the inceptual place (Derrida calls it the *archi-origine*), sexual difference drops away. Derrida notes that Elis goes toward a sexuality older than a sexuality torn or divided by sexual difference that is agonistic. The boy doesn't reside in opposition (*in einem Gegensatz*) with the being of the girl (*zum Mädchenhaften*). Rather the boy is the appearance of a much more still childhood, that which is strange. Elis is not just the appearance of a profound childhood but a being that is inceptual even to the point of being unborn. This relates to the inceptual stillness mentioned in *Beiträge* where difference in our everyday utilitarian and conflictual sense is repealed, which is to say, this speaks to a childhood ontologically ancestral to childhood as we have experienced it. In this childhood, male and female are not opposed. Heidegger writes: "The boyishness in the figure of the boy Elis does not consist in the opposite of girlishness. His boyishness is the appearance of his stiller childhood. That childhood shelters and stores within it the gentle twofold of sex, the youth and the 'golden figure of the maiden.'"[81] Derrida glosses this in terms of "die sanfte Zwiefalt der Geschlechter" (the gentle duality of the sexes) "le tendre dédoublement, la tendre ou douce dualité des sexes, donc une différence sexuelle, un deux qui ne s'est pas encore déterminé et déchaîné dans l'opposition."[82] Sexual difference is the soft or tender duality/doubling of the sexes, a twoness that is not yet determined and unloosed in opposition. This state occurs, as well, in relation to Elis's decease that constitutes a withdrawal or retreat into an inceptual state of being unborn. Here the relation between death and the state of being unborn is a strange sort of doubling in which the opposition of life/death—if not the temporality of the beginning and end of life—is neither loosened nor determined.[83]

According to Heidegger, "The stranger who has died away into earliness is the unborn one. The terms 'something unborn' and 'something strange' say the same." In the poem "Bright Spring" ("*Heiterer Frühling*") there is this line in the penultimate stanza, "And the unborn tends to its own repose," which in Heidegger's view means that the unborn "guards and watches over the stiller childhood for the coming awakening of mankindThus at rest, the early dead lives."⁸⁴ In fact, "the departed looks forward into the blue of the ghostly night."⁸⁵ The departed (*Abgeschiedenheit*), reservedness (*Verhaltenheit*), and the unborn (*das Ungeborene*) are metonymically related as synonyms for an unnameable state of inception that is aware of an awakening to come.⁸⁶

In "Die Sprache im Gedicht," it is *Geschlecht* per se that is to come, of which Derrida writes:

> This gathering of the young dead man or of the ungenerated prepares the resurrection to come of the *Geschlecht*. As the spirit of gentleness he appeases the spirit of evil, that is, of the malfeasance that reaches its zenith in the dissention [*Zwietracht*] of the sexes which now explodes, intervening even in the relation of siblings [*Geschwisterliche*], the relation between brother and sister. Sexual dissension, sexual difference as discord, as agonistic duality, is that which disturbs a serene sexual difference, that which would take place between brother and sister prior to the curse and prior to evil, the wicked flame of spirit. This *Geschwisterliche*, this relation between brother and sister, is thus not asexual, but is a sexual relation within a difference that is without dissension.⁸⁷

Derrida is addressing how Heidegger situates the reservedness or *Verhaltenheit* of the young man, Elis, in terms of a stillness or spirit of gentleness that appeases a spirit of flame that one associates with the kind of sexual passion that is characterized oftentimes by dissension or violence. Perhaps one is supposed to think a jealous or possessive spirit, one whose motivation is evil. It is in the state of reservedness associated with *dis-cès* or *Abgeschiedenheit* that Elis is the gatherer who gathers or collects (*reprend*). According to Heidegger, "the blue night, the stranger's nighting paths, the soul's nocturnal wing-beat (*Flügelschlag*) ... are gathered up into apartness, not afterward but such that apartness unfolds within their already established gathering."⁸⁸ As stranger who is apartness, Elis collects and gathers, not so much as an agency but as apartness or reservedness per se in that "apartness itself is the spirit and thus the gathering power. That power carries mortal nature back to its stiller childhood, and shelters that childhood as the kind, not yet borne to term (*nicht ausgetragenen Schlag*), whose stamp marks future generations (*der das künftige Geschlecht prägt*)."⁸⁹

Grandsons yet Unborn

The kind that is not yet borne to term (*der nicht ausgetragenen Schlag*) concerns *Verhaltenheit* wherein, in this case, future generations are marked or cast in advance by an arche-*Schlag*, an inceptual *Schlag* not yet come to term. *Ein ausgetragenes Kind* is an unborn child, and Derrida associates the unborn state to *l'archi-origine*, though he also relates it to *Tragen*, carrying as production. The word *Austrag* that in Heidegger's vocabulary refers to the carrying out of difference is discussed by Derrida as follows: "The figure or the process of carrying to term (as one says of an infant), the figure of being-carried as dif-ference, this is the *Austrag*, which comes to be a synonym for difference in the Heideggerian text."[90]

Carrying to term is yet another manifestation of genesis: the genesis of *Geschlecht* or, if one prefers, *Geschlecht* as genesis: the coming to be of kinds, sexes, peoples, generations. We normally think of generations as continuous, as one generation has to beget the next; however, in Trakl there is a withholding or retention that introduces a gap in which grandfathers have grandsons without grandfathering them. Heidegger notes this in Trakl's last poem "Grodek" when mention is made of "grandsons yet unborn." We are told that these grandsons "are not the unbegotten sons of the sons killed in battle [World War I], the progeny of the decaying generation." Heidegger comments that "the unborn are called grandsons because they cannot be sons, that is, they cannot be the immediate descendants of the generation that has gone to ruin. Another generation lives between these two. It is other, for it is of another kind in keeping with its different essential origin (*anderen Wesensherkunft*) in the earliness of what is still unborn."[91]

Does this mean that there is an ungenerated generation? Derrida writes with respect to a cited verse by Trakl ("And the ungenerated keeps to its proper repose") that "the ungenerated keep watch over and protect (*wahrt*) the more serene childhood for the coming awakening of the *Menschengeschlecht* (of the human species—or of the sex to come)."[92] Heidegger speaks of such a generation as a skipped generation. Derrida: "the ungenerated, the unengendered, are descendents because they cannot be born of sons, cannot be offshoots or direct descendents, immediate descendents of the 'fallen *Geschlecht*,' of the deposed species or sex."[93] Heidegger himself writes: "Between them and this species or sex (*Geschlecht*) there lives another generation [*Generation*, not *Geschlecht*]. It is other because it is of another order, in accord with its essentially other provenance from the dawn of the unengendered."[94]

What is this "another order" of which Heidegger speaks? And how can it be thought within the course of the generations if it is discontinuous with it, if, indeed, it is withdrawn (*Verhalten*)? The answer is that we ought to be thinking of the unborn in terms of spirit and the ghostly. The other order is, in Derrida's terms, the *fantom of the other* that is to be thought of in terms of spirit, which Heidegger identifies with apartness (*Abgeschiedenheit*). "In the way in which it flames, apartness itself is the spirit and thus the gathering power." It is this spirit that "marks future generations," and that "shelters ... the kind ... as not yet born to term." [95]

Geistig/Geistlich

Derrida's discussion of spirit in relation to "Die Sprache im Gedicht" is developed at length in *Of Spirit* where Derrida unpacks Heidegger's references to *Geist* and its various verbal derivations. *Of Spirit* reworks materials from *Fantom* and in so doing comes across as a sort of fantom limb. Readers of both texts will quickly realize that *Geist* and *Geschlecht* interrelate as idiomatic philosophemes. Both terms, for example, are monstrously polysemic, and both concern inceptual violence. *Geist*, we are told, is "divided by an internal difference,"[96] one that is characterized by avoidance on Heidegger's part, which is central to Derrida's concerns. As it happens, in *Being and Time* Heidegger initially avoids the word *Geist* explicitly, though in what Derrida calls a "second move" spirit is put within quotation marks. Hence "the word 'spirit' returns, it is no longer rejected, avoided, but used in its deconstructed sense to designate something other which resembles it, and of which it is, as it were, the metaphysical ghost, the spirit of another spirit. Between the quotation marks, through the grid they impose, one sees a double of spirit announcing itself."[97] In *Fantom*, this double of spirit is considered the fantom of something other. Of considerable significance in the Heideggerian context is how a disappropriation of spirit requires its return or reappropriation, something that speaks to "all the doublings of spirit."[98] These doublings, bear in mind, are connected with the redoubling of avoidance. For example, in the 1930s, Heidegger avoided the adjective *geistlich*, on account of its presumptive metaphysical meaning (holy, spiritual); yet, Heidegger embraces its alternative, *geistig*, as a marker for a notion of spirit that stands apart from onto-theology. However, in 1953, in "Die Sprache im Gedicht," Heidegger reverses himself and in repeating the gesture of avoidance decides to avoid the word *geistig* and privilege *geistlich* in its stead, again with the proviso that this rejects a metaphysical-Christian understanding of spirit.

> With what can look like a flagrant lack of consistency, [Heidegger] behaves as though he had not been celebrating the *Geistigkeit* of *Geist* for twenty years. This word [*geistig*], in the name of which, and from what a height, he had denounced all the forms of 'destitution of spirit,' he now inscribes in the massive and crudely typecast form of the metaphysico-Platonic tradition, the tradition responsible for or symptomatic of this *Verwesen* of *Geschlecht*: the corruption of the human race in its sexual difference.[99]

The tendency to avoid and reappropriate, to reject and return, is constitutive of Heidegger's manner of performing his discourses on spirit, each ghosting the other.

In "Die Sprache im Gedicht," Heidegger locates a certain dissension between the words *geistig* and *geistlich* in Trakl and states that "apartness is spiritual (*geistlich*), determined by the spirit (*Geist*), and ghostly, but it is not 'of the spirit (*geistig*)' in the sense of the language of metaphysics (*Die Abgeschiedenheit ist geistlich, vom Geist bestimmt, aber gleichwohl nicht 'geistig' im metaphysischen Sinne*)."[100] Peter Hertz's English translation renders *geistlich* not only as "spiritual" but as "ghostly." Derrida does not mention the ghostly possibility in *Fantom*, citing one of Heidegger's references to Trakl's poetry: "*So geistlich ergrünen/Die Eichen ...*" ("Thus the oaks turn spiritually green").[101] Derrida offers the French translation, "*Si spirituel verdoient/Les chênes*," and, in reading Heidegger closely, comments that Heidegger thinks of *geistlich* as "*l'originarité 'de ce qui depuis si longtemps est mort,' originarité (Frühe) promise par 'den Frühling der Seele.'*"[102] Which is to say, "the earliness of what for so long has been dead, an earliness promised by 'Springtime of the Soul.'" As Heidegger himself wrote: "*Er denkt an die Frühe des lang Verstorbenen, die den 'Frühling der Seele' verspricht* (He is thinking of that earliness of the long since dead which promises the 'springtime of the soul'")[103] However, this avoids reading *geistlich* in Trakl as hauntingly or ghostly, as in "Thus the oaks hauntingly turn green/Above the dead's forgotten paths." Nevertheless, Derrida does obliquely notice the *avoidance* of a fantasmatic interpretation of *Geist* when he remarks in *Geschlecht III*, "*Geist* has a value that Heidegger doesn't implement in the whole of this *Erörterung*, which is that of the fantom, of the revenant, which, however, would seem to impose and motivate the entire context."[104] Why this avoidance or disappropriation?

In finally asking, quite directly, "What, then, is the spirit (*der Geist*)?" Heidegger responds that in "Grodek" Trakl speaks of the spirit as a flame,[105] one that Heidegger underscores is both gentle and destructive, something that has its doubling in terms of the two blows of *Geschlecht*.

> Spirit or ghost understood in this way has its being in the possibility of *both* gentleness *and* destructiveness. Gentleness in no way dampens the ecstasy of the inflammatory, but holds it gathered in the peace of friendship. Destructiveness comes from unbridled license, which consumes itself in its own revolt and thus is active evil. Evil is always the evil of a ghostly spirit.
>
> [*Der so verstandene Geist west in der Möglichkeit des Sanften und des Zerstörerischen. Das Sanfte schlägt jenes Außer-sich des Entflammenden keineswegs nieder, sondern hält es in der Ruhe des Freundlichen versammelt.*

Das Zerstörerische kommt aus dem Zügellosen, das sich im eigenen Aufruhr verzehrt und so das Bösartige betreibt. Das Böse ist stets das Böse eines Geistes.]¹⁰⁶

The word "*schlägt*" is translated as "dampens" by Hertz, given that beating-down or suppressing wouldn't be gentle.

From Derrida's perspective, an inceptual double strike, the first of which is good (gentle, reserved) and the second of which is evil (destructive, pugilistic), puts *Geschlecht* into relation with *Geist* since they both require an inceptual violence that belongs to a second malign stroke without which neither can achieve a peaceful radiance of inceptuality, which is to say, of the matutinal in Trakl: a time of morning that will illumine what to Heidegger is a place of spiritual renewal. This speaks to Heidegger's master narrative, which is that of the departed journeying into the inceptual in order to return to a place, the Occident, that is now a stranger to corruption, given that it is now spiritual and its *Geschlecht* undegenerated (hence, gentle and gathered as unity, E I N). In short, the first inceptual blow supersedes the second malign stroke. Nevertheless, for Derrida there is no denying that an inceptual violence functions as the differend whereby the difference of good and evil inheres in both *Geist* and *Geschlecht*. Not incidentally, this dynamic of difference also inheres in the division between breath (*pneuma*) and fire relative to spirit.¹⁰⁷

Europe

"Die Sprache im Gedicht" is no doubt troubling insofar as it recalls fascist thinking about the spirit of Europe, something Derrida writes about in *The Other Heading (L'autre cap)*. Besides Heidegger's essay on Trakl, a major intertext for Derrida in *The Other Heading* is Heidegger's "Hölderlin's Earth and Heaven," given that it references Paul Valéry's "The Crisis of the Spirit," another tutor text for Derrida. Heidegger comments: "Perhaps Europe has already become what it is: a mere cape, yet as such, also the brain [Derrida would call it the 'head'] of the entire terrestrial body, the brain that manages the technological-industrial, planetary-interstellar calculation." Also, Heidegger is asking, "Does the occidental still exist?"¹⁰⁸ Derrida, who is thinking along these lines, writes:

> We are younger than ever [*plus jeunes que jamais*], we Europeans, since a certain Europe does not yet exist. Has it ever existed? And yet we are like these young people who get up, at dawn, already old and tired. We are already exhausted [*épuisés*]. This *axiom of finitude* is a swarm [*un essaim*] or storm of questions

[*assaut de questions*]. From what state of exhaustion must these young old-europeans who we are set out again, re-embark [*re-partir*]? Must they re-begin [*re-commencer*]? Or must they *depart* from Europe, separate themselves from an old Europe [note the Heideggerian parallel with *Abgeschiedenheit*]? Or else depart again, set out toward a Europe that does not yet exist? Or else re-embark [*repartir*] in order to return [*revenir*] to a Europe of origins [note the parallels with Heideggerian *Heimkehr* and an inceptual *Ort*] that would then need to be restored, rediscovered, or reconstituted [*restaurer, retrouver, reconstituer*], during a great celebration of 'reunion' [*au cours d'une grande fête de 'retrouvailles'*]?

Reunion [*retrouvailles*] is today an official word. It belongs to the code of French cultural politics in Europe. Ministerial speeches and documents make great use of it.[109]

Not too many pages further on, Derrida explicitly references Heidegger's "Die Sprache im Gedicht" with respect to *Ort*.

The idea of an advanced point [*pointe avancée*] of *exemplarity* is the *idea* of the European *idea* [*l'idée de l'idée* (this alludes to the "idiom of idiom" in *Fantom*)], its *eidos*, at once as *arché* —the idea of beginning but also of commanding (the *cap* as the head, the place of capitalizing memory and of decision, once again, the captain)—and as *telos*, the idea of the end, of a limit that accomplishes ... The advanced point is at once beginning and end, it is divided [*elle se divise*] as beginning and end; it is the place from which or in view of which everything takes place [*tout a lieu*]. (When Heidegger defines place, *Ort*, he recalls that in its High or Old German idiom, *Ort* refers to the point of a spear [*pointe de la lance*], there where all the forces are joined and gathered in the end; and when he says that questioning is the piety of thinking, he recalls that *fromm, Frömmigkeit*, comes from *promos*: what comes first, leads, or directs the front line [*l'avant-garde*] in a battle).[110]

These passages from *The Other Heading* reprise elements of the Trakl lectures in *Fantom*, particularly, mention of the spear or tip, and Derrida's discussion of a deconstructed circularity (a strange sort of deconstructive Eurocentrism) in the final lectures involving the ever divisible or effractive unification of beginning and end, old and young, departure and return (*re-partir, re-venir*), dis-union (dissension) and re-union (gathering) associated with exile and homecoming. At issue in *Fantom* is largely the promise of return that is given as an inceptual trait of leave taking. In going, coming back is inherently given as a promise, as an "other heading" that is always already in advance or ahead.

Drawing upon *Fantom*'s eighth lecture, Derrida speaks of Heidegger's spear, as the place as *cap* or cape, of what comes first, and of what leads us ahead. This lance is the place of a spiritual convergence or gathering of forces that in the context of modern European thinkers, Paul Valéry among them, speaks to "an advanced point, the point of a phallus if you will, and thus, once again, with a heading for world civilization or human culture in general."[111] Of course, Derrida's mention of the phallus directs us to the subject of *Geschlecht* that in this passage is latently active, given that it relates to progeny—to a people who are gathered on the advanced promontory that is Europe. That this point or cape is at once beginning and end is implicit in Heidegger for whom the stranger's apartness leads to a journey whereby beginning and end are and aren't resolved into one another.

Derrida, with *Fantom* probably in mind, takes over and develops Heidegger's more or less enigmatic remarks on the Occident in "Die Sprache im Gedicht."

> It is always in the figure of the Western heading [*du cap* occidental] and of the final headland or point [*la pointe* finale] that Europe determines and cultivates itself; it is in this figure that Europe identifies itself, identifies with itself [*s'identifie, elle-même, à elle-même*], and thus identifies its own cultural identity, in the being-for-itself [*l'être pour soi*] of what is most proper to it, in its own difference as difference with itself, close to itself [*dans sa propre différence, comme différence avec soi, différence à soi qui reste avec elle-même, auprès d'elle même*]: Yes, difference with itself [*avec soi*], with the self [*avec le soi*] that is maintained and gathered in its own difference, in its difference from with [*d'avec*] the others, if one can say this, as difference to itself, different from itself for itself [*différente de soi pour soi*], in the temptation, risk, or chance or keeping at home (with itself [*chez soi*]) the turbulence of the *with*, of calming it down [*l'apaiser*] in order to make it into a simple, interior border—well guarded by the vigilant sentinels of being.[112]

Europe as *la pointe* (whose feminine form denotes headland, tip, point) is the Heideggerian tip (or *Ort*) where identity is gathered in terms of difference. Europe's being for itself, in other words, is always already disunified in its unification, its cultural identity predicated upon taking off in pursuit of some other heading. If Europe is maintained in terms of an identity, what is most proper to that identity is gathered in terms of a "difference to itself"—i.e., a departure from itself. To return to Europe is to leave it. This speaks to a prepositional logic of the from/with. Europe as *chez soi* involves awareness of the *with* as a difference in proximity—with as *from*. In *The Other Heading*, Derrida is concerned with identity and difference in terms of a circularity in which is being performed a *dis-unification* in the sense of Heideggerian *dis-appropriation* (*Ent-eignis*). Constitutive of such *dis-unification* is the eternal return of *la différence* wherein the same as different and the different as the same are repetitiously entangled as undecidably archaic and futural.

In returning to the nationalism-cosmopolitanism divide discussed in *Fantom*, Derrida writes,

> [Europe] cannot and must not be dispersed into a myriad of provinces, into a multiplicity of self-enclosed idioms or petty little nationalisms, each one jealous and untranslatable. It cannot and must not renounce places of great circulation or heavy traffic, the great avenues or thoroughfares of translation and communication, and thus, of mediatization. But, *on the other hand*, it cannot and must not accept the capital of a centralizing authority that, by means of trans-European cultural mechanisms … would control and standardize, subjecting artistic discourse and practices to a grid of intelligibility, to philosophical or aesthetic norms, to channels of immediate and efficient communication, to the pursuit of ratings and commercial profitability."[113]

Derrida concludes, "Neither monopoly nor dispersion, therefore."[114] The Europe Derrida is contemplating is as yet to come in the deconstruction and overcoming of this choice.

In line with Heidegger, Derrida speaks of "the duty to respond to the call of European memory, to recall what has been promised under the name Europe, to re-identify Europe—this duty is without common measure." In recollecting Europe, there is the revenance of a promise, inceptual in Heidegger's case, of a Europe still to come, a place gathered and gathering that is open to an other heading (an other *Denkweg*). In "Die Sprache im Gedicht" this concerns the inceptual renewal of Europe in terms of an alternate thinking of Being detached from traditional metaphysics that the Romans degraded for the sake of their utilitarianism as a world power. For Derrida, this Europe to come will manifest an opening to the other, "it has begun to open itself, or rather to let itself open, or, better yet, to be affected with opening without opening *itself* onto an other, onto an other that the heading can no longer even relate to itself as *its* other, *the other with itself.*"[115] Certainly this can be read through the prism of political correctness (liberalism); however, it is Heidegger who posits *the promise of Europe* in terms of the figure of "the stranger," a figure of otherness taken from Trakl, a poet keen on depicting the Other, whether human or animal. "Soon fish and deer slip away./Blue soul, dark wandering."[116]

The Second Stroke

Derrida's tenth lecture expands upon the two strokes of *Geschlecht*, the first gathered and gentle, the second fractious and violent. The second stroke, apparently, is always a degradation of the first; therefore, (1) *Dichtung* is corrupted in relation to *Gedicht*, (2) the Christian-Platonic tradition is corrupted in relation to an inceptual understanding of Being, (3) dissemination is a corruption of polysemy, and (4) the sister in Trakl as uncanny, lunar, spectral, and unhoused is to be considered secondary in relation to the primacy of the brother who is spiritual, though whether this is to be seen as a corruption or not is in question. Of course, Derrida is quite aware that an incipient Platonism may be at work given that the second moment can be taken as a sort of bad copy or iteration in which the inceptual undergoes a certain manifestation. Hence *Dichtung* can be taken as the reified expression of *Gedicht*, whose violence is to be associated with the typing of *écriture*, just as dissemination can be taken as the violent repetition and manifest expression of polysemy, or the Platonic-Christian tradition can be seen as the reified iteration of what preceded it, inceptual Being. As in the case of the spiritual and the ghostly, the second stroke could be considered malign and a curse. Questionable is whether this extends to the twofold relation of the older brother to the younger sister, of Georg Trakl to his sister Margarethe. She is, after all, the lunar voice, the disembodied spirit.

Of course, Derrida's inquiry into the relation of the second stroke to the first can be mapped onto the writing/voice distinction made famous in *Of Grammatology*, and as one might expect, in *Fantom* too, Derrida goes to work on observing the deconstruction of the division or difference between the primary and the secondary that is already at work in Heidegger's treatments of identity and difference, unicity (gathering) and fragmentation (dissemination), despite his resistances to such deconstruction, as in the case of walling off the Platonic-Christian tradition as a corrupt metaphysical bulwark impervious to deconstructive possibilities. In *Fantom*, Derrida largely accepts Heidegger's later philosophy, in particular, as a species of deconstruction, albeit quite different from Derrida's own work, in that Heidegger held onto certain personal metaphysical resistances to his own overcoming of the metaphysical tradition, something Derrida explores and criticizes when he discusses the dichotomies above that form his itinerary in this tenth lecture. Recall that Derrida had stated on more than one occasion that there is never just one sort of deconstruction. "It is finally, I believe, a rather heterogeneous movement."[117] Again, "deconstructionism isn't monolithic."[118]

In turning to *Gedicht* and *Dichtung*, which analogize but also complicate the two strokes, Derrida recalls that *Gedicht* and *Dichtung* are related in terms of the unspoken being the originary site of the poem's source wherein gathering occurs—the place from which both *Gedicht* and *Dichtung* proceed. The silence of the one always already belongs to what unfolds in the second. And yet the ground tone that Heidegger imagines in the *Ein* of *Ein Geschlecht* is fundamental to *Gedicht*, not *Dichtungen*. One might say that the fundamental note isn't pronounced, but quashed. That can mean two things: that it is silent in the sense where silence belongs already to speech (*la parole*) or that, interpreted otherwise, unpronounced, inarticulate as articulated speech, it is sung in the manner of a song that, as Derrida puts it, does not return or is not reduced to articulated language (*l'articulation de la langue*). The ordinary logical opposition of what is articulated versus what is silent doesn't hold, because at the inception where a fold of *Gedicht/Dichtung* comes to pass, there is and isn't either identity or difference, a conclusion that is trivial in the absence of its being worked out along many different paths, of which the Trakl essay by Heidegger is but one. If in Heidegger's reading of Trakl the *Ein* of *Ein Geschlecht* (unicity, identity) is not pronounced and is assigned to *Gedicht*, Derrida counters by saying "I don't say it's unpronounceable" though its unpronounceability is nothing other than what the poems say.[119] That poetry is a speaking otherwise or a speaking of what cannot be spoken is hardly a novel idea; however, one needs to recognize the extent to which Heidegger radicalizes this feature of poetry.

Apropos of *Fantom*'s overarching theme of idiomaticity, Derrida poses the Heideggerian relation of an unpronounced singularity with a determinate idiom, something that Derrida considers in terms of Heidegger's reference to Old or High German where idiomaticity and the unsayable (or unpronounceable) come into contact. Derrida formulates the paradoxical adage that "His silence is German, he speaks German."[120] Returning to the theme of cosmopolitanism, Derrida wonders, if Heidegger's silence is German, whether he can ever hope to speak as an Occidental or European thinker. How can he speak from an other place than just Germany if his relation to language is marked by silence? Another way of putting this would be to ask if adopting the inceptual place of *Gedicht* is viable for philosophy. How can Heidegger assume a position as European thinker from which he can address a trans-national tradition of Platonic metaphysics or Christian theology if he does not embrace a privileged notion of place where pronouncements have been made that historically have been an important part in the spread of German philosophy beyond Germany's borders? Derrida says he hesitates to call this the assumption of a national place, though this privilege and place from which one speaks concerns what is being determined by a nation's place in the world apart from its own nationalist self-depictions. We are led to wonder: does Heidegger retreat from such a national podium when he maintains that the unpronounced is inceptual to poetry and thought and that its silence is carried along by forgotten German idioms of the Middle Ages that hold something back from being expressed? Or is Heidegger imagining that such a national place is more authentic, more Occidental when one speaks in a way that "*Son silence est allemande, il parle allemande* (His silence is German, he speaks German)?"[121] Derrida is keen on noticing that in this context *Gedicht*, *Dichten*, and *Denken* are closely related, given that it is thinking that situates the poet in relation to the place of his *Gedicht*. *Dichten*, by contrast, is related by Heidegger to the Latinate "dictation," a dictating that occurs when one dictates to an instrument, say, a typewriter.

Of course, the relation of *Dichtung* to *Gedicht* is another instantiation of the writing/voice distinction to be identified with metaphysics, if not onto-theology *tout court*. Explicitly, Derrida doesn't point out the connections with *Of Grammatology*, though anyone familiar with his work will notice the tacit critique at work whereby Heidegger is risking an onto-theological reduction in which voice even in its retreat speaks the truth of being. Since *Of Grammatology* is such a key intertext, we ought to recall that in it Derrida considers Heidegger from two perspectives. On the one hand, Heidegger is said to equate *logos* with voice. "The 'formal essence' of the sign can only be determined in terms of presence," a self-presence, in fact, that is characterized by self-identity and unity. Just as writing is said by Derrida to disrupt the Medieval "natural totality" of the "encyclopedic protection" of "the book" as a logocentric unity, writing in Heidegger (the bad stroke, as it were) disrupts thought's relation to Being.[122] In the tenth lecture of *Fantom*, Derrida speaks of this disruption in terms he imported into "Geschlecht II," that of Heidegger's identification of a "mechanical perversion" of the typewriter whereby words are being destroyed (*Zerstörung des Wortes*). The passage in question (mentioned but not quoted in the seventh lecture) occurs in Heidegger's seminar *Parmenides*.

> It is not accidental that modern man writes "with" the typewriter and "dictates" [*diktiert*] (the same word as 'poetize' [*Dichten*]) "into" a machine. This "history" of the kinds of writing is one of the main reasons for the increasing destruction of the word. The latter no longer comes and goes by means of the writing hand, the properly acting hand, but by means of the mechanical forces it releases. The typewriter tears writing from the essential realm of the hand, i.e., the realm of the word. The word itself turns into something "typed."[123]

Here we see the reappearance of the violence of the *Schlag* or stroke as a hitting and imprinting. According to Heidegger, the typed word is a degradation (or degeneration, *Verwesung*) of writing "to a means of communication." The typewriter does physical violence to the word by beating it into a genus (*Geschlecht*?) of communication that lacks spirit. This sentiment is already reflected in Derrida's observation in *Of Grammatology* that for Heidegger "what writing itself, in its nonphonetic moment, betrays, is life." As if prefiguring *Of Spirit*, Derrida writes in *Of Grammatology*:

> It [writing] menaces at once the breath, the spirit, and history as the spirit's relationship with itself. It is their end, their finitude, their paralysis. Cutting breath short, sterilizing or immobilizing spiritual creation in the repetition of the letter, in the commentary or the *exegesis*, confined in a narrow space, reserved for a minority, it is the principle of death and of difference in the becoming of being.[124]

When Heidegger complains that the typed message conceals the character of the writer by substituting itself for the signature or handwriting that one would otherwise see, he is talking about the death of what Derrida calls *le propre* as what is essential in terms of self-possession. Heidegger writes: "The typewriter makes everyone look the same." But, of course, homogenizing is what the cosmopolitan podium or international conference does as well. In other words, in order to speak across borders, the metaphysics of the proper (voice) has to be compromised by a certain violence (writing) of typifying. This dynamic refers us to the beginning of *Fantom* in which Derrida was asking whether philosophy could ever be viable as a universal discourse transcending national boundaries, given the local restrictions and identitarian particularities of linguistic idiomaticity.

If *Of Grammatology* does not explicitly consider the fold between *Gedict* and *Dichtung*, it does strongly anticipate it when Derrida comments that

> after evoking the "voice of being," Heidegger recalls that it is silent, mute, insonorous, wordless, originarily *a-phonic* [*die Gewähr der lautlosen Stimme verborgener Quellen* …]. The voice of the sources is not heard. A rupture between the originary meaning of being and the word, between meaning and the voice, between "the voice of being" and the "phone," between "the call of being'" and articulated sound; such a rupture, which at once confirms a fundamental metaphor, and renders it suspect by accentuating its metaphoric discrepancy, translates the ambiguity of the Heideggerian situation with respect to the metaphysics of presence and logocentrism. It is at once contained within it and transgresses it. But it is impossible to separate the two. The very movement of transgression sometimes holds it back short of the limit.[125]

Derrida remarks that being for Heidegger is never simply a "signified" (a reified category agreed upon in advance) and therefore "escapes the movement of the sign."

The necessary, originary, and irreducible dissimulation of the meaning of being, its occultation within the very blossoming forth of presence, that retreat without which there would be no history of being which was completely *history* and history of *being*, Heidegger's insistence on noting that being is produced as history only through the logos, and is nothing outside of it, the difference between being and the entity—all this clearly indicates that fundamentally nothing escapes the movement of the signifier and that, in the last instance, the difference between signified and signifier *is nothing*.[126]

Written long before Heidegger's posthumous works appeared, in this passage above we can see that Derrida was quite aware of Heidegger's rhetoric of dissimulation, occultation, and withdrawal (e.g., that of the *retrait*) "directed … at and beyond onto-theology in order to reach the rigorous thought of that strange nondifference [between signifier/signified; *Gedicht/Dichtung* (?)] and in order to determine it correctly."[127]

Derrida notes "Über 'die Linie'" in which the well-known crossing out of Being is a "mark of deletion" under whose strokes or imprint (*Schlag*) "the presence of a transcendental signified is effaced while still remaining legible."[128] The crossing out, in this context, broaches a "strange nondifference." In *Fantom*, once more, the relation between *Gedicht* and *Dichtung* is a variant of this theme, given that *Gedicht* could be seen as the crossing out of *Dichtung*, its retraction, even while the latter remains legible and readable (the *retrait* as a retracing). *Gedicht* is the "unheard of sense" that Derrida mentions in *Of Grammatology* when he writes that the sense of being is "a determined signifying trace" of ontological difference (being and essent, ontic and ontological, "ontico-ontological") that Derrida says derive from difference "and with respect to what I shall later call *différance*, an economic concept designating the production of differing/deferring."[129]

In *Of Grammatology*, Derrida could not develop an understanding of the inceptual in Heidegger's thinking as worked out in what was then the unpublished *Beiträge* and related posthumous manuscripts of its period. Unavailable, of course, was *Besinnung (Mindfulness)* in which Heidegger asserts that works of art are not to be considered symbolic objects, essentially, "but the clearing of Being (*Seyn*) as such which holds the decision for man's other way of being." Again, "'Artwork' now is the gathering of purest solitude unto the abyss (*Abgrund*) of Being (*Seyn*)."[130] Withdrawn from the public and the private, the work "belongs solely to inabiding the 'going under,' which alone can become the foundationally proper history that leaves behind a clearing of Being (*Seyn*)."[131] Heidegger's "Die Sprache im Gedicht" exposes this gathering of solitude, that is, the *Gedicht*, unto the abyss (*Ab-grund*) that is associated with origination and inception. This is directly in line with Derrida's reading of Heidegger in both *Of Grammatology* and *Fantom*.

By this point it should be clear that Derrida has gone far beyond thinking in terms of two separate strokes or moments in which the second is the debased imprint of the first, given that the one is invaginated within the other. This would also be true for polysemy/dissemination, which correlates to *Versammlung* (gathering) and *Zerstreuung* (scattering). Heidegger argues that despite its plurisignation, a poem by Trakl is constellated and gathered; as such, it resists the kind of disseminative scatter that would utterly destroy it. From *Of Grammatology*'s perspective, this betrays elements of a logocentric inclination, one that would prefer polysemy to the more radical dissemination or see dissemination as a bad iteration of polysemy. In *Fantom*, Derrida comments,

> If there were only gathering, the same, the unique, the place without path, then, not to mince words, this would be death. And this is not what Heidegger wants to say, inasmuch as he insists on movement on the path of the stranger, the path toward the others, and so on. It must be that between place and nonplace, between gathering and divisibility, the relationship is otherwise, a sort of negotiation and compromise that is ceaselessly in play, something that would oblige us to reconstitute the implicit logic that appears to guide Heidegger.[132]

Derrida's basic argument is that in order for place to be one of gathering, or of the gathered together, there has to be divisibility a priori. "Divisibility, deconstruction, différance, dissemination" are said to be inherent in Heidegger's vocabulary of convergence and indivisibility in which the one and the many, the gathered and the dispersed are in play.

Derrida continues:

> To say that there is divisibility does not come down to saying that there is only divisibility or division. (This too would be death.) Death lies in wait on both sides, with the phantasm of the integrity of the proper place and the innocence of a sexual difference without war, and also on the opposite side, that of impropriety or radical expropriation, or of a war of *Geschlecht* as sexual dissension.[133]

By themselves, gathering and divisibility would be death: paralysis, stasis. This means that one is then going to be concerned with the between: with the fantasy (or fantasm) of sexual difference without war and that of a proper place on one side and that of sexual dissension and radical expropriation on the other. Derrida's mention of the fantasm probably alludes to his essay "Fors" in which the place of the fantasm is that of the crypt in which both a gathering and dispersion occur, given that the crypt is the place where the fantom resides and is gathered to itself and out of which it travels forth as a spirit that haunts. Once more divisibility traverses the *geistig* and the *geistlich*, what is mental (within one) and what is out there, roaming and haunting. It is the proliferation of these states that reflects an insistence upon a particular sort of repetition—of the double *Schlag* as *Zwiefalt/Zwietracht*—that winds up disseminating across much of Heidegger's text, though by no means with a consistent outcome.

With respect to inconsistency Derrida observes, for example, that Heidegger's rejection of the Platonic-Christian tradition presupposes a bad secondariness with respect to philosophical thinking in relation to a more inceptual thinking about being such as that uncovered in pre-Socratic thinking. Heidegger's emphasis upon the two strokes inherent in, say, the *Gedicht/Dichtung* distinction is itself not entirely outside the ambit of the divided line theory of *The Republic* in which secondariness is both inferior to and more substantial than what comes before. Nevertheless, Heidegger refuses to see a negotiation with Platonism and opts for a strong dichotomy between inceptual thinking and metaphysics. That said, at issue throughout Derrida's consideration of the two strokes has been the proliferation of such a division across a number of conceptual sites, though held in abeyance is that of the good versus the bad generation or stock or race.

On Heidegger's Repudiation of Christian Onto-Theology

With respect to Trakl's poetry, Heidegger writes the following from which Derrida quotes:

> The same ambiguity of language that is determined by the site of Trakl's poetic work also inspires his frequent use of words from the world of biblical and ecclesiastical ideas. The passage from the old to the unborn generation leads through this region and its language. Whether Trakl's poems speak in a Christian fashion, to what extent and in what sense, in what way Trakl was a "Christian," what is meant here, and indeed generally, by "Christianity," "Christendom" and 'Christlike': all this involves essential questions. But their discussion hangs in a void so long as the site of his poetic work is not thoughtfully established. Besides, their discussion calls for a kind of thorough thinking to which neither the concept of a metaphysical nor those of a church-based theology are adequate.[134]

This recalls (repeats) the logic of the two strokes insofar as Trakl's poetry is identical to and different from Biblical and ecclesiastical ideas, however corrupted, that his inceptual thinking precedes and stands apart from, even as it participates in Christianity to such an extent that one has to ask if he was Christian or not. Derrida comments that "despite his discretion and prudence, such an assertion is violent enough, and I will say even one more time, dogmatic enough."[135] Derrida says that for Heidegger "metaphysics or dogmatics" is in sum "toute LA métaphysique"; that is, taken all together, "THE metaphysics."[136] This is a Christian onto-theology insofar as it translates pre-Christian Greek metaphysics. Derrida points out that Heidegger treats Platonic metaphysics and Aristotelian metaphysics similarly by supposing that the concepts of theological metaphysics or ecclesiastical dogmatics are insufficient. But, Derrida wonders, does this not impose a univocal meaning or have a plurivocal meaning that can be controlled, collected, gathered? Does this not presume that the concepts of theology, metaphysics, and dogmatics have an appointed place of which one can say this is not the place of Trakl, of Trakl's *Gedicht*, or that this is not a legitimate place relative to Trakl? What happens, Derrida asks, if we do not agree Heidegger's point? What happens if we suppose there is not a single place ("*un seul lieu*") for this thing called "THE metaphysics" or "THE theology"? What if one opts not to read Christian texts univocally and read them as one reads Trakl in a non-univocal manner? Lastly, Derrida asks about the insistence upon two blows, one good and the other bad, a point that David Krell also has pondered:

> Heidegger's strategy of distinguishing the two strokes, the good from the evil, thus seems to be entirely dependent on at least one strand of the Christian-Platonic tradition. The place of malediction or curse, and the place of the corruption of our *Geschlecht*, the place that Heidegger claims to be able to identify, will in fact be the place that has produced the tradition of metaphysics and morals.[137]

Krell's remark suggests that rejection of the Christian-Platonic tradition is what motivated Heidegger's discourse on the two strokes. Derrida thinks that if this were the case, Heidegger must have been self-deluded. He notes that the Heideggerian interpretation of the two strokes, the good and the bad, of sexual difference before and after the curse, and of all what is said of good and the bad could be mistaken to be Christian were it not for Heidegger's insistence upon something inceptual existing before the Platonic-Christian tradition from which, nevertheless, that tradition emerges. "But in this more originary situation there is nothing other than what has become Platonic-Christian. It is the status of this repetition that seems to me to be highly problematic in Heidegger."[138] Whereas Krell points out Heidegger's distance from Christian onto-theology, Derrida does not see how Heidegger can avoid operating within such a theology, how the place of Heideggerian thought can be situated outside such a theology per se.¹³⁹ This conviction will be accompanied later in the lecture by a number of general remarks on the unworkability of Heidegger's biographical speculations about why Trakl did not cry out to God on his deathbed and other instances where silence can be taken as a refusal of Christianity. Might a Christian not object that if Trakl is not explicitly Christian in his vocabulary, this does not prove that his poetry is not Christian? One need not suppose that a Christian would name God and Christ and that these words could not be left silent. But why not go and use Heidegger's own argument about silence and withdrawal? Why not talk about silence in the poem or the poem in the silence? Heidegger will not recognize the withheld in a Christian context. Derrida asks, why would Trakl speak the name of God at the end of his life, anyway? What makes it a certainty that he should? Is concealedness not applicable here? "I underline *entschiedener* Christ," Derrida specifies.¹⁴⁰ Derrida disagrees with Heidegger that in order to think Platonism and Christianity in their possibility one has to first reject them as such in order to start over. Moreover, presuming Trakl can be operationalized in order to instantiate such a rejection, departure, or turning away is rather questionable.

Brother, Sister, and Christ

Having considered the two strokes in terms of *Gedicht/Dichtung*, Plurisignation (gathering)/Dissemination (dispersal), and Inceptual/Onto-Theological thinking, we now turn to what is arguably Derrida's most suggestive discussion, which concerns the brother, the sister, and Christ. Given the various reinscriptions of the two strokes, one expects the older brother to occupy the position of the first, gentle stroke and the younger sister to reflect the second stroke of malediction that violently separates. The brother—e.g., the figure of Elis—is to be associated with what is *geistig* (spiritual) and the sister with what is *geistlich* (ghostly, lunar, uncanny). In "Strokes of Love and Death," Krell recalls that for Trakl the twosome is to be associated with the lovers, *die Liebenden*. In Trakl's lyrics they exist in a mild time of gentle embrace, glow afresh in winged things, suffer "more gently," and so on. The lovers also approach the nearness of death. "On pillows still warm,/Yellowed by incense, lovers' delicate limbs unravel."¹⁴¹ Here, incipiently, two gentle strokes, one of life and the other of death, are noticeable and appear to be repeated in Trakl's verses in a reference that is easy to escape notice, the opening and closing of eyelids. In "Abendländisches Lied" the silver eyelids of the lovers lift just before we read "E I N Geschlecht." Are the eyelids representative of the strokes, at once *Zwiefache, Zwiefalt, Zwietracht, Entzweiung*?

The figure of the sister is at times ghostly and angelic in Trakl, and Derrida wonders what it means that the poet replaces the name of Christ with that of the sister. Derrida says it may be a bit of an exercise, but that he wants to show how the figure of the sister and that of Christ can be substituted for one another explicitly in Trakl's corpus. That said,

> How are we to determine the sex of Christ and how are we to characterize, within sexual difference, the experience that is properly Christian, decidedly Christian, the experience that a man (supposing Trakl is a man ...) or a woman has by way of a relation to Christ? Son of God, Christ is the brother of all men and all women; he is simultaneously the image or the intercessor of the father. Yet he is a brother whose virility is never simply manifest or unilateral, a brother who presents himself within an aura of universal homosexuality, or in a sexual difference that has been appeased, pacified (or tender, as none other than Trakl would say), beyond all the moments of those temptations where evil is quite close, thus a brother who can be nothing other than a sister.[142]

This speaks to an inceptual effraction within *Geschlecht* as a familial marker wherein brother, sister, son, and God as father are metonymically gathered in relation to Christ as a synecdochic figure—or primal metonymy. Derrida doesn't say so, but he is, in fact, considering the family in a way that cannot exclude incest insofar as sexual difference—and the exclusionary distanciations this presupposes in terms of family relations—is inherently deconstructed from an inceptual point of view that is more originary than what one might call the social relation as formally conceived. Would that mean that incest, the specter of which haunts Trakl's biographers, could be a figure for what is most inceptual, gathered, as well as for violation, a violence done to family, generation, etc.?[143]

In the passage above, Derrida is returning to a topic considered in *Glas* that concerns the Holy Family, which in *Fantom* is being re-elaborated from the perspective of the essay "Geschlecht I" wherein Dasein is examined from the perspective of a double origin: the one sexually neutral, the other sexually differentiated. Instead of speaking in terms of *Schlag*, Derrida refers to the thrownness of *Dasein* in Heidegger that, on the one hand, establishes sexual differentiatedness and, on the other hand, breaks it up. In the passage from *Fantom* above, *Geschlecht* as primordial *Schlag* both imposes and removes sexual differentiatedness in the context of Trakl's references to brother and sister as well as to their relation to or within the Holy Family.

And if it is a matter of a son born of a virgin herself born by way of an immaculate conception, the sexual determination cannot be adequately assured to the point where one could say quite tranquilly that wherever the poet names the sister instead of Christ both he and his poem are no longer Christian. That is all the more impossible, all the more precipitous, given the fact that Heidegger himself does not fail to draw attention to the strange couple of the brother and the sister in Trakl's poems. I say "couple" because the word testifies to a sexual difference that, even though it is no longer or not yet a difference of war or dissension, that is, sexual difference as antagonism (*Zwietracht*), is nevertheless not without desire. Hegel says (with regard to Antigone) that the rapport of brother and sister is without desire, *begierdelos*: perhaps it is without manifest desire, in that space where desire instigates war, desire after the second blow, yet it is not without tender desire as a rapport with the other, a double homosexuality, a reflection of desire without an appropriation of the other, a desire in which the brother becomes the sister or the sister becomes the brother, and so on. And who may tranquilly assert that this is not the essence of a relation to Christ, the essence or at least the destination, the destined end that is sought, the destiny toward which one is under way, the entire Christian experience of the Holy Family, which is to say, or any and every family?[144]

This state of the brother and sister could be considered inceptual in the sense of what in *Beiträge* is announced as a restraint of desire "as openness for the reticent nearness of the essential occurrence of Being (*Seyn*)."[145] In this state, differences meld, where the first and second blows are not yet established in their apartness. *Ein Geschlecht* in such an inceptual instance suggests a homosexuality (the Trakl scholars speak of this as androgyny)—in which brother/sister are the same, which is theologically doubled in Christ who also eludes sexual differentiation (the hetero), since by theological definition he challenges if not inherently deconstructs difference. Here Derrida has managed to show how an inceptual or originary state of Being is Christianized without recourse to the kind of metaphysics Heidegger associated with Christian theologizing. That is, in the poetry of Trakl one sights an *other* Christianity that to date is still almost entirely hidden and unknown.

Alluding to *Glas*, where in reading both Hegel and Genet Derrida undertakes a lengthy and complicated deconstruction of sexual difference, Derrida says that the destination of Trakl's poetry is the Holy Family. Why, in fact, did Trakl, on his death bed, call out to the sister at the moment of his death when he ought to have called out to Christ? Are they too *Ein Geschlecht*?

> See *Glas*, which I allow myself to cite only because Heidegger reminds all those who make of Trakl a Christian that it is precisely at the moment of Trakl's death

that he ought to have invoked Christ and God, not the sister, the sister who is always the sister of the lunar voice (*die mondene Stimme*, the Selenic voice, as the French translation says), the voice of the moon that resounds in the spiriting night, as the final lines ... of *Geistliche Dämmerung* say, the eschatological figure of the sister. Is this Selenic figure of the sister (the *eschaton*, the nocturnal light that greets, etc.) so entirely foreign to the figure of Christ? And is the Christ, like the sister, a figure whose meaning is so decidable?[146]

In *Glas*, Derrida writes, with Heidegger in mind, that "the breast (*sein*) of this mother steals away from all names, but it also hides them, steals them; it is before all names."[147] The pun on *Sein* as Being is telling, because as in Heidegger this Being that is the breast "is before all names" and as such inceptual, which of course makes sense in terms of alluding to Melanie Klein's psychoanalytic writings, which are on Derrida's mind at various junctures in *Glas*. Again, quoting Georges Bataille, "Zeal is only unchained at the whip of the absolute past,"[148] a remark in the right column on Genet that speaks to the *Schlag* Derrida is talking about in *Fantom*, not to mention once again the inceptual. In the left column on Hegel we are told there is no monadic consciousness, no isolated sphere into which consciousness would fit, but rather the family structure. "Consciousness does not relate to itself, does not reassemble itself as totality, does not become for itself—does not become conscious—except as, except in the family."[149] Here, again, *Geschlecht* is relevant, for it is here that the "the individual contemplates himself in the other." The "two consciousnesses [within the family] structurally need each other, but they can get themselves recognized only in abolishing, or at least in relieving, the singularity of the other—which excludes it."[150] In Derrida and Heidegger's reading of Trakl, the annihilation of singularity concerns not just the incestuousness of *Ein Geschlecht* but in what Derrida views as the dismantling and deconstruction of sexual difference and with that the undoing of incest as a taboo that insists on difference and differentiation. This radicalizes Derrida's account of Hegel on the sister, though in Hegel too one glimpses at least a suspension of difference in terms of a retraction of sexual desire.

> She raises herself higher than the mother, the daughter, or the wife, but as feminine, taken in the naturalness of the sexual difference, she can have only a presentiment of the ethical spirituality. Sister, she holds herself suspended between a desire she does not experience, of which she experiences that she does not experience it, and a universal law (nonfamilial: human, political, etc.) that stays foreign to her. The fact that she is of the same blood as her brother seems to suffice to exclude desire. Appendix of the *Philosophy of Right*: "The

brother-and-sister relationship—a nonsexual relationship (*Geschwister–ein geschlechtloses Verhältnis*)."[151]

Of importance is that sexuality is held back, that the brother/sister relationship is more originary in its purity (more neutral, as "Geschlecht I" would have it) than other familial relations and, in Hegel's estimation, is most universal and ethical as a social relation. Derrida's citation of this discussion in *Glas*, which extends over several pages to *The Antigone* where Antigone is associated with the nocturnal, suggests Derrida imagined a bridge between *Glas* and *Fantom*, one that the course inflects in a way that enables us to consider Christ as a type or instantiation of an arché-inceptual figure always already taking place in the place of the brother and the sister, as if to undo the violence of the second *Schlag* and its effractions, if not the differential features that are constitutive of the earthly family (*Geschlecht*) which is but the result of a cursed second blow whose gentler more inceptual family would be that of the Holy Family in which sexual dissension is held back in, say, Christ and the Holy Virgin. One might well ask whether this holy couple is the inceptual incarnation of brother and sister in Trakl, the sacred version of an earthly couple that as brother and sister are supposed to be suspended in a desire they do not experience, but by which they are both enflamed as if by a cursed, malign stroke.

Notes

1 I attended Derrida's presentation and remember he talked about working on "Geschlecht III." The impression he gave was that this essay would appear before the end of the year.
2 Derrida, *Geschlecht III* (Paris: Seuil, 2018), 47.
3 "Time and Being," in *On Time and Being*, trans. Joan Stambaugh (New York: Harper and Row, 1972).
4 Derrida, *Geschlecht III*, 35. "Notre progression sera lente, irrégulière dans son rythme, suivant un trajet dont aucune représentation linéaire ne pourrait rendre compte. Progression, n'est-ce pas déjà trop dire d'une démarche dont on peut avoir le sentiment, irrité chez certain, qu'elle se laisse paralyser par l'insistance même: on n'avance pas, on tourne en rond, on revient sur ses pas. Apparemment sans gagner de terrain, sans occuper de position, renonçant à tout souci de stratégie discursive. Et puis tout à coup des sauts brusques, des bonds, des zigzag, chaque fois décidés, de singulières ruptures dont on ne sait pas si elles ont été minutieusement calculées ou si elles ont surpris le discours, venues à lui comme l'événement de l'autre, depuis l'autre décidées."

5   "Passions: An Oblique Offering," in *On the Name*, trans. David Wills (Stanford: Stanford University Press, 1995), 11.
6   The Loyola typescript begins with a somewhat lengthy introduction in which Derrida explains how he will be approaching Heidegger. He explains that with respect to the term *Geschlecht*, it is not easy to establish a relation (*rapport*) between what Heidegger wrote on *Geschlecht* in 1928, as detailed in "Geschlecht I," and what Heidegger has to say about it in the 1950s. How do aspects of Heidegger's corpus connect? And what does connection or relation mean in Heidegger's case? This speaks to Derrida's fascination with Heidegger's leaps and his emphasis upon leaping. The word *Geschlecht*, which in "Geschlecht II" is deemed to be not a word, is considered to be a mark whose relation or reference to a thing in terms of genus never settles into the essence of what it designates. Given the decades that intervene between Heidegger's earlier and later remarks on *Geschlecht*, Derrida imagines the locution ought to be considered in terms of a fold or duality that brings about a dissension within the mark *Geschlecht*. Derrida asks, "What does it mean to bring two texts, two places, two dates into relation?" *Geschlecht III*, 38. The issue here concerns Derrida's various analyses of *Geschlecht* across what were to be four completed essays and whether instances of what Derrida calls *Geschlecht* can be related, much less unified. Of what type is *Geschlecht*? What type of thing is it? Mention of type as genus puns on type as mark and impression, which in turn speaks to striking an impression. "A type is not only the moment or the place of the stroke, it already installs the generality of a genre" ("Un type n'est pas seulement le moment ou le lieu de la frappe, il installe déjà la généralité du genre.") 39. But what is the law of this genre? What is the law of the type that one might call a type of philosophy or thinking, and according to what law can one determine the type of thinking that is Heidegger's? Is thinking reducible to philosophy? What about thinking and poetizing? What are the limits of the type of thinking that is a thinking of the type? 40. This question leads Derrida to a consideration of place as type in Heidegger. A place only has place in terms of its limits that should be understood from the perspective of being situated, say, in terms of merely considering the locality of a text, the time of making a pronouncement, etc. The place, in other words, discloses itself as type. None of this is separable from the "typology of being" in Heidegger of which *Geschlecht* is a part. Derrida goes on to question the singularity of place, Heidegger's conception of the way or path, directionality, and Trakl's situatedness with respect to place. At this point, lecture eight in *Fantom* begins.
7   Martin Heidegger, "Language in the Poem: A Discussion of Trakl's Poetic Work," in *On the Way to Language*, trans. Peter D. Hertz (New York: Harper and Row, 1971), 159. "Die Sprache im Gedicht," in *Unterwegs zur Sprache* (Pfulligen: Günther Neske, 1986), 37.

8   See Derrida, "Sauf le nom," in *On the Name*, trans. J.P. Leavey (Stanford: Stanford University Press, 1995), 58. Here Derrida makes a clever connection he didn't make in *Fantom*: "What is the *Ort* of the *W-ort*?" The notion that the word is the place, that *Wort* = *Ort* and vice versa is an observation inherent in Heidegger that occurs as an afterthought in "Sauf le nom" which contains passages relevant to *Fantom*.
9   Die Sprache im Gedicht. Trans. Modified. Shockingly, Hertz's translation leaves out Heidegger's mention of the tip of the spear, 37 and 159.
10 Heidegger, "Die Sprache im Gedicht," 39.
11 Martin Heidegger, "Letter on Humanism," in *Basic Writings* (New York: Harper and Row, 1977), 214.
12 Ibid.
13 This remark on page 3 of lecture eight doesn't occur in the edited Loyola Typescript.
14 Derrida, *Geschlecht III*, 49.
15 Jacques Derrida, "Le facteur de la vérité," in *The Postcard*, trans. Alan Bass (Chicago: Chicago University Press, 1987), 423.
16 Ibid., 424.
17 Lacan as quoted in ibid., 425.
18 Ibid., 436.
19 Heidegger, "Language in the Poem," 160.
20 In *Geschlecht III*: "… son dire de poète (*sein dichtendes Sagen rein darin zu halten*)," 50.
21 Ibid.
22 Heidegger, "Language in the Poem," 160.
23 Ibid. *Unterwegs*, 38.
24 Derrida, *Geschlecht III*, 51. "C'est plus et autre chose qu'une métaphore."
25 Heidegger, "Language in the Poem," 160.
26 Ibid.
27 Derrida, *Geschlecht III*, 52.
28 Heidegger, "Language in the Poem," 160.
29 Dominique Janicaud, *Heidegger in France*, trans. F. Raffoul and D. Pettigrew (Bloomington: Indiana University Press, 2015), 443.
30 Krell, *Phantoms of the Other*, 145. At various points, Krell mentions the communications he had with Derrida about Heidegger/Trakl.
31 See Richard Detsch, *Georg Trakl's Poetry* (University Park: Pennsylvania University Press, 1983), 58. "As in 'Passion,' almost all of Trakl's human figures seem to be dead and yet continue to act as though they were alive in some way. His is the poetry of the living dead." Of course, this is not a very nuanced observation, but it does speak to a general awareness among the scholars of "decease" in Trakl and how dominant it is in the poetry.

32 Heidegger, "Language in the Poem," 163.
33 Ibid., 164.
34 Ibid., 166–7.
35 Ibid., 167.
36 Ibid. *Unterwegs*, 45.
37 See Mauro Senatore, *Germs of Death* (Albany: SUNY, 2018). Senatore points out that *Khōra* draws from an earlier unpublished seminar, *Theory of Philosophical Discourse: Conditions for the Inscription of the Text of Political Philosophy—The Example of Materialism (1970-71)*. Given the timing of *Khōra*'s publication, there is reason to surmise it comprises some of the sessions of *Mythos, Logos, Topos* (1985–86) that are missing in the archive.
38 Derrida, *Geschlecht III*, substitutes "décomposer, se décomposer, perdre son essence," 69. See *Fantom*, 8:19.
39 Heidegger, "Language in the Poem," 167.
40 Ibid.
41 Ibid., 170.
42 Ibid.
43 Heidegger, "Die Sprache im Gedicht," 49–50.
44 Jacques Derrida, *Khōra* in *On the Name*, trans. D. Wood and J.P. Leavey (Stanford: Stanford University Press, 1995), 111. Materials on Khōra presented in the Mythos, Logos, Topos course were subsumed into the monograph, *Khōra*, along with materials from prior lectures. In the passage cited, the emphasis on place corresponds with that of *Ort* in Heidegger.
45 Jacques Derrida, *The Problem of Genesis in Husserl's Philosophy*, trans. Marian Hobson (Chicago: University of Chicago Press, 2003), 3. Again, see Senatore who has developed this aspect of Derrida's thought in considerable detail.
46 Heidegger, "Language in the Poem," 170.
47 Heidegger, "Die Sprache im Gedicht," 50.
48 Derrida, *Geschlecht III*, 72. "Il y a donc deux coups, deux frappes, deux empreintes. Un premier coup vient frapper pour laisser son empreinte ou plutôt pour constituer de son empreinte un 'premier' *Geschlecht*. Mais le deuxième coup parait mauvais. C'est un mal, le mal."
49 Ibid., 75. In *Fantom*, the typescript reads "de mauvaise différence sexuelle, de guerre sexuelle bestiale."
50 Heidegger, "Language in the Poem," 170–1. Heidegger, "Die Sprache im Gedicht," 50.
51 Jacques Derrida, "Dissemination," in *Dissemination*, trans. Barbara Johnson (Chicago: University of Chicago Press, 1981).
52 Derrida, *Geschlecht III*, 75.
53 Heidegger, "Language in the Poem," 170–1. Heidegger, "Die Sprache im Gedicht," 50.
54 Ibid., 171; 50.
55 Ibid., 170; 50.

56 Derrida, *Geschlecht III*, 76. *Fantom*'s typescript reads: "la paix d'une duplicité simple, d'un pli sans pli, si vous voulez." That is, "the peace of a simple duality, of a fold without fold, if you like."
57 "Time and Being," in *On Time and Being*, ed. Joan Stambaugh (New York: Harper Torchbooks, 1972), 22–3.
58 *Contributions to Philosophy (from Enowning)*, trans. P. Emad and K. Maly (Bloomington: Indiana University Press, 2000), 33. *Gesamtausgabe 60. Beiträge zur Philosophie (vom Ereignis)* (Frankfurt am Main: Vittorio Klostermann, 1989), 43.
59 Ibid., 25/35.
60 Martin Heidegger, *Contributions to Philosophy (of the Event)*, trans. Rojcewicz and Vallega-Neu (Bloomington: Indiana University Press, 2012), 30.
61 Heidegger, "Language in the Poem," 172.
62 Ibid., 173.
63 Ibid.
64 *Nietzsche*, vol. 4, trans. David Farrell Krell (New York: HarperCollins, 1982), 155.
65 Heidegger, "Language in the Poem," 173.
66 Ibid.
67 Derrida, *Geschlecht III*, 84.
68 Heidegger, "Language in the Poem," 173. Translation modified. I have restored a missing sentence left out by Peter Hertz.
69 Heidegger, "Die Sprach im Gedicht," 53.
70 Derrida, *Geschlecht III*, 85.
71 Ibid.
72 Heidegger, "Language in the Poem," 173, trans. modified. Heidegger, "Die Sprache im Gedicht," 55. Derrida, *Geschlecht III*, 86.
73 Derrida, *Geschlecht III*, 86: "Que fait Heidegger? Quel mouvement, quel chemin, quelle folie, quel sens ou autre sens décrit-il, de quoi et de qui parle-t-il dans cette prétendue situation du Gedicht de Trakl?"
74 Ibid., 87. "Il parle de son lieu en parlant de lieu de l'autre, ou plutôt il est à la recherche de son lieu en suivant les pas de l'autre."
75 Ibid., 30.
76 Parvis Emad's translation. *Contributions* (2000), p. 24. *Beiträge*, 34. The two translations of Heidegger's text each have strengths and weaknesses, hence the switch to Emad's translation, in this case.
77 *Contributions*, trans. P. Emad, K. Maly (1999), 26. *Beiträge*, 36.
78 Ibid. R. Rojcewicz and D. Vallega-Neu translate *Verschlagung* as failure. But *Verschlagung* could mean deviousness.
79 Heidegger, "Language in the Poem," 175.
80 Derrida, *Geschlecht III*, 89. "Elis nommerait donc un lieu plus ancien et plus paisible que le vieux Geschlecht (vieille espèce ou vieux sexe) qui a reçu le mauvais

coup, le deuxième coup de la malédiction qui y installé le deux de la dissension, la différence sexuelle comme dissension."

81 Heidegger, "Language in the Poem," 174.
82 Derrida, *Geschlecht III*, 90.
83 In Derrida's corpus, this understanding of life/death resonates with his recently published lecture course *La vie la mort: Séminaire 1975–76* (Paris: Seuil, 2019).
84 *The Last Gold of Expired Stars: Complete Poems 1908–14*, trans. Jim Doss and Werner Schmitt (Sykesville: Loch Raven Press, 2010), 380–1.
85 Heidegger, "Language in the Poem," 175.
86 Richard Detsch, *Trakl and Heidegger*. He cites Grimm's Dictionary wherein *Abgeschiedenheit* is related to *Zurückgezogenheit, Abgesonderheit, Einsamkeit,* and *Entrücktheit*, all of which could be seen metonymically. Detsch's chapter on Heidegger and Trakl maintains that "'*Abgeschiedenheit*' is primarily the unifying principle which draws the past and the future, birth and death, into a whole. It transcends time and makes time possible, but not as something eternal or supernatural. It belongs to this world and directs all existence in the temporal order, and yet in the final analysis it remains a mystery since it has nothing to do with reality as one is accustomed to comprehend it," 78. Again, "'*Abgeschiedenheit*' as the unifying center of Trakl's poetry is appropriate if one realizes that he means death in a nonphysical sense. It is a death which in some mysterious way informs all the acting figures as well as the landscape and entire mood of Trakl's poetry. It is a death which stands not only at the end over the grave of the lovers but also at the beginning with the unborn one and the boy Elis; or, more exactly, it is a death which nullifies both end and beginning as valid concepts by creating a time-whole," 79. Even if Derrideans would dismiss Detsch's discourse as "metaphysical," it does reflect the extent to which a Trakl scholar is necessarily attracted to the very same problematics that Derrida touches upon. In some ways, Detsch might have been of use to Derrida, because he connects circularity and time with *Abgeschiedenheit* in a way that *Fantom* does not manage to do.
87 Quoted in Krell, *Phantoms of the Other*, 184.
88 Heidegger, "Language in the Poem," 177.
89 Ibid., 185. "Die Sprache im Gedicht," 66–7.
90 Quoted in Krell, *Phantoms of the Other*, 178–9.
91 Heidegger, "Language in the Poem," 184.
92 Quoted in Krell, *Phantoms of the Other*, 180.
93 Ibid., 182.
94 Ibid., 183. Krell's retranslation of Heidegger is given here.
95 Heidegger, "Language in the Poem," 185.
96 *Of Spirit*, trans. G. Bennington and R. Bowlby (Chicago: University of Chicago Press, 1989), 95.

97 Ibid., 24.
98 Ibid., 91. See also, pages 82, 83 in Derrida, *Geschlecht III*, on doubling.
99 *Of Spirit*, 95.
100 Heidegger, "Language in the Poem," 179. Heidegger, "Die Sprache im Gedicht," 59.
101 Ibid., 178.
102 Derrida, *Geschlecht III*, 81.
103 Heidegger, "Die Sprache im Gedicht," 59; Heidegger, "Language in the Poem," 178.
104 Derrida, *Geschlecht III*, 82. "Il y a une valeur de *Geist* que Heidegger ne met pas en oeuvre dans toute cette *Erörterung*, c'est celle de fantôme, de revenant, qui pourtant semblerait s'imposer et <se> motiver par tout le contexte." See also, Krell, *Phantoms of the Other*, 174. "Yet Derrida expresses his astonishment that Heidegger avoids altogether the relation between *Geist* and ghost, spirit, and *le revenant, le fantôme*. Such avoidance is clearly what lends the entire seminar its title, *le fantôme de l'autre*."
105 David Krell relates how the Old High German word *gheis* functions as the root of *Geist* and (in English) ghost, "apparently pre-Teutonic in origin and related to the Sanskrit *hedas*, 'anger, fury,' which might of course get us eventually to fire and flame." Relevant too is the Gothic *usgaisjan*, "to drive one outside oneself" and the Old Nordic *geisa*, "to rage." Related is the ek-static. See Krell, *Phantoms of the Other*, 100.
106 Heidegger, "Language in the Poem," 179; Heidegger, "Die Sprache im Gedicht," 59–60.
107 In terms of inceptual violence, Krell's discussion of *gheis, hedas, geisa*, and *usgaisjan* discussed in footnote 105 refers to a violence that in Heidegger's text is performed in terms of the linguistic effraction of the word *Geist* itself. In short, it is with language that language is beaten and split apart (note Heidegger's well-known use of the hyphen to break words up). As we have seen, *Geist* is effracted into *geistlich*, spiritual/ghostly, and *das Geistige* "of the spirit" ("*de l'esprit*"). In his writing on Trakl, Heidegger associates *das Geistige* with the intellect as "suprasensuious noeton," something that is to be opposed to the sensuous *aistheton*, and as such pertains to a Platonic and Christianized division that the word *geistlich* avoids—at least, in Heidegger's intended deployment of the word. One can see in this instance that *geistlich* in its sense of the ghostly challenges *das Geistige* as rational intellection, which is why Heidegger identifies *geistlich* with the strange, the uncanny, and separation (apartness), whereas *das Geistige* reflects what is proper (and canny) as *noeton*. Of course, both *geistig* and *geistlich* are still German cognates for the word "spiritual," which, of course, problematizes them in terms of their identity in difference and difference in identity. They are, in effect, the split up protons or etyms of *Geist*, a word that the *Langenscheidt* dictionary defines generally as spirit, mind, intellect, wit, genius, morale, but also ghost, specter, apparition, phantom,

and, in terms of *der Böse*, the Evil One. Noticeable to Derrida is that the splitting up of *Geist* into conflictual subsets doesn't result in a stable configuration of relations but concerns an avoidance or suppression that is accompanied by a return—in this case, of spirit—that performs revenance. Of significance to Derrida in both *Of Spirit* and *Geschlecht III* is the Heideggerian performance of disappropriation and reappropriation in terms of a return that is always uncanny and disorienting, as in the case of revalorizing the opposition of *geistig/geistlich*. It is in this sense that spirit always returns fantasmatically as something other, say, the lunar voice of the sister that haunts the brother. That the brother-sister relation is *geistig*—rationally comprehensible in the intellect as entirely normal—but also unnatural and unearthly (given the incestuous relations between them, however spiritual) speaks to a certain strange *geistlichkeit*. Derrida doesn't say so explicitly, but one can presume that in Trakl there is a connection being made between the unnatural and the supernatural and that this concerns what one would ordinarily call the strange. However, Heidegger avoids that sense of strange (*Fremd*) in favor of *Fram*, which transposes the strange from what is uncanny to what is ek-statically external or removed (i.e., from what is normal, natural, ordinary). Trakl's verse "Something strange is the soul on the earth" speaks mainly to this disembodied *ek-stasis*, though the trace or trait of the uncanny and the unnatural (*geistlichkeit as fantasmatic*) is not entirely suppressed. Although a broader reading of *Of Spirit* is outside our purview, it cannot be overlooked that its opening line, "Je parlerai du revenant, de la flame et des cendres" ("I shall speak of ghost, of flame, and of ashes"), speaks to the horror of what is unnatural and *geistlich* in terms of fire and ash when transposed from what could be a natural setting of simply burning wood to the unnatural setting of the Shoah, to which Derrida is alluding, where *Geschlecht* (race) is clearly at issue for reasons the National Socialists equated with *Geist*, a term foundational for fascisms generally in Europe leading up to the Second World War.

108 Martin Heidegger, "Hölderlin's Earth and Heaven," in *Elucidations of Hölderlin's Poetry*, trans. K. Hoeller (Amherst: Humanities, 2000), 201.
109 Jacques Derrida, *The Other Heading*, trans. Pascale-Anne Brault and Michael B. Naas (Bloomington: Indiana, 1992), 8. *L'autre cap* (Paris: Minuit, 1991), 14–15.
110 Ibid., 24–5. *L'autre cap*, 29.
111 Ibid., 24.
112 Ibid., 26.
113 Ibid., 39.
114 Ibid., 41.
115 Ibid., 76.
116 Georg Trakl, "Autumn Soul," ver. 2, in *The Last Gold of Expired Stars: Complete Poems 1908–14*, trans. Jim Doss and Werner Schmitt (Sykesville: Loch Raven Press, 2010), 117.

117 Jacques Derrida, "Deconstruction in America," *Journal of the Society for Critical Exchange* 17 (Winter 1985), 6.
118 Jacques Derrida, "Some Statements and Truisms," in *States of Theory*, ed. David Carroll (New York: Columbia, 1990), 88.
119 Derrida, *Geschlecht III*, 102.
120 Ibid.
121 Ibid.
122 Jacques Derrida, *Of Grammatology*, trans. G.C. Spivak (Baltimore: Johns Hopkins University Press, 1976), 18.
123 Martin Heidegger, *Parmenides*, trans. Andre Schuwer and Richard Rojcewicz (Bloomington: Indiana University Press, 1992), 80–1.
124 Derrida, *Of Grammatology*, 25.
125 Ibid., 22.
126 Ibid., 22–3.
127 Ibid., 23.
128 Ibid.
129 Ibid.
130 Martin Heidegger, *Mindfulness*, trans. Parvis Emad and Thomas Kalary (London: Continuum, 2006), 28. Translation slightly modified.
131 Ibid., 29. Translation slightly modified.
132 Derrida, *Geschlecht III*, 106–7; Krell's trans. in *Phantoms* slightly revised, 189.
133 Ibid.
134 Heidegger, "Language in the Poem," 193.
135 Derrida, *Geschlecht III*, 108. "Malgré sa discrétion et sa prudence, une telle assertion reste assez violent, et je dirai une fois de plus assez dogmatique."
136 Ibid.
137 Krell, *Phantoms of the Other,* 190. This corresponds to *Geschlecht III*, 109.
138 *Geschlecht III*, 110 "Mais dans cette situation plus originaire, il n'y a rien d'autre que ce qui est devenu platonico-chrétien. C'est le statut de cette répétition qui me paraît hautement problématique chez Heidegger."
139 The important intertext here is the section "Fallenness and Thrownness" in *Being and Time* (I.5) in which Heidegger begins to posit two moments, an inceptual moment of ontological differentiation in which Dasein is held back followed by a supplementary moment in which Dasein undergoes a fall into the everyday where entities are differentiated into distinct kinds. Krell's chapter on "Geschlecht I" in *Phantoms of the Other* examines various texts in Heidegger where these two moments are at issue and argues that Derrida is drawn to Heidegger's essay on Trakl, "Die Sprache im Gedicht," in order to engage with the history of Heidegger's two-stroke conception. This is a seminal explication.
140 Derrida, *Geschlecht III*, 112.

141 Trakl's "Nearness of Death (version 2)," quoted in and translated by David Krell, "Strokes of Love and Death," in *Intimations of Mortality* (University Park: University of Pennsylvania Press, 1986), 168–9.

142 Quoted in Krell, *Phantoms of the Other*, 192. Derrida, *Geschlecht III*, 114.

143 The Brenner version of "Passion" by Trakl would be key to working through the remarks being made by Derrida on brother, sister, and Christ. "Passion" references "Die Schwester, dunkle Liebe/Eines wilden Geschlechts"—The sister, dark love, of a wild race. The poem is a complex intertwining of figures that wouldn't ordinarily be imagined to be related. It is presided over by Orpheus who is mourning the dead Eurydice in the evening garden, a typological figure for both paradise and Gethsemane ("O, that more piously the night would come, Christus"). Mary, the suffering mother, cloaks her "holy dishonor," having witnessed the incest of brother and sister, perhaps. (Is she their mother whose stock [*Geschlecht*] they are defiling?) Mention is made of a boy (the brother?). The boy's nativity is considered negative in relation to Christ's. Certainly the boy and Christ overlap. But Christ can also be identified with Orpheus, and Eurydice can be associated with the sister. All of these figures seem to merge, something that is underscored by the incest of brother and sister. "Zwei Wölfe im finsteren Wald/Mischten wir unser Blut in steinerner Umarmung/Und die Sterne unseres Geschlechtes fielen auf uns."—"Two wolves in the dark forest/We mixed our blood in stony embrace/And the stars of our race fell on us." The animalism of the lovers might have interested Derrida had he examined "Passion," in part because it suggests Trakl was thinking in terms of dismantling the differences between man, god, and animal as well as between life and death, as in the line when the deceased lovers are said to look on themselves on the crossroad. Hence the falling stars. It's unfortunate that both Heidegger and Derrida ignore this poem, probably far more so in Derrida's case given its extreme relevance and radicality in terms of deconstructing identity and difference in ways that go beyond any theological-metaphysical recuperation. Ethically, Trakl yokes the holy together with what is most unholy and in so doing conflates them even while splitting them up. At the end of "Passion," a rosy angel of morning steps out from the grave of the incestuous lovers. Derrida will consider the matinal at length toward the end of his commentary on Heidegger, which again makes this poem quite relevant. Last, "Passion" ambiguates paganism and Christianity in a way that inflects the poetry toward Heidegger's allergy to Christian metaphysics, something that could have been of interest to Derrida. See Detch on "Passion" in *Georg Trakl's Poetry*, 13–15, and Hans Esselborn, "Poetologische Leitfiguren Georg Trakls" in *Autorschaft und Poetik*, ed. Uta Degner et al. (Salzberg-Wien, Otto Müller Verlag, 2016). Another missing facet in both Heidegger and Derrida is consideration of *Geschlecht* in the context of Otto Weininger's theories of sexuality that had some influence on Trakl, according to

the Trakl scholars. See "Georg Trakl und Otto Weininger" in Alfred Doppler, *Die Lyrik Georg Trakls,* Band XXI Trakl-Studien (Salzberg: Otto Müller Verlag, 2001).
144 Quoted in Krell, *Phantoms of the Other,* 192–3. Derrida, *Geschlecht III,* 114–15.
145 *Contributions to Philosophy (Of the Event)*, trans. R. Rojcewicz and D. Vallega-Neu, 30. *Beiträge,* 35–6.
146 Quoted in Krell, *Phantoms of the Other,* 193.
147 Jacques Derrida, *Glas,* trans. John P. Leavey and Richard Rand (Lincoln: University of Nebraska Press, 1986), 133b.
148 Ibid., 134b.
149 Ibid., 136a.
150 Ibid.
151 Ibid., 149a.

7

Of Promise and Return

The eleventh, twelfth, and thirteenth lectures of *Fantom* focus on the philosophical nationalism of *patrie* in Heidegger. These lectures relate to the course that is to come in the following year, *Mythos, Logos, Topos*, in which *patrie* factors far more broadly in terms of Ancient Greek thinking (Plato's *Menexenes* and *Timaeus*) as well as in terms of Medieval conceptions of sovereignty, blood, and soil. Exceptional for Derrida is that Heidegger's reading of Georg Trakl in "Die Sprache im Gedicht" can be taken as an allegory of how to deconstruct *patrie* by way of a negative theology of nationalism and of homeland, a deconstruction that has to factor in the effractions of the two strokes discussed at length in earlier lectures as an inceptual violence that vexes distinctions between identity and difference even as it demands their separation. In this context, it can be said that difference (differentiation, differentiatedness, etc.) holds open the possibility of identity (gathering, collecting, assembling, unifying, etc.) and that identity does the same for difference. Toward the end of *Fantom* Derrida will discuss *patrie* from the perspective of an open circularity that concerns promise and re-turn, themes that recall earlier lectures from the first half of the course where exile and return are highlighted quite prominently.

The eleventh lecture begins by addressing the possible objection that the course seems to have drifted off topic. "Certain among you are asking yourselves perhaps if the somewhat meticulous and microscopic attention that we bring to the letter of a text by Heidegger on a poet over several weeks doesn't distance us from our subject and the great questions of nationality or of philosophical nationalism."[1] Derrida adds that if this is what people think, they are wrong, because the places for considering the great and burning questions have never been abandoned. That said, Derrida notes that he will be speaking of country (in French, *pays*, in German, *Land*). This will not only concern the poetry of Trakl but of Hölderlin, as well, who stands behind Trakl as a precursor of thinking about a return to the land or country. This question of *retour*, of coming back, will inform much of what is developed in the last three lectures of *Fantom* and relates to the earlier lectures in the course on exile and return in the contexts, especially, of Arendt and Adorno for whom the feeling of being a stranger on the earth, or as someone who has departed, carries a quite different valency from what Derrida considers in Heidegger. Still, Adorno's sense of himself as being looked upon as a specter who had turned up in Germany after the Second World War can't be ignored.

Of initial interest to Derrida is Heidegger's remark in "The Letter on Humanism" that

> What throws in projection is not man but Being itself, which sends man into the ek-sistence of Da-sein that is his essence. This destiny comes to pass as the lighting of Being, as which it is. The lighting grants nearness to Being. In this nearness, in the lighting of the *Da*, man dwells as the ek-sisting one without yet being able properly to experience and take over the dwelling.[2]

Derrida points out that living in terms of the nearness requires one to think nearness ("*penser la proximité*") because in the absence of thinking about nearness one cannot think about country, nation, and language. Nearness in Heidegger is a privative marker that negates the philosophical metaphysics of nation, nationhood, and nationality. In Heidegger's reading of Trakl that negation is everywhere being signaled by means of emphasis upon the inceptual where lighting (*Lichtung*) grants nearness.

Heidegger himself follows the passage above from "The Letter" on nearness with the observation that "In [my] lecture on Hölderlin's elegy 'Homecoming,' this nearness 'of' Being, which the *Da* of Dasein is, is thought ... from the experience of the oblivion of Being [as] the 'homeland' (*Heimat*)."[3] This statement takes distance from vulgar modern-day nationalist-political conceptions of one's relation to place. If *Heimat* (*patrie*) is thought in an essential sense, it is not done so in a patriotic or nationalist sense. Derrida notes that the essence of *Heimat* is to be associated with the intention of thinking the *absence* of modern man's *patrie*. In "The Letter on Humanism" Heidegger writes, with Hölderlin in mind, that "the word [homeland] is thought here in an essential sense, not patriotically or nationalistically but in terms of the history of Being. The essence of the homeland, however, is also mentioned with the intention of thinking the homelessness of contemporary man from the essence of Being's history." Heidegger continues, "When Hölderlin composes *Homecoming* he is concerned that his 'countrymen' find their essence. He does not at all seek that essence in an egoism of his nation. He sees it rather in the context of a belongingness to the destiny of the West."⁴ In a subsequent passage that recalls Fichte's cosmopolitanism, Heidegger writes that

> "German" is not spoken to the world so that the world might be reformed through the German essence; rather, it is spoken to the Germans so that from a fateful belongingness to the nations they might become world-historical along with them. The homeland of this historical dwelling is nearness to Being.⁵

Heidegger wants to distinguish this from "the mere cosmopolitanism of Goethe" insofar as Hölderlin's "relation to Greek civilization is something essentially other than humanism. When confronted with death, therefore, those young Germans who knew about Hölderlin lived and thought something other than what the public held to be the typical German attitude."⁶ At issue is Heidegger's inceptual notion of Being that at once enables him to exceed the limitations of mere nationalism and simultaneously reject the cosmopolitanism of humanism.

Derrida, who largely expects his auditors to read these passages on their own, comments that for Heidegger man must decide an essence for himself that is not reducible to classical humanism wherein man is but a rational animal, one that can reason anywhere. Derrida points out that Heidegger's notion of man is more originary than that of the humanist whose values derive from the pragmatism of the Romans. Rejected is mere anthropologism. "Every nationalism," Heidegger writes, "is metaphysically an anthropologism and as such subjectivism. Nationalism is not overcome through mere internationalism; it is rather expanded and elevated thereby into a system."⁷ Derrida comments that according to Heidegger in the "Letter," homeland is not supposed to be thought of in nationalistic or patriotic terms, because one is thinking in terms of the history of Being, which is apolitical. Heidegger is imagining the absence of *patrie*, which risks a certain homelessness. Hölderlin comes home to a home that is not that of a nationality or of a people. He does not want to enter into the egoism of a people and therefore considers what it means to belong to the destiny of the Occident (*Zugehörigkeit des Abendlands*). Derrida notes that because Heidegger rejects the reduction of place to a region or regionality, even *Abendland* (Occident) is to be avoided conceptually, because place is related to the emergence of being, the origin, and our proximity to it. This is not Europe per se. Heidegger explains this as follows:

> When Hölderlin composes *Homecoming* he is concerned that his "countrymen" find their essence. He does not at all seek that essence in an egoism of his nation. He sees it rather in the context of a belongingness to the destiny of the West. But even the West is not thought regionally as the Occident in contrast to the

Orient, nor merely as Europe, but rather world-historically out of nearness to the source.[8]

In the essay "Remembrance," from *Elucidations of Hölderlin's Poetry*, Heidegger says that "the homeland withdraws from [the] desire to grasp it." In this context, however, Heidegger speaks of spirit, not man or *Dasein*. "The spirit is present as spirit even in its beginning, and already open to the open; otherwise it would not be spirit. For that reason, the homeland too also comes toward the spirit's knowing will, right from the beginning. But because it is the origin, it comes necessarily in such a way that it conceals itself."[9] Hence the spirit has to abide *near* the origin that is called homeland. This concerns belonging to something destinal, which is what Derrida views as the replacement for a nationalist conception of identity with place. Homeland is not an identitarian but a proximate concept concerning one's proximity to the *Da* of *Da-sein*, a nearness that manifests lack.

In this context, Derrida's interest in Heidegger's "Letter on Humanism" concerns what one might call an attempt to dismantle the nationalist/cosmopolitan divide, since both terms are at bottom symmetrical versions of the same humanist metaphysics. This is a schema, Derrida says, that has been verifiable in earlier lectures without having to refer to Heidegger. What one has, Derrida says, is *an appeal to go beyond* race, territory, the state, and even a particular language spoken by a people in order that the nation can escape its isolationism, which disempowers it. To be liberated from the abstract, conceptual restrictions that particularize and isolate the state, one has to consider a non-empirical understanding of the national, which presumably is to be found in Hölderlin and Trakl, because they have intimations of that other beginning crucial to the history of Being. Yet, Derrida clarifies that shockingly right after discussing an inceptual history of Being, Heidegger makes the leap of naming Germany. "*Il nomme l'Allemagne, il nomme l'Allemand, la germanité, das 'Deutsche' entre guillemets ce qui est mal traduit par 'la réalité allemande …'* (He calls Germany, the German, and Germanness, das 'Deutsche', between quotes, that which is badly translated by 'the German reality …')."[10] This, as Derrida explicitly points out, speaks to "the Fichtean gesture" in the *Addresses to the German Nation* wherein the German calling—indeed, the very fact of being German—makes one a people of the world. Fichte, we are told, does not just speak to anyone, but to the nation of a German people, a nation that has not as yet even come into being as a concrete entity and, as such, is still being asked to reflect philosophically. Fichte's discourse, we are told, is a precursor to Germany as a nation and as such has not yet arrived or come into being as a nationalist discourse but rather as one that has a universal horizon, that of spiritual freedom ("*liberté spirituelle*"). According to the logic of the double stroke demonstrated at length in the prior lecture, one ought to be thinking of *das Deutsche* as what precedes the curse of the second stroke, *Deutschland*, which is metaphysically reified.

A complicating factor is that although Heidegger wants to think Germany non-empirically and even non-regionally, he cannot simply deny *patrie*, because that would give in to an empty, abstract universalism along the lines of Fichtean discourse. That would result in a cosmopolitanism that would be the symmetrical inverse of nationalism. In the "Letter," Heidegger appears to be aware that cosmopolitanism (universalism) and nationalism would be two versions of the same humanist metaphysic. Derrida says that Heidegger could not escape rejecting the formality of such a schema of inversion on account of the inceptual history of being, reflected in Heidegger's conception of *Dasein*. In "Die Sprache im Gedicht," it is place rather than *Dasein* that is stressed.

Certainly, when Heidegger deplores homelessness as the effect of metaphysics or the destinal consequence of a historically established empirical orientation to world, he is rejecting subject-centered notions of place, habitation, and belonging that are politically, economically, and socially utilitarian and expedient. When Heidegger cites Hölderlin's *Andenken* as disclosing a place that is both more inceptual and futural at once, he introduces a temporality that cannot be supported by mere historicality wherein a locale is defined in terms of a simple timeline of events running from past to present. Hence one encounters Hölderlin's circular logic regarding the most original as the most futural, which informs Trakl's narrative of the departed going under in order to return to an inception that is temporally at once earlier and later, both back and forward in time. This is endemic to "Die Sprache im Gedicht" where the notion of place is not metaphysically grounded in a familiar, linear historical temporality.

Autumn Soul

In turning to part three of Heidegger's "Die Sprache im Gedicht," Derrida says he closes a circle whereby one returns to the last strophe of Trakl's "Autumn Soul" ("*Herbstseele*") cited at the outset of Heidegger's text in order to further the interrogation of place and departure. In the poem, the fleeing of the fish and other prey already speaks to departing. The dark wandering too reflects leave taking and parting. "*Départ de l'autre, de l'Aimé*" (Trakl: "Parted us from loved ones, others"). Here Derrida cites Heidegger on the poem's third stanza that "speaks of those wanderers who follow the stranger's path through the ghostly (*geistliche* [spiritual]) night in order that they may 'dwell in its animate blue.'" Heidegger speaks to the notion of place when he says immediately, "An open region that holds the promise of a dwelling, and provides a dwelling, is what our language calls a 'land' (*Den freien Bereich, der ein Wohnen verspricht und gewährt, nennt unsere Sprache das 'Land'*)."[11] Derrida is quick to note Heidegger's perhaps chauvinistic locution "*unserer Sprache*" that carries the implication not only that it is German and "ours," but that in its naming the land something is promised and reserved. Derrida notes that if the word "land" is a word of *our* (German) language, it is a word whose promise belongs to us.[12] Derrida observes that for Heidegger there is a distinction to be made between land and country, a difference that recalls the two strokes from the previous lecture in which the first is at peace, the second at war.

Having reappropriated the word "land," Heidegger adds something decisive, which is that "the land into which the early dead goes down is the land of this evening. The location of the site that gathers Trakl's work into itself is the concealed nature of apartness, and is called 'Evening Land,' the Occident (*Abendland*)."[13] Here the nature of apartness and its place is instantiated by Trakl's *Gedicht*, which is to say, its *Abgeschiedenheit*. Although *Abend* means evening, Derrida adds that in Spanish evening means late. "(La tarde *en espagnol) le soir, c'est le tard.*" In Sanskrit "sr" means to go, to follow. Was Heidegger thinking of *Abend* in such terms of wandering, following, and being late? The etymologies hardly contradict Trakl's lyric. Not just a matter of lateness, one is to think of delay or belatedness in the sense of a holding back (*Verhaltenheit*).[14] The land or place is belated, tardy, held back. The country (*le pays*) in which the young deceased declines is that of such an evening—of a lateness or tardiness, a place where habitation is promised, the land as "tard-pays" (the late-country). What promises is the delay. In this sense, place is akin to language that "holds back its own origin and so denies its being to our usual notions."[15] Indeed, Derrida connects language and place when he says that the locality of place gathers into itself the *Gedicht* of Trakl. Is *Dichtung* delayed in its coming to pass? Is a poetry worthy of the name characterized by belatedness, delay, lateness? In some of Trakl's lyrics the human figures appear to be born too late, to have been born into a largely vanished or departed world of remnants of what once has been, a world slow to return.

The region, land, or place of evening is key to Derrida's remarks in these last lectures, because this so-called land of descent is an inceptual locale where logical oppositions are dis-composed, for example, the binary oppositions of night/day, late/early, death/birth, end/beginning. When Heidegger says that "this land is older, which is to say, earlier and therefore more promising (*darum versprechender*),"[16] he is not being paradoxical, merely, but speaking on the hitherside of paradox where oppositionality has long been deconstructed and deconstituted, as if the logical clamps of paradox had been pried open and broken apart, subjected to some sort of hammer *Schlag*. Time is no longer linear and hardly obeys its famous arrow. Philosophically, land has little to do with a physical plot somewhere that someone occupies (it is just a metaphor in Trakl), but is a transcendental (in the sense of archaic) site that gathers. Time and space are strange, spooky, because they run counter to our commonplace Newtonian understanding of the world. The Trakl scholars have been well aware of how beginning and end are subjected to a circular development as in "Dark Stillness of Childhood" ("*Dunkle Stille der Kindheit*") in which that stillness refers to both the beginning and the end as if to abolish the arrow of time. For Derrida of significance is a logic of circularity whose repetition grinds away at dualisms: descent/ascent, early/late, evening/morning, exile/return. Here once more difference and identity are at issue.

Inceptual Temporality

Heidegger acknowledges the stranger's act of departing more as an inclination or draw to the inceptual than as a decision of opportunity or choice, though for Heidegger it does have the significance of a political rejection of the state of post-war Europe. All that kept to the side, Heidegger tells us that the stranger "unfolds human nature forward into the beginning of what is yet to be borne."[17] This concerns a temporality in which "the end—being the end of the decaying kind (*verwesenden Geschlechtes*—precedes the beginning of the unborn kind (*ungeborenen Geschlechtes*). But the beginning, the earlier earliness (*die frühere Frühe*), has already overtaken the end."[18] Such "earliness preserves the original nature—a nature so far still veiled—of time." This nature of time will be concealed as long as one is conditioned by an Aristotelian notion of time, "still standard everywhere." In contrast, "true time, however, is the arrival of that which has been. This is not what is past, but rather the gathering of essential being (*Versammlung des Wesenden*), which precedes all arrival in gathering itself into the shelter of what it was earlier, before the given moment." Time as a chronological progression from past to present to future is "gathered up into apartness" and unfolds in a way that gathers temporalities differently; hence, "the end precedes the beginning."[19]

The poetry of Trakl brings us to a gathering and brings us to a site in which the logical parameters of metaphysical thinking are exceeded in terms of an apartness/gathering whose difference is not just undecidable but effracted. Is it possible to bring apartness itself before our mind's eye, to contemplate it as the poem's site? This is what Heidegger's essay is attempting to do, though it engages in the very kind of splitting and enfolding (or gathering) that contributes to a certain incomprehensibility that a close reader is certain to notice in the many exchanges wherein one poem substitutes vertiginously for another and major themes (patience, pain, spirit, flame, evil, home, death, *Geschlecht* [as generation, kind, kin, race, etc.]) both converge and pull away from one another.

Ethos

It probably occurred to those of Derrida's students who had done their homework in reading "The Letter on Humanism" that there might have been a commentary by Derrida to come on a crucial passage about ethics in which Heidegger explains that in ancient Greek "*ethos* means abode, dwelling place." Heidegger explains, "The word (*ethos*) names the open region in which man dwells. The open region of his abode allows what pertains to man's essence, and what in thus arriving resides in nearness to him, to appear. The abode of man [his *ethos*] contains and preserves the advent of what belongs to man in his essence."[20] In "Die Sprache im Gedicht," this abode or ethos is the place to which the stranger journeys as he declines into inceptual earliness where "the power to still," which is inherently ethical, manifests itself in terms of withdrawal, holding back, delay.[21] In "The Letter on Humanism" this ethics is reflected in the story Heidegger tells of Heraclitus humbly warming himself in front of a stove. Speaking to visitors who had expected an exalted thinker with gaudy philosophical trappings, Heraclitus (in his role as the stranger) says, "for here too the gods are present." Apartness gathers.[22]

In the lecture we are considering, Derrida quotes two very long passages from "Das Wesen der Sprache" ("The Nature of Language") in which Heidegger discusses proximity and the neighborhood of poetry and thinking in which the two are drawn to one another on account of nearness. What determines the neighborhood to be a neighborhood, and if it is nearness that determines, what is nearness? Moreover, how does nearness enable remoteness to come to the fore? When Heidegger in the "Letter" associates the abode with nearness, does that expose the ethical as the neighborly? In "Geschlecht IV" Derrida will discuss *Mit-Sein* in Heidegger, and one might well wonder if the interest in nearness anticipates that later discussion. In this eleventh lecture, the question of nearness is kept open for later elaboration, though the tutor texts have been quoted at length.

Throughout the last lectures of *Fantom* of much interest to Derrida is that a promise abides in the nearing of an abode (*ethos*), the event (*événement*) of the coming of a place. Derrida's neologism for this is "*vénement*." That promise or arrival of the abode of man (*ethos*) is sent whenever there is engagement, calling, and decision, a sending that is the performativity of the promise thought inceptually as a broaching or intimation of what is to be. Derrida notes that it would be required here to open a whole detour on the discreet but essential role of speech as promise. If Heidegger thinks that the promise is implicit in engagement, decision, and calling (*Heissen*), from Derrida's point of view this relates not just to the performativity of a promise, but to the dispatch of a social contract, which Heidegger considers to be ontologically inceptual in the land. Does the word *Geschlecht* come to instantiate that social contract as socially/politically realized? Derrida says that ideally one would want to explore the promise in Heidegger from different angles: (1) that of the promise and the oath of the hand, the hand as "*une forme de la promesse*"[23]; (2) the promise as speech act; (3) the use of *Verheissen* as in *Land der Verheissung* (land of promise) and *Versprechen*, which can mean to promise, but also to misstate (*sich versprechen*, one's having misspoken); and (4) the use of the word "promise" in the sense that the land promises habitation, that the land has promise, but also that the land has been promised to a people, a *Geschlecht* (and by extension a nation?). Otherwise, how could the land be thought to belong to an us?

The idea that something has been promised to a people is inherent in the idea that the land has promise, that it is promising (propitious). *Verheissung* leads to *Versprechen*.[24] This promise, in its double sense, moreover is to be considered more inceptual than the promise of salvation (religious, ethical, educational, technical, cultural) that stems from a Platonic-Christian understanding of the Occident. Because it is more originary and matinal, *Abendland* is more authentic in terms of its promise (and promising) of a future to come.

Heidegger himself insists that Trakl is "the poet of the yet concealed evening land ... older, which is to say, earlier and therefore more promising than the Platonic-Christian land, or indeed than a land conceived in terms of the European West. For apartness is the 'first beginning' of a mounting world-year, not the abyss of decay." Furthermore that "the land into which the early dead goes down is the land of this evening. The location of the site that gathers Trakl's work into itself is the concealed nature of apartness and is called '*Abendland*', the Occident."²⁵ This refers to a trait of union in the absence of its being posed, Derrida cautions. Place, poem, promise, apartness, the world-year, the sun's diurnal course, withdrawal and reemergence, and the "one single call that the right *Geschlecht* [genus, sex, race …] may come to be, and to speak the flame of the spirit into gentleness"²⁶ are all traits of union, or, if one prefers, of *Erörterung*.

Abendländisches Lied

The twelfth lecture of *Fantom* is bridged with the previous lecture by mention of a revolutionary or cyclical promise of the day or year that is more matinal and primordial than the earliest morning. It is the evening in Evening Land (*Abendland*) that declines into what is most inceptual. Derrida comments that in *Fantom* we have followed the path of taking a step beyond, of a crossing over toward the inception which is hidden in the country that is the Occident. He continues by noting that this crossing over or step beyond in *What Is Called Thinking?* relates to Nietzsche's *Übermensch* who transcends beast and rational animal. This crossing is the advent of a post-human condition of man, though Derrida doesn't specifically reference the post-human per se. In *What Is Called Thinking?* Heidegger recalls Nietzsche's teaching that "man's essential nature is not yet determined—it has neither been found nor been secured."²⁷ As noted earlier, this point was taken up in "Die Sprache im Gedicht." If man is the rational animal, Nietzsche argues that man's reason only exists in order to look down upon and subject the animal. Furthermore, Nietzsche argues that the division between sensuousness (ascribed to the animal) and rationality (ascribed to humans) is merely a metaphysical opposition enabling humans to pass beyond the physical in order to be supra-sensual. Man himself is the metaphysical, Heidegger notes. Here, of course, Derrida is on familiar terms with hierarchical metaphysical oppositions, and in his later courses in his career he will return to the animal/man distinction at quite some length, a subject that has been much written about by Michael Naas and others.

More immediately of note is Heidegger's understanding that Nietzsche's conception of the superman needs to be thought in terms of "(1) the passing over; (2) the site from which the passage leaves; and (3) the site to which the passage goes." Zarathustra "overpasses man as he is" and is to be considered "a transition" or a "bridge." "The superman, strictly understood, is the figure and form of man to which he who passes over is passing over."²⁸ Once more, foundational is the philosopheme of departure or *Abgeschiedenheit* that characterizes Zarathustra's going over and also his place of dwelling in a cave on a mountain apart from the world of mankind. There is also the thematic of the matinal in *Also Sprach Zarathustra*. As quoted in Heidegger: "One morning he rose with the dawn, stepped before the sun, and spoke to it."[29]

Not to be overlooked is that in contrast to Trakl's wanderers, madmen, and strangers, Zarathustra doesn't incline but decides by force of will. Also, whereas Trakl's figures step back into the inceptual, Zarathustra's teachings cross over into the futural. In "Who Is Nietzsche's Zarathustra?" Heidegger explains "the superman—taking the word literally, is that human being who goes beyond prior humanity solely in order to conduct such humanity for the first time to its essence, an essence that is still unattained, and to place humanity firmly within that essence."[30] Zarathustra's teaching, Heidegger says, involves tomorrow, "not merely today."[31] And his teaching of the superman "proceeds beyond prior and contemporary humanity; thus he is a transition, a bridge."[32] By contrast, Trakl's stranger does not teach; he does not even speak. He does not attempt to encounter, as any teacher must, but withdraws. Yet he too is on a mission to place humanity firmly within its essence. Are the stranger and Zarathustra two dimensions of the same phenomenon? Derrida doesn't say.

Discussion of Nietzsche was briefly started toward the end of the eleventh lecture and has been carried over to the early part of the twelfth lecture, whereupon Derrida turns to his main agenda: a return to an interrogation of *"Ein Geschlecht"* in terms of the *coup* or blow (singular but also plural) that both unifies and divides. In so doing, Derrida will mount a more intense and expanded analysis of the inceptual violence of *Schlag*, beginning with Heidegger's commentary on Trakl's *"Abendländisches Lied,"* one of a number of poems on the Occident. Not mentioned by Derrida—and this is something of a meaningful oversight, given the first half of *Fantom*—is that a poem called *"Abendland"* ("Occident") was dedicated to a Jewish poet and dramatist, who would later become quite well known as a major figure in her own right. Trakl's dedication reads: "To Else Lasker-Schüler, with admiration." One might well keep this in mind considering that what makes *"Abendländisches Lied"* overtly controversial—and again, Derrida remains silent on this point—is Trakl's invocation of "E i n Geschlecht" with the odd spacing of "Ein" that when juxtaposed to the title of the poem may be read National Socialistically as a racist injunction, not that Trakl meant it that way or that he himself harbored racist ideas or, more specifically, anti-Semitic feelings, given the friendship with and admiration of Lasker-Schuler. Indeed, none of this might matter if Heidegger himself had not substituted the phrase *"des rechten Schlages"* for *"E i n Geschlecht."* Heidegger writes: "Trakl's poem sings of the land of evening. It is one single call that the right or proper race may come to be, and to speak the flame of the spirit into gentleness (*Trakls Dichtung singt das Land des Abends. Sie ist ein einziges Rufen nach dem Ereignis des rechten Schlages, der die Flamme des Geistes ins Sanfte spricht*)."[33] *Schlages* is the word being used for race, rather than *Geschlecht*, most likely because it is more inceptual, a point underscored by Heidegger's use of the word *Ereignis*, which the translator has rendered in terms of coming-to-be. The poem, Heidegger is saying, is a unique calling for or after the ap-propriation (or en-owning) of the proper or right kind, type, or race. The quote also specifies that as such the poem is speaking in and as the gentleness of the flame of spirit, expressed in Trakl as a kind of serenity that can erupt suddenly into something fiery and violent: the flaring up of spirit/intellect that metaphorically burns (destroys) what has come before.

In light of Nazi ideology about spirit and the bringing about of a proper or right race, Trakl is in danger of being read anachronistically by Heidegger or his readers in terms of a historical context with which the poet had nothing to do. Odd is that this is the consequence of a retroactive reading undertaken in the early 1950s that distances itself from National Socialism (Trakl himself was repudiated by the Nazis as degenerate) even as traces of its ideology surface. Again, as is usual, Derrida may have expected his audience to be aware of such a controversy, even if he himself did not take pains to frame these issues in this way.

Somewhat related to the suspension point above is that Derrida's interrogation of Heidegger on Trakl relates tangentially to Derrida's "Shibboleth" on Paul Celan which Derrida gave as a lecture in 1984, the year in which he delivered the beginning of *Fantom*. Celan, of course, is in the role of fantom of the other throughout much of the lectures on Trakl/Heidegger, and particularly in the later ones, because at issue is circularity (the anniversary of the date in Celan) and what Derrida calls archaeology and eschatology. "[Celan] gives himself over to the inscription of invisible dates: anniversaries, rings, constellations, and repetitions of singular and unrepeatable (*unwiederholbar*) events."[34] The invisible in Celan concerns the unwritten: *Gedicht*. In Celan, as in Trakl, "discontinuity is the law; discontinuity and that which nonetheless gathers in the discretion of the discontinuous, that which gathers in the caesura of the relation to the other, in the interruption of address."[35] Celan is indebted to Trakl's attenuated poesis, his disaggregation within aggregation, a characteristic that enables Heidegger to jump from verse to verse within Trakl's corpus. However, the more major point here is Derrida's own retroactive reading of Trakl and Heidegger via Celan that reinflects the history of National Socialism from a certain Jewish point of view active in the shadow of Trakl's poetry as interpreted by Heidegger, and reflected in *Of Spirit* when Derrida starts out with the striking Celanian statement recalling the Holocaust: "*Je parlerai du revenant, de la flame et des cendres* (I shall speak of revenance, of flame, and of ashes)." That is to say, he will speak of the specters of mass murder in a way that Heidegger avoids: "... *et de ce que, pour Heidegger, éviter veut dire* (and of what, for Heidegger, *avoiding* means)." One might well wonder if Heidegger's abstract appeal to a proper or right race or type concerns such avoidance even as it serves as a racial marker.

Avoidance and Suspension

Not only did Heidegger publicly avoid mention of the Holocaust, with very rare exceptions, but, as was noted earlier, he also avoided mention of the social or society. Methodologically in his readings of poetry he also avoided the most basic literary critical protocol of gathering sufficient evidence for an interpretation. This latter "method" of avoidance (*Vermeidung*), as Derrida understands it, is most acute in the twelfth lecture, given that Heidegger only cites two lines from "*Abendländisches Lied*" ("Occidental Song").[36] Here it is not just the method of avoiding the poem in its entirety that is at stake, though this is what Derrida emphasizes, but the fact that Heidegger has but one overriding issue that catches his interest: that of the double stroke of *Schlag/Geschlecht*. "What interests us in all this is a certain thinking of the two, of difference as duality and the interplay between these dualities."[37]

Line one of "*Abendländisches Lied*" reads "O nocturnal wing-beat of the soul: (*O der Seele nächtlicher Flügelschlag:*)." Between this and the next verse of interest to Heidegger are two colons, the first following line one, the second following line twenty. Derrida points out that the first colon leaves the wingbeat suspended ("*laissent suspend ce 'coup,' ce* Schlag").[38] For Heidegger the text that appears between the colons is *avoidable*, merely "everything that follows, even to the transition from descent to ascent." However, what commands attention is mention of "*E i n Geschlecht*." This puts enormous pressure on Flügel*schlag* (wing-beat) and the one *Geschlecht* for which Heidegger will substitute the words "*des rechtes Schlages*." Even the very ending of the poem seems negligible to Heidegger who replaces the figure of "the lovers" with "the tribes of mankind" that are restored by means of the "*one* generation" (if not sex, kin, or race) to "the stiller childhood." The blow or stroke that unifies *Geschlecht* "prompt[s] the soul to set out toward the 'blue spring'" that is mentioned in a poem cited by Heidegger entitled "In the Dark" ("Im Dunkel").³⁹

Derrida notes that Heidegger has no other interest than in the *Schlag*, which is why Heidegger ignores the poem's composition and the figures that form or displace one another. If there is an exception, it would be the double colons, which Derrida thinks relates to the two wings of the bird and its beat (*Schlag*).

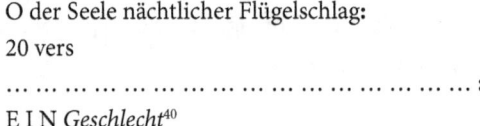

O der Seele nächtlicher Flügelschlag:
20 vers
… … … … … … … … … … … … … … … … :
E I N *Geschlecht*⁴⁰

Derrida wonders, are the two colons really one? In other words, should we superimpose them so that "E i n Geschlecht" immediately follows "*Flügelschlag*"? And should we not then consider these two words to be like the wings themselves beating up and down? There's more: the wing-beat is to be identified with the number two (the two strokes discussed earlier in the course), whereas the one *Geschlecht* obviously denotes oneness. Juxtaposed they posit the paradox of two being one and one being two, something that is inherent in the colon as signifier, mark, type. Does the *E I N Geschlecht* respond to the more inceptual *Flügelschlag*? Derrida thinks so and remarks that we need to pay attention to the dualities of two wings, two colons, two words for race, and the two lovers as a gamut of doubles.

Most important, of course, is Derrida's continued emphasis upon there always being two strokes separated by a hiatus, which in "*Abendländisches Lied*" Derrida locates in the suspension indicated by the colons (the double points). The soft wingbeat of the bird—or initial stroke—is followed by the making of a *Geschlecht* that implies a certain violence by means of a second stroke, whether it be sexual congress, bearing children, disciplining familial relations, discriminating between endogamy and exogamy, wherein difference holds open identity. It is in this context that the importance of Trakl's title is to be noted, namely that the title names the place or *Ort* where the one kind is located, a place that is itself of the right kind: "*des rechtes Schlages*." It is in this place that the lovers are situated as one *Geschlecht* (generation, gender, race, kind).

At about this point Derrida transitions to the thesis of "Geschlecht I" about Heidegger's avoidance of the topic of sexuality, something that is confirmed yet once again in Heidegger's commentary on "*Abendländisches Lied*" insofar as Heidegger skips over and thereby *avoids* the lovers in the final stanza.

O, the bitter hour of decline,
When we behold a stony countenance in black waters.
But in radiance the lovers lift the silver eyelids:
O n e gender. Incense flows from rosy pillows
And the sweet song of the resurrected.

O, die bittere Stunde des Untergangs,
Da wir ein steinernes Antlitz in schwarzen Wassern beshaun.
Aber strahlend heben die silbernen Lider die Liebenden:
E i n Geschlecht. Weihrauch strömt von rosigen Kissen
Und der süße Gesang der Auferstandenen.[41]

Jim Doss and Werner Schmitt in their helpful inclination to translate, more literally than not, offer the word "gender" for *Geschlecht*, which of course is at variance with the plurisignatious suggestion of "right kind" and the term Derrida is offering, namely "sex," not that this exhausts the possibilities as suggested above in parentheses. That the lovers are one is, of course, a familiar trope in lyrics where mystical union, as in the metaphysical poetry of John Donne, is affirmed in a context that marries Christianity with Neo-Platonism. In such poetry, sexual, corporeal difference melts away as the lovers achieve spiritual unity, at least, insofar as they are embracing one another in the act of making love.

Trakl's poem, however, can hardly be considered a love lyric, merely because it is largely a poem about bygone times, "times of peaceful stillness and golden autumns/When we peaceful monks pressed the purple grape." There is talk of what seem to be ghostly warriors "awakened out of wounds and starry dreams," "the ancient tone of the cricket," of shepherds who once "moved along dusking forests (*dämmernden Wäldern*)." Stanza four summarizes by apostrophizing the "bitter hour of decline" wherein is contrasted a stony or petrified profile, appearance, or look of a face or visage—whether animal or man is left ambiguous—with the radiance of the lovers who open their eyes. Precisely what "one gender, race, sex, tribe, or kind" has to do with any of the preceding is a matter of free association as is so much in Trakl's poetry wherein narrative cohesion is as illusory and subject to disaggregation as it is persuasively compelling as a sustained reverie, fantasy, or dream.[42] Indeed, that Derrida didn't offer a lecture on Trakl's *Traumdeutung* or dreamwork in a Freudian key (Trakl and Freud were both writing their best work in the 1910s) is surprising, given that Heidegger readily engages in free associations that repress sexuality, even as there is a conspicuous return of the repressed in the word *Geschlecht* in which sex and race can't be entirely dissociated. That said, the contrast of the stony appearance with the radiant lovers is perhaps readable enough in terms of promise: that of the renewal of the land in contrast to what of the past has been memorialized in memory and stone. To put it most directly, the lovers represent rebirth. In that context, "o n e race" or one (national) people, to extrapolate a bit, would be the logical denotation for what the lovers are to inaugurate and set in motion as future generations. For Heidegger, however, this would be too crudely inceptual and therefore not inceptual enough, which is probably why he ignores the lovers altogether from the perspective of his own reworking of the history of Being.

What matters to Heidegger is the wing-beat or double stroke inherent in *Geschlecht* that both unifies and divides it. What matters is *Schlag* as/and *Geschlecht*, to say nothing of "das E I N."

> The emphatic "one *Geschlecht*" contains the key note in which Trakl's poetic work silently sounds the mystery. [*Dieses betonte 'Ein Geschlecht' birgt den Grundton, aus dem das Gedicht dieses Dichters das Geheimnis schweigt.*] The unity of the one kinship [*einen Geschlechtes*] arises from the race [*Schlag*] which, along "the lunar paths of the departed," gathers together and enfolds the discord [*Zwietracht*] of the generations into the gentler two-fold [*Zwiefalt*]—which does so in virtue of its apartness [*Abgeschiedenheit*], the stiller stillness reigning within it, in virtue of its "forest sagas," its "measure and law." [*Die Einheit des einen Geschlechtes entquillt dem Schlag, der aus der Abgeschiedenheit her, aus der in ihr waltenden stilleren Stille, aus ihren "Sagen des Waldes" "aus ihrem" "Mass und Gesetz" durch "die mondenen Pfade der Abgeschiedenen" die Zweitracht der Geschlechter einfältig in die sanftere Zwiefalt versammelt.*]

Heidegger continues:

> The "one" in "one *Geschlecht*" does not mean one as opposed to two. Nor does it mean the monotony of dull equality. "One *Geschlecht*" here does not refer to a biological fact at all, to a "single" or "identical" gender [*Eingeschlechtlichkeit, Gleichgeschlechtlichkeit*]. In the emphatic "one *Geschlecht*" there is hidden that unifying force which unifies in virtue of the ghostly night's gathering blue [*der versamelnden Bläue der geistlichen Nacht einigt*]. The word speaks from the song wherein the land of evening is sung. Accordingly, the word "*Geschlecht*" here retains the full manifold meaning mentioned earlier. For one thing, it names the historical generation of man, mankind as distinct from all other living beings (plants and animals). Next, the word "*Geschlecht*" names the races, tribes, clans, and families of mankind. At the same time, the word always refers to the twofoldness [*Zwiefalt*] of the sexes.

> The blow [*der Schlag*] which marks the tribes of mankind as the simple oneness of "*one Geschlecht*," and thus restores them and mankind itself to the stiller childhood, acts by prompting the soul to set out toward the "blue spring." [*Der Schlag, der sie in die Einfalt des "Einen Geschlechts" prägt und so die Sippen des Menschengeschlechtes und damit dieses selbst in das Sanfte der stilleren Kindheit zurückbringt, schlägt, indem er die Seele den Weg in den "blauen Frühling" einschlagen läßt.*][43]

Peter Hertz's translation is awkward from the standpoint of Derrida's close reading of Heidegger's German in which versions of *Schlag* appear and in which there is yet another double or pair instantiated by the words *Zwietracht* and *Zwiefalt*, discord and twofold, terms that are themselves deconstructively interlaced. Of importance to Derrida is how discordance and twofoldedness relate to the *Schlag* or *coup* in terms of an inceptual violence that inceptually deconstitutes the difference of one and two (really, the one and the many) and that is also undecidably destructive and gentle, differentiating and gathering. In that sense the blow or *coup* conforms to what in the 1960s Derrida called "la différance."

Consequently, Derrida asks yet again how to think the unity of the E i n *Geschlecht*, given that it is so internally divided (hence the spacing of the letters in *ein*), and not only that, but divided by an inceptual violence that can be localized as a blow or even two blows. Of course, this violence is not quite so easily contained, given that it inheres in de-cease, setting apart, departing, twofoldedness (*Flügelschlag*), the dissension of the sexes, serenely as the break of day, and so on. *Der Schlag* is the strike that stamps or casts a people (but perhaps also brother and sister) as "*one Geschlecht*" (one generation) and as such is said to restore them to what Heidegger references as the stiller childhood, one in which, by way of Trakl, we are to understand a social relation innocent of pernicious dissension (i.e., of the social per se as we live it). But does that then presuppose homogeneity (of kin, generation, race, etc.) to be a social and individual panacea? Is *one Geschlecht* but a synonym for homogeneous being-in-the-world? Does this realize a political longing for the elimination of "others" who by their very interestedness introduce discord? This might well be so were it not for the fact that *Geschlecht* isn't etymologically homogeneous nor even singular, given its synonym, *Schlag*, a point Heidegger incipiently stresses with the implication that there is no peace within *Geschlecht*, even if peacefulness is thinkable. In thinking along these lines, Derrida writes of peacefulness and dissension:

> The stroke or lineage, *der Schlag* [*Le coup, ou la souche, der Schlag*], is thus that which gathers (and therefore constitutes the place). It gathers simply, into simplicity [*einfältig*], the dissension (the agonistic duality) into the gentle and

tender duality. The stroke gathers the *Zwietracht* [dissension] into a *Zwiefalt* [two-fold]. It is thus the stroke that beats two times two, two dualities or differences of *Geschlecht*, two sexual differences, albeit not only sexual, and the signification of sexuality is enveloped here in the polysemy of *Geschlecht*.[44]

Recall the statement in "Geschlecht II" that Derrida wasn't sure whether *Geschlecht* was a word or not. In the passage above, *Geschlecht* is seen less as a word than as a mark or sign for a (dis)appropriative occurring whereby beings are gathered under the stamp of a particular genus as *one* kind that is internally divided into two genders: male and female. Of importance is that accord and discord characterize not just a state of being but a social state of existence in terms of which the social relation is established, something Derrida explores at length in his later lecture course on the politics of friendship where the friend/enemy distinction of Carl Schmitt comes into play. That the social relation is "given" or "posited" inceptually within Heidegger's handling of *Schlag* is something Heidegger himself characteristically resists, which may be why he is so interested in Trakl wherein the social relation undergoes decease, suspension, or abandonment. Metaphorically, the animals that scatter upon being approached would be quite indicative of social avoidance.

Derrida continues:

> It is perhaps when the sexual sense separates itself and determines itself as only sexual that discord appears, discord and the war of the sexes. It is the simplicity and the tenderness of the difference that is announced as the future of what is very old in the departure or the *dis-cès*, moving beyond the Platonic-Christian Occident. The gentle difference, insofar as it is tied up with a stroke [*un coup*], and also because it is bound up with a lineage [*une souche*], is an imprint [*une empreinte*]. This imprint coins the one [*cette empreinte frappe le un*]—the unity of the one into the two—and we come to see that the one is not opposed to two, and truth to tell, cannot even be distinguished from it.[45]

Derrida takes this a step further in suggesting that the blow also "coins the word that gathers into one, into the very gathering unity of the word *Geschlecht*, its multiple significations, from which, in one single mark, all the strokes come, one single word, a word which itself says gathering."[46] The "*Ge*" of *Geschlecht*, Derrida suggests, is itself a stroke of the pen that speaks gathering. Given Derrida's discourse, it is clear that invoking *one Geschlecht* as simple homogeneity is not a viable conceptual option.

Derrida will take up a notion of dividedness as fold in order to argue that *Zwiefalt* and *Einfalt* are neither the same *nor* different as well as *both* the same and different in a manner that follows the logic of a negative theology, which Derrida himself invokes. Then too there is recourse to paronomasia: "*Der Schlag schlägt ... die Sprache spricht ... das Ereignis ereignet* (the stroke strikes ... language languages ... the event eventuates)."[47] This requires one to carry over identity into difference and difference over into identity and could be said to mark the time of a certain wingbeat that keeps such words up in the air, as if hovering in suspension. "Every predication on the subject of *Schlag* presupposes some sort of striking," a repetition of beating. Such beating suggests to Derrida that the unity of the one is not a given or a fact; rather, it is viewed as a movement if not a desire. Not one or a unity of one, there is unifying movement. Is this striking a pulse, like the wingbeat, a keeping of percussive sounds in suspension as that which hovers or is kept aloft? If so, questions about temporality could be asked. If the *Schlag* is a pulse that keeps time, one might wonder if the generations temporally mark the wingbeats of a division into kinds.

The Path, the Circle, the Revenant

Derrida doesn't launch into a discussion about time. Rather, he will make three broad points about *Schlag* within which there are many opportunities for expansion. (1) Derrida will discuss the *Schlag* in terms of opening up. He speaks about how the strike strikes, and says that the blow (*frappe*), contrary to what we might think, doesn't sign or seal in the sense of sealing up, enclosing, or concluding, because the blow is, in fact, a broaching or opening up, *un frayage* (breaking open the way; *Bahnung* in German). Its violence or at least its force exerts itself as the piercing through of the way, the breaking open, which is to say, the fracture, the effraction in light of a passage and a perspective of a passage way, or *Weg*.[48] Opening the way is a liberation, Derrida says, initiated by a violence (really, an originary violence) that sets the soul on the path toward the land of evening. Putting the soul on the path by means of a *Schlag* is to be considered an impressing of movement and its track on the soul as it goes toward the "blue spring." However, by means of such an opening the fixity of the imprint on the soul is relieved: lifted.

(2) Derrida's second point touches on circularity. Derrida says that according to the problematic figure of the circle of which he spoke the last time, the path, once opened up, leads back to a primeval or inceptual moment whose earliness always already precedes the early.[49] This can be symbolized by Trakl's "blue spring" or by thinking in terms of a dawn before dawn. More than what is most

matinal, the matutinal is itself a broaching or opening up, a consequence of *Schlag*, that is promising and as such is a promise open to the future, one that will lead back to inception.

In order to comprehend what is gathered inceptually, Derrida invokes the French idiom of *la veille*: "a good word here for gathering, in French, all of these significations."[50] There is *veiller* in the sense of guarding and protecting in the safety of a certain vigilance or "watch," or *veiller* in the sense of what has happened yesterday, the most matinal of yesterday's morning. *Veiller* would include the evening coming to the *Abendland*, the place and time where one is on nightwatch. *Veiller* also means eve and therefore relates to, say, a time such as Christmas Eve where one is on watch for what will happen at and after the break of day in terms of a promise of what is to come, no doubt, eschatologically, though Derrida doesn't say so. The return or *retour*, Derrida says, signifies the relations between *les veilles*. Derrida is quite perceptive in seeing that *veiller* as a word embraces *earliness* (the eve before), *vigilance* (the watch), but also *sheltering* (in Heidegger's vocabulary, concealment). Indeed, the break of day is being considered a *Schlag* insofar as it instantiates an opening that differentiates night from day, hence temporalizing *la veille* in terms of a reference to yesterday (to what comes before) as well as to a vigilant futural watching for the return of what is paradoxically most early: the inceptual trait or *An-fang*. Hence the circularity of Heidegger's path.

(3) Derrida's third point about *Schlag* circles back to *Fantom*'s preoccupations with nationalism. Here Derrida opens up an issue to which he will return in the lecture course of the following year on *Mythos, Logos, Topos* wherein he engages with writings by Nicole Loraux on Athenian funeral orations in *Children of Athena* and Ernst H. Kantorowicz's *The King's Two Bodies*. This concerns the nation or *patrie* in terms of "rassemblement en retour," gathering in terms of returning: the king's return after death in which his spirit gathers people together as a national people. This theme will later occupy Derrida's reading of *Hamlet* in *Specters of Marx* in which the return of the murdered king *fails* to gather or assemble a people. In *Hamlet* the return of the ghost signifies *Unfug*: chaos, the out of joint, the moral collapse of the state, the need for political rectification that Hamlet will ultimately fail to bring about.[51] Whereas in Shakespeare the return of the king is relatively an individual matter (that of Hamlet and his compatriots), in the context of Kantorowicz's book, the spiritual return of the king is a public matter absolutely foundational to a conception of the nation that like the king's two bodies is divided into a physical and spiritual opposition. We can even see this in Fichte, hardly a Medieval thinker, whose *Addresses* invoke a

spiritual German nation that is inherently one in contrast to a physical collection of many individual principalities. Fichte's *Addresses* are, of course, meant to deliver a blow to what he considers to be German consciousness, to introduce a blow whereby the German spirit returns in order to pull a people and a land together.

In *Mythos, Logos, Topos*, Derrida speaks of return in the context of the death of the king and his lost body. Because the king is eternal, one doesn't confuse him with the empirical body, that is, with the possible disappearance of his empirical body, because living or dead this possible disappearance is the very structure of royalty, of the royal function as the condition of the national estate. The king may be dead and his body lost, but he always returns. This is not contradictory, but consistent with *"le roi ne meurt jamais."* When one says the king never dies, one means that the function of the monarch (of what is royal) is incarnate and imperishable, as a principle of inalienability of property, and of national sovereignty. The person can die, but royalty never, which means that the king dies as empirical individual, but not as king. "*Le roi est mort, vive le roi* (the king is dead, long live the king)." Fundamental to the national, then, is an eternal return of that which cannot die that has disappeared, an eternal return from a condition of absence (decease) fundamental to many of Trakl's lyrics that are holding vigil in order to witness return. In *"Abendländisches Lied,"* that witnessing concerns observing the opening of the lovers' silver eyelids.

The Decline of Spirit

In "The Letter on Humanism," discussed by Derrida in the previous lecture, it was already made quite clear that the concept of the modern nation-state is precisely what Heidegger rejects on the grounds that it is metaphysical and also technological in the sense of being an apparatus established for the sake of dominating the earth, which Heidegger repudiates. In *What Is Called Thinking*? Heidegger explicitly insists that the men and women of his time are not up to the task of husbanding the earth, given that they are merely capable of engineering (*praxis*). In *Introduction to Metaphysics*, which may have been somewhat influenced by Ortega y Gasset's *Revolt of the Masses* of a few years earlier, Heidegger writes that "the spiritual decline of the earth has progressed so far that people are in danger of losing their last spiritual strength, the strength that makes it possible even to see the decline [which is meant in relation to the fate of 'Being'] and to appraise it as such."[52] In such instances, Heidegger is speaking to the world as a thinker of the world, not just of the German region of Baden. His complaint about "the reduction of a people to a mass" (Ortega's chief complaint) is spoken from a cosmopolitan perspective, though it is inflected from the position of being a German thinker who supposedly can think more authentically (inceptually, truly) on account of embodying the German language whose linguistic heritage is up to the task.

Derrida is well aware that Heidegger's repudiation of the nation-state and the spiritual decline of the earth put him at odds with both nationalism and cosmopolitanism, the one based on a metaphysics of place, the other on a metaphyics of the human. Moreover, Heidegger's *"valeur de retour"* and *"rassemblement en retour,"* gathering in turn, in return(ing), relate to a so-called schema of return that in the Heideggerian context Derrida will not flatly identify with nationalism, though he notes that the schema of return invokes the word "*Heimkunft* without which nationalism is difficult to imagine."[53] One could push this further, say, into issues of expansionism and colonization, he says, but time is limited.

In accord with Derrida's resistance to equate Heidegger's discourse with nationalism or the nationalistic, there has been and continues to be an avoidance of equating *Schlag* with that of *souche* (stock, kin, kind, and, by extension, race). This avoidance may be reminiscent of the rubric Derrida himself formulated as the title for an essay, "How to Avoid Speaking: Denials" (1986), in which avoidance and postponement are correlated. One avoids saying something in order to return to it later. Not reading *Schlages* as a word pregnant with the word *Schlag* may well be the kind of avoidance that avoids and postpones a certain identification. To bring out this feature of Derrida's exegesis, it is worth noting Hertz's translation of a passage that Derrida renders in French with a considerable number of asides in parentheses. Hertz's translation reads:

> Trakl's poem sings of the land of evening. It is one single call that *the right race* may come to be, and to speak the flame of the spirit into gentleness.[54]

The French translation by Jean Beaufret and W. Brockmeier, copiously amended by Derrida, reads as follows:

> La poésie de Trakl [dit Heidegger] chante *das Land des Abends* [le pays du soir]. Elle [*die Dichtung*] est un unique appel [*ein einziges Rufen*] à l'appropriation [mais c'est aussi l'événement; nach dem *Ereignis*] de la juste frappe [*des rechten Schlages*] qui transfigure [dit la traduction étrangement pour "spricht"] la flamme de l'esprit en douceur apaisée [*der die Flamme des Geistes ins Sanfte spricht*].[55]

Clearly, the translation Derrida adapts *makes no mention whatsoever of race*, whereas Hertz evidently thought that Heidegger must have been talking primarily about "the right race." Earlier in the course, as we saw, Derrida left Heidegger's invocation of "the right kind or race" in abeyance. But here one can't help noticing that Derrida himself is speaking and translating in a way *that is actively avoiding the mention of race*. Above, Derrida equates "*des rechten Schlages*" as a transitive and transformative event. Was this intended to repeat Heidegger? Notice that in "Die Sprache im Gedicht" Heidegger engages in denial when he insists that "*one Geschlecht*" "does not refer to a biological fact at all" or to a single gender. Rather "one *Geschlecht*" is to be considered a trait in which is hidden "that unifying force which unifies in virtue of the ghostly night's gathering blue."[56] The one *Geschlecht* is therefore not to be considered a word with ostensive reference but something more inceptual akin to the *logos*, discussed in numerous other texts by Heidegger, that concerns an appropriative eventfulness of gathering and unification. This modality of "one *Geschlecht*" speaks to the just, initial stroke. However, Heidegger does inherently acknowledge what Derrida identifies as the malign second stroke or curse whereby a *Geschlecht* is ex-pressed that has the capacity to name "the races, tribes, clans, and families of mankind," if not the "twofoldness of the sexes." Is the first stroke the denial and/or withdrawal of the second? Is the retreat from affirming race always already given in the first stroke?

Certainly, the two strokes recall the division between *Gedicht* and *Dichtung* wherein the first takes priority over the second in terms of muting it. Derrida, in translating "*des rechtes Schlages*" as "*la juste frappe*" (the just stroke or blow), considers this to be an inceptual stroke that transitively transfigures the flame of spirit ("*la flamme de l'esprit*"), which can become incendiary and evil, into something gentle, peaceful, and good. In the historical context of race, the Jew, and the German, which concerned Derrida considerably in the 1980s, the avoidance of Hertz's readerly interpretation of *des rechtes Schlages* as the right race by means of favoring an inceptual just stroke obviates a violence of flame and ash that could be associated with racism. This, then, is itself a moment wherein something terrible is being transformed and countered by an inceptual gentleness wherein social division is withdrawn, suggesting an inceptual stepping back from manifestations of genocide. Yet, isn't this inceptual moment an event (i.e., an *Er-eignis*) in which violence, however gentle, is destined?

Inceptual Language

As if to change the subject, in alluding to remarks made earlier in the course on Fichte with respect to the ambiguities of the nationalism-cosmopolitanism divide, Derrida asks if it would be an abuse to ask if "*cette juste frappe*" in its association with all that is gentle might not have an essential relationship with the possibility of language, and, in particular, German, which now could be considered an inceptual *Sprache* or language relative to the *Abendland* (or Europe) insofar as it precedes any specific nationalist identity. Such an inceptual notion of language relates once more to *Gedicht*, "*cette parole silencieuse*" (this silent speech) that concerns German as unsaid. "*L'Allemagne comme ce qui est tu par cette parole silencieuse, comme ce qui est chanté*" ("German as that which is silenced [left unsaid] by this silent speech, as that which is sung").[57] In other words, the singing associated with the poem withdraws into a silence or not-saying that is linguistically inceptual, though not to such a point where what one could identify as German is eradicated. Paradoxically, even as Heidegger posits an inceptual notion of language in whose eventfulness of appropriation Europe is invoked most authentically anterior to any metaphysics or Christianity, let alone any sort of nationalism, it is still the *German* language that is at issue, inceptually. This is reminiscent of Fichte's conundrum whereby one wants to have one's nationalism and one's cosmopolitanism too without risking contradiction.

Derrida implicitly justifies Heidegger's invocation of German by emphasizing the performativity of language as a creative, constitutive force as opposed to a medium of representation. What Derrida in the essay "Envoi" calls the "gathered sending of Being" concerns a transitive movement that in *Fantom* linguistically performs the sending as a poetry that must return to "a more originary and powerful envoi." As Derrida puts it, "No doubt … in the gathering of the *envoi* and of destinality, the *Geschick* does not have the form of a *telos*, still less of a certainty (whether Cartesian or Lacanian) of the arrival at destination of the envoi. But at least there is (*es gibt*) an envoi, a sending."[58] The performativity of sending, in other words, avoids the kind of representationality that would presuppose an identity, system, or structural end point. "The *Geschick*, the *Schicken*, and the *Geschichte* of which Heidegger speaks are not sendings of the representative type. The historiality they constitute is not a representative or representable process, and in order to think it, we need a history of Being, of the *envoi* of Being that is no longer regulated or centered on representation."[59] This Heideggerian principle, if we can call it that, is foundational to Derrida's reading of "Die Sprache im Gedicht" insofar as the performativity of *Geschlecht* and *Schlag* elude static, preconceived representations that are formally concretized, given that such words are not words, quite, but rather transmissions of the gathered sendings of Being. In a passage where Derrida once more attempts to define the type of word that *Geschlecht* is, he says that *Geschlecht* resembles at the very least a sort of negative theology, one that negates a logic of S is P.[60]

Returning to the Return

The thirteenth and final lecture of *Fantom* begins with the announcement that this will be the last lecture before Easter and that Derrida will go abroad. Playing on the phrase *"je dois me rendre à l'étranger"* ("I must go abroad"), Derrida somewhat humorously puts himself in the role of the stranger in Trakl who journeys and who will inevitably return to the homeland—in Derrida's case, Paris. His reference to Easter is also motivated in that it is meant to broach a Christian dimension in Trakl's poetry concerning resurrection that Heidegger has been so eager to avoid and deny. At issue in this lecture, then, will be the motif of return, "the motif that I have emphasized so much last time."[61] In returning to the return in the closing pages of Heidegger's "Die Sprache im Gedicht," Derrida is going to finish his exegesis of Heidegger without contextualizing it in terms of *Fantom* as a whole in which the themes of the stranger, return, and homecoming are so relevant generally—e.g., in terms of Adorno and Arendt. Of course, the stranger who returns in Trakl is hardly the Jewish stranger coming back to his or her former homeland, but in *Fantom* this Jewish context is inherently relevant to "Die Sprache im Gedicht" insofar as it emphasizes themes such as race, the stranger, exile, return, and homeland, if not the malign *Schlag* that Heidegger calls a curse. More than likely, Derrida was already thinking about aspects of what in a later course he calls the problematic of "the Jew, the German," which in the twelfth lecture we noticed had already included a certain allusion to or correspondence with Paul Celan, given how much the contemporaneous essay "Shibboleth" dovetails with *Fantom* in terms of the motif of circularity and return: the importance of the anniversary in Celan and of the return to the homeland in Heidegger. In contrast to Celan, however, the return in Heidegger is that of a return to an understanding of *patrie* (*Heimat*), no matter how much Heidegger wants to distance this from *Patriotismus*.[62]

As he does elsewhere, Derrida outlines an itinerary of subjects to be covered, one that he presents here in three main parts.

1. Derrida considers the promise (*Versprechen*) as (a) the determination of *das Land*, (b) the appeal to "la juste frappe" or proper stroke that is inceptual and gentle, (c) of a sexual difference without fold (*sans pli*)—which is to say, *différance*, (d) the gentleness of a break of day that manifests a return (its messianic dimension denied by Heidegger), and (e) the performativity of an injunction or assignation of God's speaking as a *Zusprechen* or assignation. Notable is Heidegger's mention that "God's speaking is the speaking which assigns to man a stiller nature ... (*Gottes Sprechen ist das Zusprechen, das dem Menschen ein stilleres Wesen zuweist*)."[63]

2. Derrida speaks of a return to the *Heimat*, which has to be taken idiomatically as a return to a more inceptual understanding of German than nationalists would be capable of imagining. Here German is related to place, though this place (*lieu*) needn't be identified with a national territory. What Heidegger attempts, according to Derrida, is a regaining of the *Heimat* through the step or *Schritt* and the hand (*Hand-Werk*). This entails an appropriation of the *Heimat* that goes beyond mere speaking.

3. Lastly, Derrida wants to justify yet another engagement with Heidegger, this time in the context of a course on nationalism and philosophical nationality ("*le nationalisme et la nationalité philosophique*"). Derrida clarifies that of interest to everyone should be not only Heidegger's propositions about speech, Christianity, Platonism, sexual difference, history, homeland, poetry, place, etc., but the method of Heidegger's reading: his manner of proceeding, interceding, and so on. We need to be mindful of Heidegger's interrogation of philosophy by means of considering the interlocution between thought and poetry and why such an interlocution requires "cette Allemagne-là," this here Germany. Not only does Derrida acknowledge that Heidegger interrogates philosophy but that he deconstructs it as well ("*et la déconstruit*").[64] Derrida acknowledges that his auditors may well be tired of such a slow exegetical march across Heidegger's essay on Trakl, not to mention Derrida's returning to Heiddegger over and over. Nevertheless, Derrida exclaims, "Encore Heidegger!"

In this last lecture, some of what has been noted in the itinerary above will be set aside, though there will be much discussion of notions of return and promise, especially since the inevitability of the return is connected with the fulfillment of the promise. Initially, however, Derrida wonders whether the place to which one returns is ever the same. Or if the person who returns is the same. Derrida has "the returns" of Heidegger in mind—before, during, and after the Second World War—in terms of intellectual prominence and moral infamy, certainly, but more importantly, for Derrida, in terms of philosophical relevance. Derrida, for example, has himself "returned" to Heidegger's invocation of *Geschlecht* at different times in his career and wants to know if this returning isn't itself as internally divided as the Heidegger who comes back, the one who in France made his appearances before and after the war. In 1985, Derrida says, the political questions that relate to Heidegger have changed, the corpus has altered, given publication of posthumous work, and so on. Hence once glimpses "*de nouveaux paysages*."

What is revealed and what is eclipsed (Derrida refers to "*ses eclipses*")?[65] Here one has to consider the fixity of a radiant solar presence versus the lunar blocking out of the sun, both of which speak to an eternal return or *ricorso*. That the thought of someone like Heidegger will return after each eclipse—say, that of the Heidegger affair, which was raging at the time—speaks to its promise and hence to a certain messianism: that despite attempts to forget or ban him from consideration, his work will reemerge at a future time because of its redemptive capacities, however those may be perceived. "Coming out from under a cloud, the same text, the same legacy (*legs*) is no longer the same, it turns about itself and again surprises us once more."[66] Derrida takes from Heidegger the idea that a thinker who does not accept the law of this eclipse and who does not calculate with it is not a thinker but merely a calculator who cannot calculate with the non-calculable. The point, of course, is that whereas the circularity of return ought to be calculable, as in the case of calculating the time of dawn each morning, that in fact one cannot predict the time when a body of work comes out of the state of being eclipsed (repudiated, forgotten, destroyed), if in fact it does reemerge at all. In the latter case, one would be speaking of the thinker as stranger in absolute terms as someone who does not return.

Trakl's lyrics are a meridinal writing, which is why Heidegger was so strongly attracted to him. "All thought is meridinal, Paul Celan had said, but it is meridinal either diurnally or nocturnally; it is to be found in the indecisive balance of the hours, within their milieu."[67] This quotation is not by Derrida or Heidegger, but by Alain Badiou who meditates on the diurnal at length in the opening pages to his seminal lecture course *Lacan: l'antiphilosophie 3* where he considers Hölderlin, Hegel, Nietzsche, Mallarmé, Valéry, Claudel, and Celan. For Mallarmé, we are told, midnight is a time of suspension in which something is anticipated and welcomed, in a way not unrelated to promising, when a waking is destined to come about within sleep. For Hölderlin the night is a time of setting to work. "This night is a recollection, a memory, which is the place where waking and sleeping reside edge to edge."[68] For Nietzsche's Zarathustra, midday is the time of truth when shadows are extinguished by the sun direct overhead. Hegel's well-known owl of Minerva takes flight only at dusk, says Badiou, because philosophy occurs when the events of day are over. If philosophy is the midnight of the thinker's day, it is so as the *après coup* of what has come to light regarding the truth of being.[69] Taking Badiou into account, one quickly realizes that Derrida's exploration of the meridinal in Trakl and Heidegger is part of a much larger constellation of writings requiring exposition and development. By way of a reading of Jean Beaufret, Badiou considers Heidegger as a thinker for whom the radiance of presence carries darkness and night within it in terms of a withdrawing of the truth at the moment of its bursting forth. This is quite in line with what Derrida was developing in the decade before Badiou gave his seminar and would be hardly surprising to painters such as Rembrandt, Poussin, and Georges de la Tour, or writers such as Virgil, Dante, Tasso, or Milton, for whom the absolutes of dark and light never obtain, given their ever transitioning temporality (see, for example, John Milton's "L'Allegro" and "Il Penseroso").

In terms of the transitioning of light and dark, Derrida himself was stating that Heidegger's thinking passes into and out of eclipse. "It's another surface of inscription, an other textual power ... linked to idiom" that cannot be ignored, because it is untranslatable even if paradoxically it is translatable enough.[70] Here clarity is always mixed with obscurity according to a certain circularity that may nonetheless be held open to the extent that the return is not assured: that a thinker's lifework might not reemerge from the dark.

Remembering, Gathering, Going Back

If Hölderlin and Hegel associated night with recollecting and remembering, Derrida thinks of memory, legacy, and the archive as returning after night has passed, a return to a new text of some sort that is preserved in memory as not just one but many inscriptions, many translations, each taking up the other by means of relay. This accumulation of traces in the same engram at once ecliptical and elliptical constitutes remembering. That man returns to something in thought in the morning by way of remembering involves the *Schlag*, the stamp of an imprint. Is this merely a matter of technique, purposely committing something to memory, or the result of something that weighs on memory? This speaks to a division familiar to readers of Marcel Proust: voluntary versus involuntary memory. The force of memory is its ability as *Schlag* to inscribe or write itself in many places simultaneously, to occupy many surfaces of mnemonic inscription, surfaces that return upon waking or after a time of being in eclipse.

In *What Is Called Thinking?* Heidegger associates memory with man, implying that memory marks an essential difference between man and animal.

> Memory is the gathering and convergence of thought upon what everywhere demands to be thought about first of all. Memory [*Gedächtnis*] is the gathering of recollection [*die Versammlung des Andenkens*], thinking back. It safely keeps [*birgt bei sich*] and keeps concealed [*verbirgt*] within it that to which at each given time thought must be given before all else, in everything that essentially is, everything that appeals to us as what has being and has been in being.[71]

Heidegger immediately continues by asserting that "thinking back to what is to be thought" is "the source and ground of poesy. This is why poesy is the water that at times flows backward toward the source, toward thinking as a thinking back, a recollection."[72] Stones and deer are not poets, but human beings may be, given their capacity to remember in a way that flows back to the source.

Previously in the seventh lecture of *Fantom*, Derrida had openly refuted *What Is Called Thinking?* on the man/animal distinction. In the final lecture we are considering, he is dubious that one could make a separation based on the determination that man remembers, whereas the animal does not. The doubt is introduced by way of citing the ending of Trakl's "End of Summer" ("*Sommersneige*").

> The green summer has grown
> So quiet; and the stranger's footstep
> Rings through the silver night,
> May a blue deer remember his path,
>
> The harmony of his spiritual years!
>
> [Der grüne Sommer ist so leise
> Geworden und es läutet der Schritt
> Des Fremdlings durch die silberne Nacht.
> Gedächte ein blaues Wild seines Pfads,
>
> Des Wohllauts seiner geistlichen Jahre!][73]

In Trakl it is the blue deer that is gathering and recollecting, perhaps even coursing toward the source of the spiritual year. The deer is the performative that commemorates. "It is this limit between two memories, as between animal and human, that is constantly coming into question in our seminar."[74] In laying some of the groundwork for *Of Spirit*, which considered the philosophemes of animal, technology, the question, and spirit, Derrida broaches issues of biological, technological, mental, and artificially programmed mnemonic structures, all of which concern a circular coming back or return.

The Stroke as Envoi

By way of another outline, this time very sparse, Derrida mentions (1) the experience of territory, (2) "of sexual territory," and (3) of return and *patrie*.

He then comes back to finishing the by now voluminous commentary on "Die Sprache im Gedicht," beginning with a consideration of Heidegger's summation that "Trakl's work sings the song of the soul, 'something strange on the earth,' which is only just about to gain the earth by its wandering, the earth that is the stiller home of the homecoming generation (*Trakls Dichtung singt den Gesang der Seele, die 'ein Fremdes auf Erden,' erst die Erde als die stillere Heimat des heimkehrenden Geschlechtes erwandert*)."[75] As noted earlier, counter to Plato and Christian theology, the soul returns to the earth, not to heaven, and in so doing has a salvific destiny. Derrida wants us to notice that it is to the earth and not to a nation that the soul returns. If there is mention of *Heimat*, it is not in nationalist terms ("patrie *n'a évidemment pas de sens nationale* [evidently *patrie* has no national sense or meaning]"),[76] but rather in terms of "*des heimkehrenden Geschlechtes*," the homecoming generations or peoples. Is this but a synonym for the coming back of a *Volk*? Derrida does not ask. *Heimat*, he argues, has the sense of *Geschlecht* that is not bound by a formal territory such as a nation-state, but rather to idiom and an inceptual place (*Ort*). Here, again, overlap with Fichte's *Addresses* is alluded to, for in Fichte the nation state is something as yet to come, something promised by *Geschlecht*. Given the contexts in Heidegger and Fichte, Derrida is quite keen on linking *Geschlecht* to a specific idiom of *Heimat* related to a history of destinal sending as opposed to humanity in an ahistorical universalizing sense.

Geschlecht is at issue precisely when "God's speaking (*Sprechen*) is the speaking (*ist das Zusprechen* [exhortation, consolation, encouragement]) which assigns to man a stiller nature, and so calls on him to give that response (*Entsprechung*) by which man rises from what is authentic ruin (*eigentlichen Untergang*) up into earliness (*die Frühe*)."[77] This repeats the trope of the two strokes in which the first mutes the second. In this case, the first stroke, which is gentle, is associated with inception, morning, the early. Indeed, the second stroke of division and ruin (death) even leads back to this inceptual stillness (rebirth). Related is Heidegger's statement that "the 'evening land' (*das 'Abendland'*) conceals the rising of the dawn of the '*one* generation (*birgt den Anfang der Frühe des* 'Einen *Geschlecht*)."[78] That is, the *Abendland* holds and conceals within itself the return of the one *Geschlecht*, which one could easily translate as sex, race, generation, and so on. However, because *Geschlecht* is itself defined in terms of a circularity or return, it strongly suggests generation. The statements above by Heidegger are central to what Derrida sees as a sort of master narrative that informs Heidegger's understanding of Trakl's corpus in which a return to the matinal plays a messianic role wherein a promise is both given and fulfilled.

Also of primary concern is the following statement by Heidegger.

> [Trakl's] poetry has no need of historical 'objects.' Why not? Because his poetic work is historical in the highest sense. His poetry sings of the destiny which casts mankind in its still withheld nature, that is to say, saves mankind.[79]

This last sentence by Heidegger, to which Derrida will return more than once, is of major importance, given its emphasis in German on *Schlag* and *Geschlecht*: "*Dichtung singt das Geschick des* Schlages, *der das* Menschengeschlecht *in sein noch vorbehaltenes Wesen* verschlägt, d. h. rettet." A more helpful English translation from the Derridean point of view might be: "His poetry [in the sense of *Dichtung* as opposed to *Gedicht*] sings the sending and dispensation of the *Schlag* [the blow, strike, knock] that saves humankind by driving it into its still withheld essence."[80]

Derrida will take his time in approaching this last sentence by means of going back to remarks by Heidegger concerning the stranger's footfalls (*schritte des Fremdlings*) on the earth. These steps resound in harmony (*tönen*) and in accordance with the softly sounding spirit (*"leisen Geist"*) of the ancient forest legend that represents the primeval forest. This legend, Derrida says, is that of a buried account or story about the country. What Derrida translates as *l'esprit des forêts* relates to the death of the generation (*Geschlecht*) of the fathers (alternatively, "*morte de la race des pères, ou le sexe des pères*"—death of the race or sex of the fathers), something that anticipates the lecture course of the following year, *Mythos, Logos, Topos*, in which Derrida will define *patrie* in terms of the return of the dead King: "the King is dead, long live the King!" In other words, Derrida already sees in Heidegger's reading of Trakl the impossibility of the death of the fathers who are buried in legend and the extent to which country is defined in terms of such an impossibility whereby an eternal return of the fathers' generation is inevitable.

Trakl's four versions of "*Abendland*," in fact, are strewn with the apparitions of ghostly figures, often in the form of shadows. In the lengthy second version of "Abendland," specters, shadows, angels, mere shapes (apparitions), and echoes are everywhere to be found as a metaphorical blossoming of the land. "Often this is love:/A blossoming thorn bush/Stirs the cold fingers of the stranger."[81] Relative to such blossoming, Derrida cites the beginning of part 3 of version 2: "So quiet are the green forests/Of our homeland." There too wanderers encounter the "thorny hedge." The homeless are, paradoxically, most at home insofar as they are in search of the inceptual where "the heart is reconciled in green silence" wherein the inceptual (*Ur-sprung* as *Ur-Schlag*?) is withdrawn and disclosed. Figures such as "the green silence" disclose a destiny other than that of the cities. For "mighty are the cities constructed/And stony on the plain;/ But the homeless one follows/The wind with open forehead (*Mit offener Stirne dem Wind*),/The trees at the hill."[82] Unlike the cities, the hills have their natural, proper measure. This speaks to Derrida's theme of monstrosity from "Geschlecht II" that in Heidegger's passage above takes issue with the great stone cities that have benefitted from the progress of a monstrous technology that one might call *unheimlich* (unhomely, uncanny). In Trakl it is as if the homeland is unhomely: *geistlich* (spooky).

In contrast, Heidegger invokes the *Abendhugel* (*coline du soir*, evening hill), which embodies *Abendland*. Derrida remarks that this insistence on *patrie*, as well as on the very old legend of the forest and on the loss of measure relative to technology, shows that Trakl is attentive to a certain historicity, though for Heidegger, Trakl rejects both the concepts of *Geschichte* and *Historie*: history as the occurring of events, and history as the representation of the past (*Vorstellen des Vergangenen*). Instead of such historical conceptions, Heidegger invokes the historical in terms of Trakl's singing the destinal. Derrida observes that for Heidegger poetry has no use for historical objects or historical representations, because its *Gedicht* merely opens the *possibility* for representation. The song, in other words, precedes *Vorstellungen*. The song does not represent objects as such but is a "historial" form of silently broaching events. Historically, as previously quoted, "*Seine Dichtung singt das Geschick des Schlages, der das Menschengeschlecht in sein noch vorbehaltenes Wesen verschlagt, d.h. rettet.*"[83] Trakl's poetry sings the sending, the envoi and the destiny, the dispensation. That which is assigned is signified in the gesture of sending, destining and addressing. This is the mission as emission: that which sends and destines a blow, a strike, and the resultant mark or imprint. At the beginning, Derrida says with an eye to other texts by Heidegger, is the sending of the mark, the strike or blow, as a gift or giving that comes even before being. Derrida then amends a French translation of Heidegger's sentence italicized above. "*Sa poésie chante [insister] l'envoi destinal de la marque, de la frappe, du coup, de l'empreinte qui* verschlägt (*qui frappe en séparant, en 'spécifiant' dit la traduction française*)."[84] Derrida adds that here it is a matter of a strike that separates in order to give its specificity, its originality, its proper (essential) mark, which is to say, its idiomaticity. At issue, is separation or division into kinds (*Geschlechter*) that concerns the casting of humankind (*Menschengeschlecht*).[85] In so doing, the *frappe* or *Schlag* bestows being in terms of *Wesen* (nature, essence, quidditas) and as such produces human race, a type or particular that wasn't in existence before. Putting matters slightly otherwise, it can be said that the *Schlag* as inceptual violence, however gentle, is the prime mover of differentiation, of what elsewhere Derrida spoke of in terms of dif-ference.

> "*Verschlägt*, d.h. rettet (*frappe de différence, c'est à dire sauvé*), sauvé le Menschengeschlecht." Ce coup sauve le propre de l'homme ... à la fois archi-originaire et à venir (selon le cercle ouvert dont nous parlions les fois dernières).
>
> ["*Verschlägt*, that is to say, saved (the blow of difference, that is to say, saved), saving humankind." The blow saves the proper of man, at once archi-originary and to come (according to the open circle of which we have spoken at previous times)].[86]

Earlier we recall how Derrida emphasized the two blows, the one gentle, the other harsh. In the passage above by Heidegger, Derrida notices the repetition of beating: *Schlag ... Verschlägt*. Because the first blow, stroke, or strike is inceptual (archi-original) it has the capacity to save the proper of mankind presumably because it holds something back in the *arché* to which one returns in order to be saved from ruination, as the stranger does in Trakl's poetry. Unclear is whether Derrida thinks this primordial stroke preserves the essence of the race, however gently, or whether it conceals or retreats from race as made externally manifest by means of the second stroke or blow that causes social division and strife.

In glossing the very end of Heidegger's statement concerning the saving of mankind's essence, Derrida avers that if the sending of the blow or mark bestows *le propre de l'homme*, it is to be considered a bestowal that saves and as such is more historial (inceptually historical) than any history insofar as it precedes and precludes the rhetoric of recounting histories. In other words, "*Ce salut est archi-originaire*," the dispensation of the blow is arche-originary. Here one has to pay attention to Derrida's French translation whereby the condition of being *Verschlägt* is associated with *salut* as a salvific term. *Salut* refers to blessing, rescuing, saving, as well as to release. The *salut* can be viewed as deliverance, which speaks to both giving and dispatching. This is one of those instances in which for Derrida a French translation illuminates a key word in Heidegger that otherwise remains obscure. The *salut* saves by conferring that essence whereby *Geschlecht* is held apart *in sein noch vorbehaltenes Wesen*, which is to say, reserved both inceptually (secretly, concealedly) and futurally (in terms of the promise, the sending, the destinal). Derrida notes that this speaks to the circularity incipient in "Die Sprach im Gedicht." What is kept in reserve as a sort of secret anticipates the promise associated with the *salut* that releases and saves. Derrida says there is no difference (no interval of time, distinction, break) between "*Verschlagen* and *Retten: frapper de différence et sauver.*" In other words, the cast saves. *The sending of the blow saves the human race in its being already held back in the promise of what is to come.* The song (*Flügelschlag*) of the poet participates in this event of reserving, dividing, dispatching, promising, and saving. Does the poetry of the poet instantiate a certain *Verschlagenheit* in the sense of a throwing off course—say, words such as *Geschlecht* and *Schlag*—due to some blow or *salut*? Derrida doesn't ask this question; rather, he focuses on the poem in terms of *Heimkehr*, a return to home.

The song of the poet, we are told, takes the form of a return back from the futural to the originary that was initiated inceptually in terms of the blow, the promise, and the *salut*. The movement toward the future is a return to the inception. Derrida cautions that the return isn't an accidental predicate or supplementary notion of habitat or *Heimat*, but the essential movement which constitutes or institutes originally the *patrie* or the *pays* as *promesse d'habitat*. *Heimat* isn't a place that one inhabits originally and to which one day, having left, one desires to return. *Heimat* (land, country) never appears as such but rather as the *promesse du retour*, even if in fact one hasn't really left it at all. This is what an inceptual notion of country announces: the return as promise, the return promised that is also necessarily and irreducibly a return of the promise. And this is what is sung in terms of "*la frappe de la différence comme salut: événement de la promesse même,*" the blow of difference as deliverance: event of the promise itself. Hence the phrase "*verschlägt d.h. rettet*" whereby one is destined to return no matter how far one has been blown off course, a meaning Derrida may well have had in mind. For, as Derrida puts it, the poetry of Trakl sings (as *Gedicht*) the soul which, as stranger to the earth, receives it in terms of its migration: the earth as "*patrie plus sereine,*" a *patrie* more peaceful, more serene. Does this constitute a right of return? This remains unexamined.

Springtime of the Soul

Derrida's final lecture closes around the notion of the early (*Früh*) as orient/ orientation, as the originary moment of an orientation to which one comes back. Heidegger's "Die Sprache im Gedicht" ends with consideration of Trakl's "Springtime of the Soul," which Derrida takes to be a return to an inception: primacy, commencement, spring. Spring in particular signifies a yearly opening and a promise, a greeting (*salut*) of the future. Its inception, Derrida notes, comes even before Spring, the season. This Spring or commencement also can be viewed as coming at the end of the seasons, as well. This is why, Derrida says, Heidegger distinguishes between *Verfall* and *Untergang*, fall and descent. The soul as stranger on the earth does not fall but declines on his trek to a point where there is an inclining that conducts one into what is early, *in der Frühe*—Spring.

> The poet sees the soul, "something strange," destined to follow a path that leads not to decay [or fall], but on the contrary to a going under [*Untergang*]. This going under yields and submits to the mighty death [*gewaltigen Sterben*] in which he who died early leads the way [*das der in der Frühe Verstorbene vorstirbt*].[87]

Derrida cites Heidegger's last phrase in French as "*meurt en montrant la voie*," "*mourir que meurt d'avance*," and also offers "*pré-meurt*" for "*meurt*" in order to access the undecidability of ending/beginning that holds open and in suspense, as it were, the closing of a circle. This death, insofar as there is one, Derrida says, is itself Spring ("*cette mort-là est le printemps*") and is that which comes and will come again in the future.

Acknowledging that the lyric is intoned by *Gedicht*, Derrida turns to the *Dichtung* of the personage who according to Heidegger is singing, namely the figure of the brother, the one who sings of dying a mighty death and whose power speaks to the accomplishment of an end that is also a beginning. Derrida notes that this death does not happen in Spring but is to be associated with the Spring as inception; hence, death is the moment of that which arrives and returns to the future. "Spring which comes at the end because it is at the beginning (according to the anniversary, the version of the year, the revolution of the seasons) ... and thus the opening of the year. It transfigures death or mourning into promise and in so doing greets/saves the future."[88] Moreover, the calling of the song belongs to the promise and the calling calls an essential event of poetizing essential to speech (poetically, *Dichtung*) that draws upon the transitive silence of *Gedicht*. The brother who sings the song dies powerfully (*gewaltig*), which means he goes under in order to arise. Derrida views this as messianic, a *theologeme* he has raised before in relation to Heidegger's eternal returning. It is the brother who accomplishes death in and as Spring (renewal, resurrection).

> There would be a lot to say from this point of view concerning the fact that the figure of the brother is the only one who gathers up this song [*la seule rassembler ce chant*]: neither the sister nor anyone else (not the father, the mother, the son, or the daughter). Would that be to say that all these 'familial' figures are specific figures of the brother [*sont des figures spécifiant le frère*], that not only father and son are brothers, which a certain kind of evidence could confirm, but

that mother and sister too are brothers, and above all those who do not belong [*n'appartiennent pas*] to the "generic" or genealogical family are brothers, the brother thus marking the rupture [*marquant ainsi la rupture*] with the family structure, the rupture or the surpassing [*dépassement*] or the emancipation, the friend following the brother (a figure of the fatherland [*patrie*] or, beyond the fatherland, of the brotherland [*la patrie dans la fratrie*])? Natality, naturality [*naturalité*], nationality, or else the contrary, the beyond of all that [*ou son au-delà*]? A question I leave in suspense.[89]

The main question, in other words, has turned to that of *ein Geschlecht* as family in terms of a withdrawal of differentiatedness required for a certain gathering of relations not just by the figure of the brother but *as* the brother, given that he is most primordial, the one who marks or inscribes a rupture not with the family but with its differentiated structure and in so doing is the principle of the one in and *as* whom all are assembled and identified. Does the figure of the brother surpass the fatherlandish? And is he thereby emancipated from nation and nationality? He is insofar as one cannot think of the brother as a citizen or inhabitant: that is, as an independent social subject. Rather the brother is sent as that ap-propriation within which the structure of the family is both withheld and expressed, given that the brother is the relative within whom identity and difference are most inceptually related. At least, this is the hypothesis that Derrida leaves in suspension. In "Geschlecht IV" Derrida will consider friendship in the context of *Mitsein* and *Mitdasein* in a way that may well recall the emphasis on brotherliness with which "Geschlecht III" came to a close. Just as "Springtime of the Soul" speaks of the song of the brother, in "Geschlecht IV" Derrida discusses the voice of the friend of which Heidegger speaks in *Being and Time*.

Relevant to the close of *Fantom*'s last lecture is that in the essay "The Way to Language," included in *On the Way to Language*, Heidegger points out that poetic saying is an abode that grants the quiet of mutual belonging (friendship? brotherliness?) in which the distinction between things yields to an eventfulness of appropriation whereby differences are suspended. Derrida sees this suspension in terms of an interchangeabilty of familial relations (brother for sister, etc.), though in "Springtime of the Soul" there is a yielding to gathering and identity of all things intoned by the ringing of the dark bell. Here the quiet of mutual belonging speaks to *ein Geschlecht*, one that has the authority of law. "*Das Ereignis ist das Gesetz, insofern es die Sterblichen in das Ereignen zu ihrem Wesen versammelt und darin hält*" (The event of appropriation is the law insofar as mortals are gathered into the appropriateness [or ownness] of their nature and there holds them)."[90]

Like many other of his lecture courses, *Fantom of the Other* does not end with a recapitulation but stops in *medias res* with a certain unstated promise that nothing that was said will be forgotten and not taken up at some later point. The suspicion (or hypothesis, to put it more plainly) that Nazism is written in the letter of philosophical nationalism will be taken up the following year in coming back to the issue of home and placed in the context of the Athenian understanding of *chora*, which Derrida, after Nicole Loreaux, views as a nationalist philosopheme that presupposes a blood and soil mythos of the Athenian hero as autochthonous countryman. There, too, being of one *Geschlecht* is paramount, though Derrida does not mention the German term. However, he does seize on a passage in Plato's *Menexenus* in which there is talk of the departed and their return to what Heidegger would have called the *Ort* of the inceptual. Quoting Aspasia's funeral oration, Socrates tells us,

> For they were good because they were sprung from good fathers ... And first as to their birth. their ancestors were not strangers, nor are these their descendants sojourners only, whose father have come from another country, *but they are of the children of the soil, dwelling and living in their own land.* And the country (*chora*) which brought them up is not like other countries, a stepmother to her children, but their own true mother; *she bore them an nourished them and received them,* and in her bosom they now repose. It is meet and right, therefore, that we should *begin by praising the land which is their mother* ... The country is worthy to be praised, not only by us, but by all mankind—first, and above all, as being dear to the gods. [...] The second praise which may be fairly claimed by her is that at that time when the whole earth was sending forth and creating diverse animals, tame and wild, *she our mother was free and pure from savage monsters, and out of all animals selected and brought forth man,* who is superior to the rest in understanding, and alone has justice and religion.[91]

Socrates goes on to remark, "for woman in her conception and generation is but the imitation of the earth."[92] Hence she is in essence like the earth who brings forth being. The earth as mother, however, is the one who has "out of all animals selected and brought forth man," a *Geschlecht* superior to other beings. Derrida's citation of this passage in *Mythos, Logos, Topos* is hardly accidental, given how strongly it interconnects with the lectures on Trakl without ever mentioning this fact. This new lecture course will dwell at length on conceptions of "khōra" that Derrida published separately as a short monograph by that name. There, once more, Derrida returns to the topic of genesis as a problematic of the inceptual conditions of producing kinds. In that context, *Khōra* is analogous to *Geschlecht* as *Schlag* in terms of producing kinds. In *Menexenus* this production of kinds is always already bound up with the kind of philosophical nationalism that presupposes exceptionalism, superiority, and the sanctity of place. As to the Athenian people, they are to be considered elect, not only as being human as opposed to being merely animal, but as a superior race of men (*Genos*). Not only that, but their particular exceptionality is thought to be something that would have to be universally accepted, a point Derrida makes in *Mythos, Logos, Topos* wherein he ties much of this material back into the opening sections of *Fantom* on the national-cosmopolitan. Here, for the time being, Heidegger will be eclipsed, not that his burning flame won't cast shadows on much that Derrida will be delivering in this new term of 1985–86 wherein the problematics of *Fantom* will be recast and recast again as if by heavy philosophical blows.

Notes

1 Derrida, *Geschlecht III* (Paris: Seuil, 2018), 119. "Certains d'entre vous se demandent peut-être si cette attention un peu méticuleuse et microscopique que nous portons à la lettre d'un texte de Heidegger sur un poète depuis quelques semaines ne nous éloigne pas de notre sujet et des grandes questions de la nationalité ou du nationalisme philosophiques."
2 Martin Heidegger, "Letter on Humanism," in *Basic Writings* (New York: Harper, 1977), 217. Derrida excerpts from this passage: *Geschlecht III*, 121.
3 Heidegger, "Letter on Humanism," 217.
4 Ibid.
5 Ibid., 218.
6 Ibid.
7 Ibid., 221.
8 Ibid., 218.
9 "Remembrance," in *Elucidations of Hölderlin's Poetry*, trans. Keith Hoeller (Amherst: Humanity Books, 2000), 116.
10 Derrida, *Geschlecht III*, 123.
11 Heidegger, "Language in the Poem"; in *On the Way to Language*, trans. Peter D. Hertz (New York: Harper, 1971), 194. *Unterwegs zur Sprache*, 77. Hertz's translation is modified as he leaves out reference to "our language" that by implication is the German language.
12 Ibid., 194.
13 Ibid.
14 Derrida cites p. 186 of the Neske publication of *Unterwegs zur Sprache* ("Das Wesen Der Sprache") in which Heidegger speaks of language and withholding. "If

language everywhere withholds its nature in this sense, then such withholding is in the very nature of language. Thus language not only holds back when we speak it in the accustomed ways, but this holding back is determined by the fact that language holds back its own origin and so denies its being to our usual notions" (Hertz trans., 82). This indicates once again that Derrida realized the relation between the inceptual in Heidegger and withholding/withdrawing. Given that he had read *Parmenides*, he had probably gained considerable context for this dynamic.

15 Martin Heidegger, "The Nature of Language," in *On the Way to Language*, 81.
16 Heidegger, "Language in the Poem," 194.
17 Ibid., 175.
18 Ibid., 176.
19 Ibid.
20 Heidegger, "Letter on Humanism," 233. Note that ethics is not defined socially in terms of relationships among people, something that underscores my earlier point about Heidegger's allergy to the social.
21 Heidegger, "Language in the Poem," 174.
22 Heidegger, "Letter on Humanism," 233.
23 Derrida, *Geschlecht III*, 134.
24 Derrida mentions that *heißen* isn't meant by Heidegger to mean to give an order but in the sense of protecting and conserving. To call has to do with drawing something near.
25 Heidegger, "Language in the Poem," 194.
26 Ibid., 195. The question of what the flame is seems to defy definition. Derrida discusses it in *Of Spirit* wherein spirit's association with the flame is identified already by Heidegger with evil. Derrida makes a connection with Old Testament Hebrew in which *ruah raa* is associated with an evil spirit. However, Derrida doesn't go into the lengthy associations of fire with holiness, purity, wrath, punishment, etc. In *Of Spirit*, fire appears to metaphorically stand for the dynamism of difference in its most effractious and consuming form of manifestation. There one gets the strong impression that for Derrida *zoe, pneuma, psyche, nous, esprit, Geist* (and its variants) are combustible, given that they concern passion: inflaming. Such in-flaming is, presumably, "beyond good and evil." Of course, fire is inceptual in Heraclitus and in antiquity was understood as both creatively life giving and catastrophically destructive: a good and an evil.
27 Martin Heidegger, *What Is Called Thinking?*, trans. J. Glenn Gray (New York: Harper and Row, 1968), 58.
28 Ibid., 60.
29 Ibid., 63.
30 Martin Heidegger, *Nietzsche*, vol. 2, trans. David Farrell Krell (San Francisco: Harper, 1979), 215.

31 Ibid., 216.
32 Ibid., 217.
33 Heidegger, "Language in the Poem," 195. "Die Sprache im Gedicht," 79.
34 Jacques Derrida, "Shibboleth," in *Midrash and Literature*, ed. G. Hartman and S. Budick (New Haven: Yale University Press, 1986), 308.
35 Ibid., 309.
36 Georg Trakl, "Abendländisches Lied," in *The Last Gold of Expired Stars: Complete Poems, 1908–14*, trans. Jim Doss and Werner Schmitt (Sykesville: Loch Raven Press, 2010), 128–9. This is a dual language publication in German/English.
37 Derrida, *Geschlecht III*, 143. "Ce qui nous intéresse dans tout cela, c'est une certaine pensée du deux, de la différence comme dualité et le jeu entre plusieurs dualités."
38 Ibid.
39 "Im Dunkel," 2nd version in Trakl, *The Last Gold of Expired Stars*, 154–5. "*Es schweigt die Seele den blauen Frühling* (The soul silences the blue springtime)." As in the case of Friedrich Hölderlin, Trakl's poems have been published in their different versions that can differ considerably.
40 Derrida, *Geschlecht III*, 143.
41 Trakl, *The Last Gold of Expired Stars*, 130–1.
42 In this context, polysemy and dissemination relate to Trakl's poems generally as gathering-dispersal. Illusory is the sense one has that any given poem is a whole that when decoded will be coherent when, in fact, individual lines pull away from each other or resist synthesis in a way that risks aggressive dissociation and dehiscence.
43 Heidegger, "Language in the Poem," 195. "Die Sprache im Gedicht," 79. Translation modified.
44 Derrida, *Geschlecht III*, 147. Translated in David Krell, *Phantoms of the Other* (Albany: SUNY, 2015), 204.
45 Ibid. Krell's "coins" could be translated more literally as "strikes."
46 Ibid.
47 Ibid., 207.
48 Derrida, *Geschlecht III*, 151.
49 Ibid.
50 Ibid. "La vielle est un bon mot ici pour rassembler, en français, toutes ces significations …."
51 Jacques Derrida, *Specters of Marx* (London: Routledge, 2006).
52 Martin Heidegger, *Introduction to Metaphysics*, trans. Gregory Fried and Richard Polt, 2nd ed. revised (New Haven: Yale University Press, 2014), 42. Brackets supplied by editors.
53 Derrida, *Geschlecht III*, 152.
54 Heidegger, "Language in the Poem," 195.

55 Derrida, *Geschlecht III*, 156.
56 Heidegger, "Language in the Poem," 195.
57 Derrida, *Geschlecht III*, 156.
58 "Envoi," in *Psyche: Inventions of the Other*, vol. 1, trans. Peggy Kamuf and Elizabeth Rottenberg (Stanford: Stanford University Press, 2007), 121.
59 Ibid., 110.
60 Derrida, *Geschlecht III*, 148–9.
61 Derrida was about to go to Chicago to deliver "Geschlecht II" at Loyola University, which was holding a conference on March 22–23, 1985. "Motif sur lequel j'ai beaucoup insisté la dernière fois." *Geschlect III*, 159.
62 Derrida, *Geschlecht III*, 160.
63 Heidegger, "Language in the Poem," 196. "Die Sprache im Gedicht," 79.
64 Derrida, *Geschlecht III*, 161.
65 Ibid.
66 Ibid., 162. "Sortir du nuage, et le 'même' texte, le même legs n'est plus le même, il tourne sur lui-même et surprend encore."
67 Alain Badiou, *Lacan: Anti-Philosophy 3*, trans. Kenneth Reinhard and Susan Spitzer (New York: Columbia University Press, 2018), 9. *Lacan: L'Antiphilosophie 3 1994–1995* (Paris: Fayard, 2013), 20. "Tout pensée est meridienne, aurait dit Paul Celan, mais elle est méridienne diurne ou nocturne; elle est dans la balance indécise des heures, le milieu des heures."
68 Ibid., 10. "Cette nuit est une souvenance, une mémoire, qui est le lieu où l'éveil et le sommeil sont bord à bord," 21.
69 Ibid., 13. In French, 23.
70 Derrida, *Geschlecht III*, 162. "… une autre surface d'inscription, une autre puissance textuelle … liée a l'idiome."
71 Heidegger, *What Is called Thinking?*, 11. *Was Heisst Denken?* in *Gesamtausgabe* I:8 (Frankfurt am Main: Klostermann, 2002), 13.
72 Ibid., 23. In German, 26.
73 Trakl, *The Last Gold of Expired Stars*, 148.
74 Quoted in Krell, *Phantoms of the Other*, 216. Derrida, *Geschlecht III*, 164.
75 Heidegger, "Language in the Poem," 196. "Die Sprache im Gedicht," 80.
76 Derrida, *Geschlecht III*, 165.
77 Heidegger, "Language in the Poem," 196. "Die Sprache im Gedicht," 79.
78 Ibid. Hertz's translation has "holds" in place of "conceals."
79 Ibid.
80 Heidegger, "Language in the Poem," 195. "Die Sprache im Gedicht," 79.
81 This is version 2 of the poem. Trakl, *The Last Gold of Expired Stars*, 433.
82 Ibid., 431.
83 "Die Sprache im Gedicht," 80.

84 Derrida, *Geschlecht III*, 169. French translation of Heidegger: "La parole dans l'élément du poème, Situation du Dict de Georg Trakl," in *Acheminement vers la parole*, trans. J. Beaufret, W. Brokmeier, and F. Fedier (Paris: Gallimard, 1976), 81. In English as cited earlier, "His poetry sings of the destiny which casts mankind in its still withheld nature—that is to say, saves mankind." Heidegger, *Language in the Poem*, 196.

85 Derrida, *Geschlecht III*, 170.

86 Ibid.

87 Heidegger, "Language in the Poem," 197. "Die Sprache im Gedicht," 80.

88 Derrida, *Geschlecht III*, 174. "*Frühling* qui vient à la fin parce qu'il est au début (selon l'anniversaire, la version de l'année, la révolution des saisons) *est donc l'ouverture de l'année … il transfigure la mort ou le deuil en promesse et en salut de l'avenir.*"

89 Derrida, *Geschlecht III*, 176, trans. David Krell, *Phantoms of the Other*, 222. French text has been added in brackets for reference.

90 Heidegger, "The Way to Language," 128. In *Unterwegs zur Sprache*, 259. Translation modified.

91 Plato, *Collected Dialogues*, ed. Edith Hamilton and Huntington Cairns (Princeton: Princeton University Press, 1975), 237 b, c, d, p. 189. Italics mine.

92 Ibid.

Bibliography

Adonis. *Selected Poems*. Translated by Khalid Mattawa. New Haven: Yale University Press, 2010.

Adorno, Theodor. "Education after Auschwitz." In *Critical Models*. Translated by Henry W. Pickford. New York: Columbia University Press, 1998.

Adorno, Theodor. "Im Flug erhascht." In *Gesammelte Schriften*. Vol. 20. No. 2. Edited by Rolf Tiedemann, Gretel Adorno, Susan Buck-Morss, and Klaus Schultz. Frankfurt am Main: Suhrkamp, 1970–86.

Adorno, Theodor. *The Jargon of Authenticity*. Translated by Knut Tarnowski and Frederic Will. Evanston: Northwestern University Press, 1973.

Adorno, Theodor. "On the Question: 'What Is German?'" In *Critical Models: Interventions and Catchwords*. Translated by H.W. Pickford. New York: Columbia University Press, 1998.

Alain Badiou, *Lacan: Anti-Philosophy* 3. Translated by Kenneth Reinhard and Susan Spitzer. New York: Columbia University Press, 2018.

Arendt, Hannah. "On Humanity in Dark Times: Thoughts about Lessing." In *Men in Dark Times*. New York: Harcourt Brace, 1968.

Arendt, Hannah. *The Origins of Totalitarianism*. New York: Harcourt, 1968.

Arendt, Hannah. "Was bleibt? Es bleibt die Muttersprache." In Günter Gaus, *Zur Person: Porträts in Frage und Antwort*. Munchen: Feder Verlag, 1965.

Arendt, Hannah. "'What Remains? The Language Remains': A Conversation with Günter Gaus." In *Essays in Understanding: 1930–54*. New York: Schoken, 1994.

Arendt, Hannah and Martin Heidegger. *Letters 1925–1975*. Translated by Andrew Shields. New York: Harcourt, 2004.

De Peretti, Cristina et al. *Derrida Lecteur de Heidegger (après les Cahiers noirs)*. Coimbra: Palimage, 2018.

De Tocqueville, Alexis. *Democracy in America and Two Essays on America*. Translated by G.E. Bevan. London: Penguin Books, 2003.

Derrida, Jacques. *The Beast and the Sovereign*. Edited by Michel Lisse, Marie-Louise Mallet, Ginette Michaud. Translated by Geoffrey Bennington. Chicago: Chicago University Press, 2009.

Derrida, Jacques. "Des Tours de Babel." In *Difference in Translation*. Edited and translated by Joseph F. Graham. Ithaca: Cornell University Press, 1985.

Derrida, Jacques. "Deconstruction in America." *Journal of the Society for Critical Exchange* 17 (Winter 1985): 1–33.

Derrida, Jacques. "Envoi." In *Psyche: Inventions of the Other*. Vol. 1. Translated by Peggy Kamuf and Elizabeth Rottenberg. Stanford: Stanford University Press, 2007.

Derrida, Jacques. "Le facteur de la verité." In *The Postcard*. Translated by Alan Bass. Chicago: Chicago University Press, 1987.

Derrida, Jacques. "Fichus: Frankfort Address." In *Paper Machine*. Stanford: Stanford University Press, 2005.

Derrida, Jacques. "Force of Law: The Mystical Foundation of Authority." In *Deconstruction and the Possibility of Justice*. Edited by Drucilla Cornell, Michel Rosenfeld, and David Gray Carlson. Translated by Mary Quaintance. New York: Routledge, 1992.

Derrida, Jacques. "From General to Restricted Economy: A Hegelianism without Reserve." In *Writing and Difference*. Translated by Alan Bass. Chicago: University of Chicago Press, 1978.

Derrida, Jacques. "Geschlecht I: Sexual Difference, Ontological Difference." In *Psyche: Inventions of the Other*. Vol. 2. Stanford: Stanford University Press, 2007.

Derrida, Jacques. "Geschlecht II: Heidegger's Hand." In *Deconstruction and Philosophy*. Edited by John Sallis. Translated by John P. Leavey, Jr. Chicago: University of Chicago Press, 1987.

Derrida, Jacques. *Geschlecht III: Sexe, race, nation, humanité*. Edited by Geoffrey Bennington, Katie Chenoweth, and Rodrigo Therezo. Paris: Seuil, 2018.

Derrida, Jacques. "Geschlecht IV: Heidegger's Ear, Philopolemology." In *Reading Heidegger*. Edited by John Sallis. Translated by John P. Leavey. Bloomington: Indiana University Press, 1993.

Derrida, Jacques. *Given Time: I. Counterfeit Money*. Translated by Peggy Kamuf. Chicago: Chicago University Press, 1992.

Derrida, Jacques. *Glas*. Translated by John P. Leavey and Richard Rand. Lincoln: University of Nebraska Press, 1986.

Derrida, Jacques. *Of Grammatology*. Translated by G.C. Spivak. Baltimore: Johns Hopkins, 1976.

Derrida, Jacques. "Honoris Causa." In *Points: Interviews 1974–94*. Translated by Peggy Kamuf. Stanford: Stanford University Press, 1995.

Derrida, Jacques. *Khora*. In *On the Name*. Translated by David Wood and J.P. Leavey. Stanford: Stanford University Press, 1995.

Derrida, Jacques. "Living On: Borderlines." In *Deconstruction and Criticism*. Translated by James Hulbert. New York: Seabury Press, 1979.

Derrida, Jacques. *Monolinguism of the Other*. Translated by Patrick Mensah. Stanford: Stanford University Press, 1998.

Derrida, Jacques. "Onto-Theology of National-Humanism (Prolegomena to a Hypothesis)." Translated by Geoffrey Bennington. *Oxford Literary Review* 14, no. 1 (1992).

Derrida, Jacques. *The Other Heading*. Translated by Pascale-Anne Brault and Michael B. Naas. Bloomington: Indiana, 1992.

Derrida, Jacques. *Parages*. Edited and translated by John P. Leavey et al. Stanford: Stanford University Press, 2011.

Derrida, Jacques. "Passions: An Oblique Offering." In *On the Name*. Translated by David Wills. Stanford: Stanford University Press, 1995.

Derrida, Jacques. *The Politics of Friendship*. Translated by George Collins. New York: Verso, 1997.

Derrida, Jacques. *The Post Card: From Socrates to Freud and Beyond*. Alan Bass. Chicago: Chicago University Press.

Derrida, Jacques. *The Problem of Genesis in Husserl's Philosophy*. Translated by Marian Hobson. Chicago: University of Chicago Press, 2003.

Derrida, Jacques. "The Retrait of Metaphor." In *Psyche: Inventions of the Other*. Vol. 1. Translated by Peggy Kamuf and Elizabeth Rottenberg. Stanford: Stanford University Press, 2007.

Derrida, Jacques. "Sauf le nom." In *On the Name*. Translated by J.P. Leavey. Stanford: Stanford University Press, 1995.

Derrida, Jacques. "Shibboleth: For Paul Celan." In *Sovereignties in Question*. Edited by Thomas Dutoit and Outi Pasanen. New York: Fordham University Press, 2005.

Derrida, Jacques. "Some Statements and Truisms about Neo-Logisms, Newisms, Postisms, Parasitisms, and Other Small Seismisms." In *States of Theory*. Edited by David Carroll. Translated by Anne Tomiche. New York: Columbia, 1990.

Derrida, Jacques. *Specters of Marx*. Translated by Peggy Kamuf. London: Routledge, 1994.

Derrida, Jacques. *Of Spirit*. Translated by Geoffrey Bennington and Rachel Bowlby. Chicago: University of Chicago Press, 1989.

Derrida, Jacques. "At This Very Moment in This Work Here I Am." In *Psyche: Inventions of the Other*. Vol. 1. Translated by Peggy Kamuf and Elizabeth Rottenberg. Stanford: Stanford University Press, 2007.

Derrida, Jacques. "Transfer Ex Cathedra: Language and Institutions of Philosophy." Vol. 2 of *The Right to Philosophy*. Translated by Jan Plug et al. Stanford: Stanford University Press, 2004.

Detsch, Richard. *Georg Trakl's Poetry*. University Park: Pennsylvania University Press, 1983.

Doohm, Stefan Müller. *Adorno: A Biography*. Translated by Rodney Livingstone. Cambridge: Polity, 2005.

Faulkner, William. *Light in August*. New York: Vintage, 1990.

Fichte, J.G. *Addresses to the German Nation*. Translated by Gregory Moore. Cambridge: Cambridge University Press, 2008.

Fichte, J.G. *Reden an die deutsche Nation*. Berlin: Holzinger, 2014.

Foucault, Michel. "My Body, This Paper, This Fire." In *History of Madness*. Edited by Jean Khalfa. Translated by Jonathan Murphy and Jean Khalfa. London: Routledge, 2009.

Foucault, Michel. *Society Must be Defended*. Translated by David Macey. New York: Picador, 2003.

Graziano, Frank. "A Biocritical Introduction." In *The Dark Flutes of Fall, Critical Essays on Georg Trakl*. Edited by Eric Williams. Columbia, South Carolina: Camden House, 1991.

Habermas, Jürgen. *The Structural Transformation of the Public Sphere*. Translated by Thomas Burger. Cambridge: MIT, 1989.

Harries, Karsten. "Language and Silence: Heidegger's Dialogue with Georg Trakl." *Boundary 2*, 4, no. 2 (1976).

Janicaud, Dominique. *Heidegger in France*. Translated by F. Raffoul and D. Pettigrew. Bloomington: Indiana University Press, 2015.

Heidegger, Martin. "Building, Dwelling, Thinking." In *Poetry Language, Thought*. Translated by Albert Hofstadter. New York: Harper and Row, 1975.

Heidegger, Martin. "Concerning 'The Line.'" In *The Question of Being*. Translated by William Kluback and Jean T. Wilde. New Haven: College and University Press, 1958.

Heidegger, Martin. *Contributions to Philosophy (From Enowning)*. Translated by Parvis Emad and Kenneth Maly. Bloomington: Indiana University Press, 1999.

Heidegger, Martin. *Contributions to Philosophy (of the Event)*. Retranslated by Richard Rojcewicz and Daniela Vallega-Neu. Bloomington: Indiana University Press, 2012.

Heidegger, Martin. "Evening Conversation." In *Country Path Conversations*. Translated by B.W. Davis. Bloomington: Indiana University Press, 2005.

Heidegger, Martin. *Gesamtausgabe 94: Überlegungen II–VI (Schwarze Hefte 1931–38)*. Edited by Peter Trawny. Frankfurt am Main: Vittorio Klostermann, 2014.

Heidegger, Martin. *Gesamtausgabe 95: Überlegungen VIII–XI (Schwarze Hefte 1938–39)*. Edited by Peter Trawny. Frankfurt am Main: Vittorio Klostermann, 2014.

Heidegger, Martin. "Hölderlin's Earth and Heaven." In *Elucidations of Hölderlin's Poetry*. Translated by K. Hoeller. Amherst: Humanities, 2000.

Heidegger, Martin. *Introduction to Metaphysics*. Translated by Gregory Fried and Richard Polt, 2nd ed. revised. New Haven: Yale University Press, 2014.

Heidegger, Martin. "Language in the Poem." In *On the Way to Language*. Translated by Peter Hertz. New York: Harper and Row, 1971.

Heidegger, Martin. "Letter on Humanism." In *Basic Writings*. Edited by David Farrell Krell. Translated by Frank A. Capuzzi et al. New York: Harper and Row, 1977.

Heidegger, Martin. *Letters to His Wife: 1915–70*. Translated by R.D.V. Glasgow. Cambridge: Polity, 2008.

Heidegger, Martin. *Nature, History, State*. Translated by Gregory Fried and Richard Polt. London: Bloomsbury, 2013.

Heidegger, Martin. *Nietzsche*. 4 vols. Translated by David Farrell Krell. New York: HarperCollins, 1982.

Heidegger, Martin. "Origin of the Work of Art." In *Poetry, Language, Thought*. Translated by Albert Hofstadter. New York: Harper and Row, 1975.

Heidegger, Martin. *Ponderings II–VI: Black Notebooks 1931–38*. Translated by Richard Rojcewicz. Bloomington: Indiana University Press, 2016.

Heidegger, Martin. *Ponderings VII–XI: Black Notebooks 1938–39*. Translated by Richard Rojcewicz. Bloomington: Indiana University Press, 2017.

Heidegger, Martin. "Remembrance" in *Elucidations of Hölderlin's Poetry*. Translated by Keith Hoeller. Amherst: Humanity Books, 2000.

Heidegger, Martin. "Die Sprache im Gedicht: Eine Erörterung von Georg Trakls Gedicht." In *Unterwegs zur Sprache*. Pfulligen: Günther Neske, 1986.

Kant, Immanuel. *Anthropology from a Pragmatic Point of View*. Edited by R.B. Louden. Cambridge: Cambridge University Press, 2006.

Killy, Walther. *Über Georg Trakl*. Göttingen: Vandenhoeck und Ruprecht, 1960.

Krell, David Farrell. *Intimations of Mortality*. University Park: Pennsylvania University Press, 1986.

Krell, David Farrell. *Phantoms of the Other*. Albany: SUNY, 2015.

Lacan, Jacques. "Seminar on the Purloined Letter." In *Ecrits*. Translated by Bruce Fink et al. New York: Norton, 2002.

Librett, Jeffrey S. *The Rhetoric of Cultural Dialogue*. Stanford: Stanford University Press, 2000.

Marx, Karl and Friedrich Engels. *The German Ideology*. Amherst: Prometheus Books, 1998.

Norton, Robert. *Secret Germany: Stefan Georg and His Circle*. Ithaca: Cornell University Press, 2002.

Plato. *Collected Dialogues*. Edited by Edith Hamilton and Huntington Cairns. Translated by F.M. Cornford et al. Princeton: Princeton University Press, 1975.

Rajchman, John and Cornel West. *Post-Analytic Philosophy*. New York: Columbia, 1985.

Rapaport, Herman. "Performativity as Ex-Scription: Adonis after Derrida." In *Performatives after Deconstruction*. Edited by Mauro Senatore. London: Bloomsbury, 2013.

Riecke, Jörg, ed. *Duden: Das Herkunftwörterbuch, Etymologie der deutschen Sprache*. Vol. 7. 5th ed. Mannheim: Dudenverlag, 2014.

Sauermann, Eberhard. *Die Rezeption Georg Trakls in Zeiten der Diktatur*. Vol. 12. Brenner Forum Innsbruck: Studien Verlag, 2016.

Schlegel, Friedrich. "On Philosophy. To Dorothea." In *Theory as Practice: A Critical Anthology of Early German Romantic Writings*. Translated by Jochen Schulte-Sasse et al. Minneapolis: University of Minnesota Press, 1997.

Schlegel, Friedrich. "Über die Philosophie An Dorothea (1799)." In *Kritische Ausgabe*. Vol. 8. Edited by Ernst Behler and U. Struc-Oppenberg. Munich: Ferdinand Schöningh Verlag, 1975.

Schmölzer, Hilde. *Dunkle Liebe eines wilden Geschlechts*. Tübingen: Francke, 2013.

Senatore, Mauro. *The Germ of Death: The Problem of Genesis in Jacques Derrida*. Albany: SUNY, 2018.

Therezo, Rodrigo. "Preface." In *Geschlecht III*. Paris: Seuil, 2018.

Trakl, Georg. *The Last Gold of Expired Stars: Complete Poems 1908–14*. Edited and translated by Jim Doss and Werner Schmitt. Sykesville, Loch Raven Press, 2010.

Weber, Max. *Wirtschaft und Gesellschaft*. Tubingen: Mohr, 1956.

Wittgenstein, Ludwig. *Culture and Value*. Translated by Peter Winch. Chicago: Chicago University Press, 1984.

Wittgenstein, Ludwig. *Notebooks 1914–1916*. Translated by V.E.M. Anscombe. 2nd ed. Chicago: University of Chicago Press, 1979.

Wittgenstein, Ludwig. *Tractatus Logico-Philosophicus*. Translated by D.F. Pears and B.F. McGuinness. London: Routledge and Kenan Paul, 1974.

Index

Adonis (Esber, Ali Ahmed Saïd) 4–5, 12, 69–76, 83–5, 98
Adorno, Theodor 4–5, 7–8, 12–13, 35, 40, 63, 68–9, 74, 83–4, 91–2, 98, 146, 194, 217
  "Im Flug erhascht" ("Caught in Flight") 56
  Jargon of Authenticity, The 41–2, 60
  Minima Moralia 25
  nationalist ideology 40–2
  "On the Question 'What Is German'?" 47–8
  Philosophy of New Music 57
Arendt, Hannah 4–5, 7–8, 12, 25, 31, 42, 47, 56, 63, 66, 69, 74, 83–92, 94, 97–8, 146, 194, 217
  Lessing Prize speech 84–6, 90
  Men in Dark Times 84
  Origins of Totalitarianism 90–1

Badiou, Alain 219–20
Bataille, Georges 110, 180
Baudrillard, Jean 63
Beaufret, Jean 122, 143, 214, 219
Beethoven, Ludwig 51
Benjamin, Walter 7–8, 83, 106
Bonaparte, Louis Napoleon 65
Brokmeier, Wolfgang 143, 214
Buber, Martin 7, 83

Celan, Paul 7, 11, 83, 204, 217, 219
Chamberlain, Houston Stewart 127
Cohen, Hermann 7, 83

Derrida, Jacques
  Answering for the Secret 1
  "At This Very Moment in This Work Here I Am" 7
  Beast and the Sovereign, The 1, 13 n.2, 43 n.17, 65
  Death Penalty 1
  Eating the Other (Rhetorics of Cannibalism) 1, 61, 115

Force of Law 7, 106
"Fors" 11, 174
"Geschlecht I" 6, 103, 106, 108, 112, 120, 122, 178, 181, 206
"Geschlecht II" 5–6, 50, 103, 107–8, 110, 113, 117, 119, 121–3, 135–6, 138, 148, 150, 159, 171, 210, 224
"Geschlecht III" 6, 103, 106, 135–6, 164, 228
"Geschlecht IV" 6, 103, 200, 228
Given Time: I. Counterfeit Money 116
Glas 178–81
Of Grammatology 23, 94, 97, 169, 171–4
Hostility and Hospitality 1
"How to Avoid Speaking: Denials" 214
Kant, the Jew, the German 1, 7, 25
Khōra 146–8, 229
Language and the Discourse of Method 17, 20, 63
"Le Facteur de la vérité" 140
"Living On: Border Lines," 72–3
"Loyola Typescript" 5, 117, 135
Mythos, Logos, Topos 1–3, 24, 193, 212–13, 223, 229–30
Onto-Theology of National-Humanism (Prolegomena to a Hypothesis) 5
Other Heading, The 165–8
Perjury and Pardon 1
Philosophical Nationality and Nationalism 1, 20
Politics of Friendship 1–2, 86, 90, 104, 210
Post Card, The 9, 11–12, 14 n.15, 116
Problem of Genesis in Husserl's Philosophy, The 148
Questions of Responsibility 1
Retrait of Metaphor 105
"Shibboleth" 7, 204, 217
Specters of Marx 2, 11–12, 56, 113, 212
Of Spirit 6, 29, 31, 78, 103, 121, 136, 163, 172, 221
Testimony 1

Theological-Political, The 1, 7, 24, 31, 83, 109
Descartes 19, 63–4, 68, 95
  Discourse on Method 18
Dilthey, Wilhelm 95
Dōgen, Master 22
Doohm, Stefan Müller 54–6, 59

Emad, Parvis 143, 153
Engels, Friedrich 48, 52, 83, 109
  German Ideology, The 9, 35–6, 38, 41

Feuerbach, Ludwig 37, 39
Fichte, Johann Gottlieb 42, 47–51, 56, 60, 64, 66–70, 72, 75–8, 83, 91, 109, 127, 139, 158, 195, 215–16
  Addresses to the German Nation 3–5, 8–9, 24, 26–7, 29, 31, 37–8, 108, 112, 196–8, 212–13, 222
  on national identity 24–35
Foucault, Michel 63, 96–7, 104–5
  History of Madness 95, 100 n.33

Gasset, Ortega y 214
  Revolt of the Masses 213
Gaus, Günter 84, 88–91
Goethe, Johann Wolfgang von 19, 51, 83, 195
Grün, Karl 35, 37, 39–41, 52, 83

Hegel, Georg Wilhelm Friedrich 19, 39, 80, 83, 179–80, 219–20
  Phenomonlogy of Spirit 59
  Science of Logic 59
Heidegger, Elfride 87–8
Heidegger, Martin 66, 69–70, 83, 96–7, 114
  Being and Time 31, 36, 114, 119, 163, 189 n.139, 228
  Black Notebooks, The 28, 30–1, 93, 94, 107, 126, 171
  "Building, Dwelling, Thinking" 105
  Christian Onto-Theology 175–9
  Contributions to Philosophy (of the Event) 126–7, 143
  Introduction to Metaphysics 8, 30, 213
  "Letter on Humanism" 31, 139, 194, 196–7, 200, 213
  Nietzsche II 151, 154
  "Origin of the Work of Art" 105

Parmenides (seminar) 75, 119, 171
Elucidations of Hölderlin's Poetry 196
Specters of Marx 2, 11–12, 56, 113, 212
"Time and Being." 136
What is Called Thinking? 59, 113, 115–16, 119, 136, 145, 202, 213, 220–1
"Who Is Nietzsche's Zarathustra?" 203
Heine, Heinrich 40
Hertz, Peter 123, 146, 164–5, 209, 214–15
Hess, Moses 37, 39
Hölderlin, Friedrich 11–12, 19, 28–9, 36
  Andenken 197
  Homecoming 194–5
Holocaust 5, 205
Horkheimer, Max 54–5, 59
Hume 52–3

Immendorf, Georg 26
  Café Deutschland series 26, 50

Janicaud, Dominique 143–4
Jaspers, Carl 41, 88
Jean-Luc-Nancy, *L'absolu littéraire: Théorie de la littérature du romantisme allemande* 75

Kafka, Franz 7
Kant, Immanuel 77, 83, 88
  Anthropology from a Pragmatic Point of View 51, 53–4
  Fichte *versus* 51–4
Kantorowicz, Ernst H.
  The King's Two Bodies 212
Kiefer, Anselm 26
Klein, Melanie 180
Krell, David Farrell 6, 129, 143–4, 176–7
  Intimations of Mortality 129
  Phantoms of the Other 6, 14 n.12
  "Strokes of Love and Death" 129, 177, 190 n.141
Kristeva, Julia 63

Lacoue-Labarthe, Philippe, *L'absolu littéraire: Théorie de la littérature du romantisme allemande* 75
Leavey, John P. 123–4
Loraux, Nicole
  Children of Athena 212

Maly, Kenneth 143, 153
Man, Paul de 2
Marx, Karl 48, 52, 56, 74, 83, 109, 113, 212
   German Ideology, The 9, 35–6, 38, 41
Mendelssohn, Dorothea 25, 34, 75–7

Nietzsche, Friedrich 7, 11, 35, 37, 109, 145
   Ecce Homo 83
   Übermensch 37, 202
   "Who Is Nietzsche's Zarathustra?" 203, 219

Proust, Marcel 220

Rosenzweig, Franz 7, 83
Rousseau 19, 23, 77, 83

Sartre, Jean-Paul 41, 96
   Anti-Semite and Jew 96
Schelling, Friedrich Wilhelm Joseph 39, 83
Schiller, Friedrich 19, 28, 83
Schlegel, Karl Wilhelm Friedrich 4, 19, 25, 34, 76–80, 83–4, 91, 128
   "On Philosophy. To Dorothea" 75

Schleiermacher, Friedrich 19, 95
Schmitt, Carl 83, 86, 210
Scholem, Gershom 7, 83, 88, 106
Second World War 49–50, 108, 194, 218
Semmig, Hermann 37–8
Serres, Michel 63
Socrates 147–8, 229
Sonnemann, Ulrich 60
Spinoza, Baruch 7, 31, 106

Tel Quel 63
Tocqueville, Alexis de 4–5, 9, 12, 23, 63–9, 83
   Democracy in America 65–6

Valéry, Paul 167, 219
   "The Crisis of the Spirit" 165
Voltaire 19, 77, 83

Wagner, Richard 53–4, 83, 127
Weber, Max, *Economy and Society* 104
Wittgenstein, Ludwig 4–5, 7–8, 37, 63, 83–4, 91–8
   Culture and Value 84, 92, 97
   Tractatus Logico-Philosophicus 97

www.ingramcontent.com/pod-product-compliance
Lightning Source LLC
Chambersburg PA
CBHW072145290426
44111CB00012B/1985